MARTYRDOM: A GUIDE FOR THE PERPLEXED

T&T Clark Guides for the Perplexed

T&T Clark's Guides for the Perplexed are clear, concise and accessible introductions to thinkers, writers and subjects that students and readers can find especially challenging. Concentrating specifically on what it is that makes the subject difficult to grasp, these books explain and explore key themes and ideas, guiding the reader towards a thorough understanding of demanding material.

Guides for the Perplexed available from T&T Clark

De Lubac: A Guide for the Perplexed, David Grumett
Christian Bioethics: A Guide for the Perplexed, Agneta Sutton
Calvin: A Guide for the Perplexed, Paul Helm
Tillich: A Guide for the Perplexed, Andrew O'Neill
The Trinity: A Guide for the Perplexed, Paul M. Collins
Christology: A Guide for the Perplexed, Alan Spence
Wesley: A Guide for the Perplexed, Jason E. Vickers
Pannenberg: A Guide for the Perplexed, Timothy Bradshaw
Balthasar: A Guide for the Perplexed, Rodney Howsare
Theological Anthropology: A Guide for the Perplexed, Marc Cortez
Benedict XVI: A Guide for the Perplexed, Tracey Rowland
Eucharist: A Guide for the Perplexed, Ralph N. McMichael
Process Theology: A Guide for the Perplexed, Bruce Epperly
Sin: A Guide for the Perplexed, Derek R. Nelson

Forthcoming Titles:
Political Theology: A Guide for the Perplexed, Elizabeth Philips

MARTYRDOM:
A GUIDE FOR THE PERPLEXED

PAUL MIDDLETON

t & t clark

Published by T&T Clark International
A Continuum Imprint
The Tower Building,   80 Maiden Lane,
11 York Road,   Suite 704,
London SE1 7NX   New York, NY 10038

www.continuumbooks.com

British Library Cataloguing-in-Publication Data
A catalogue record for this book is available from the British Library

ISBN: 978-0-567-03217-1 (Hardback)
        978-0-567-03218-8 (Paperback)

Typeset by Newgen Imaging Systems Pvt Ltd, Chennai, India
Printed and bound in Great Britain

In Memoriam

Fiona E. T. Hutchison (1954–2006)
Lizzie McQuade (1919–2008)
Nigel Yates (1944–2009)
Elizabeth Middleton (1946–2009)

The souls of the righteous are in the hand of God, and there shall no torment touch them. In the sight of the unwise, they seemed to die . . . but they are in peace (*Wisdom of Solomon* 3.1–3).

Sterben werd' ich, um zu leben!
(Klopstock, 'Resurrection Ode')

CONTENTS

PREFACE

When I began my PhD studies in September 2000 at the University of Edinburgh, the world was a different place. I had already decided to study the phenomenon of 'radical martyrdom', as I termed it, in early Christianity, arguing that the early Christians were generally more enthusiastic about seeking out opportunities for martyrdom than commentators had been willing to admit. I argued that early Christians made sense of their experiences of persecution by spiritualizing Jewish Holy War ideology, casting themselves in the role of cosmic warriors engaged in battle with Satan. Their deaths were the means by which they conquered, and so the logical choice for those who saw life as death and death as life was to seek out martyrdom. Many early Christians not only provoked their own deaths, but even took their own lives in order to hasten their victory over the forces of the devil. A version of my PhD thesis, *Radical Martyrdom and Cosmic Conflict in Early Christianity*, was published by T & T Clark in 2006. Some of my arguments are represented in this volume in Chapters 2 and 3.

One year after I commenced PhD studies, martyrdom became a topic of global significance. Most people will be able to recall where they were when they heard the news of the attack on the Twin Towers on Tuesday, 11 September 2001. I was at home working on martyrdom in the gospel of Mark. It just so happened I had the BBC News channel on in the background when news of the first plane hitting the North Tower broke. As the horrors of the day unfolded, I could not help but compare the actions of these Islamicist suicide bombers and the Christians of the first three centuries who also appeared to demonstrate a 'lust for death'.

The world has changed in the ten years since the events of 9/11. Martyrdom has become one of the most pressing, yet still relatively neglected issues in theology and religious studies. My thesis covered Jewish and Christian martyrology from the Maccabees to the Decian persecutions, and only touched on contemporary events in the introductory chapter. However, since I had set early Christian martyrdom in the context of Jewish Holy War, I was always aware of the potential for fruitful comparison of martyrdom between the three Abrahamic religions. This short volume begins that conversation. Aimed at the educated non-specialist, I have tried to keep endnotes to a minimum, and have instead suggested additional bibliography at the end of the book.

While I cover martyrdom in Judaism, Christianity, and Islam, this is not a 'Book of Martyrs'; and readers who hope to find their favourite martyr mentioned will almost certainly be disappointed. Although many are mentioned, I am more interested in the contested nature of martyrdom, particularly the way martyrs are created by the retelling of their stories. I have paid no attention to any official canonization of Christian martyrs; those who follow my argument will come to see that no institution has the ability to determine who is and who is not a martyr.

Inevitably, there are wide gaps in such a small, yet ambitious volume. In response to the potential charge that I have not covered areas considered by some to be of particular importance, I plead lack of space. I have devoted more space to early Christian martyrdom, since that is my particular area of expertise, and I use that material to develop the intellectual framework for the treatment of martyrdom in other traditions and time periods. In this volume, as well as guiding the reader through what may be unfamiliar material, I also hope to begin a conversation among the small but growing band of specialists in martyrdom.

I am grateful to Thomas Kraft of Continuum not only for suggesting I contribute to the *Guides for the Perplexed* series, but also for his extraordinary patience as countless deadlines passed. His colleague, Dominic Mattos, has never been slow to point out the latest volume in the series at the various conferences we've attended, shaming me into productivity. However, in my defence, to cover martyrdom in three major religions from their beginning to the present day was always going to be a tall order.

Colleagues at both the University of Wales Lampeter, and then Chester University have been encouraging, sympathetic, and supportive, especially Augustine Casiday, Rob Warner, Nigel and

Paula Yates, Kathy Ehrensperger, Bill Campbell, Wendy Dossett, Mohammad Seddon, Tom Greggs, Wayne Morris, Hannah Bacon, and Berni Hunt (who provided the index) I was given sabbatical leave by Lampeter, and spent four months as a visiting fellow at the University of Edinburgh, and greatly appreciated the collegiality of Hans Barstard, Larry Hurtado, David Ferguson, Hannah Holtschneider, Michael Barnes, Paul Foster, George Newlands, and especially Helen Bond; a bottle of malt whisky is riding on whether or not this book is out before her (equally overdue) *Jesus: A Guide for the Perplexed*!

Ruth Russell-Jones and David Cowie have been invaluable as 'perplexed' proof readers. As representatives of those for whom the book is aimed, they have offered important insights and suggestions. Ruth, in particular, as well as correcting some of my misunderstandings of English history, has spotted some real typographical howlers, not least my description of the Iranian government's attempts to ban public displays of 'mounting'. While I'm sure they would indeed wish to ban such activity, I did mean to write 'mourning'!

Friends and family have always been important to me, and in the years it has taken to complete this book, four close friends and family members have died, and it is to their memory I dedicate this work. In my first book, I acknowledged the many friends who were sources of conversation, support, and coffee. One of the principle providers of all three was the Rev. Fiona Hutchison. Fiona was as good a friend as anyone could wish for. Lively, wise, and hospitable, her untimely death in 2006 robbed the Church of Scotland of one of its most talented ministers.

Professor Nigel Yates, a former colleague at the University of Wales Lampeter, was a historian of considerable distinction, and a friend and inspiration to a great many people. Robust, and never afraid to vocalize his opinion, no matter how controversial, he was as high up the Anglican candle as one could be without disappearing into the clouds (of incense). Such was his dedication to his students that when he was diagnosed with prostate cancer, he planned his own spectacular requiem mass in meticulous detail, and ordered that it be videoed as a teaching aid for students on what a 'proper' Anglo-Catholic funeral should look like.

My gran, Lizzie McQuade, was born not long after the end of the First World War. Her hilarious and vivid accounts of what was often a difficult life, especially raising a family during and after the

Second World War, displayed an effortless clarity of expression. In my own writing, and especially in this book, I try to remember that academic work is principally communicating a story.

Finally, the loss of my mum, Elizabeth Middleton, in April 2009 was a devastating and unexpected blow. I will always be grateful for her encouragement, support, and the many sacrifices she made as my brother, sister, and I were growing up. This book is offered as a small and inadequate gesture in return.

Epiphany 2011

LIST OF ABBREVIATIONS

A. H.:	Irenaeus, *Against Heresies*
Antiquities:	Josephus, *Antiquities of the Jews*
De Fuga	*De Fuga in Persecutione*
Ep.:	Cyprian, *Epistle*
Eth. Nic.:	Aristotle, *Nicomachean Ethics*
Exhortation:	Origen, *Exhortation to Martyrdom*
H. E.:	Eusebius, *Historia Ecclesiastica*
M. Agape:	*The Martyrdom of Agape*
M. Apollonius:	*The Martyrdom of Apollonius*
M. Carpus:	*The Martyrdom of Carpus, Papylus, and Agathonice*
M. Conon:	*The Martyrdom of Conon*
M. Fructuosus:	*The Martyrdom of Fructuosus and Companions*
M. Ignatius:	*The Martyrdom of Ignatius*
M. Justin:	*The Martyrdom of Justin and Companions*
M. Lyons:	*The Letter to the Churches of Lyons and Vienne (The Martyrs of Lyons)*
M. Marcellus:	*The Martyrdom of Marcellus*
M. Perpetua:	*The Martyrdom of Perpetua and Felicitas*
M. Pionius:	*The Martyrdom of Pionius*
M. Polycarp:	*The Martyrdom of Polycarp*
M. Potamiaena:	*The Martyrdom of Potamoiaena and Basilides*
M. Ptolemaeus:	*The Martyrdom of Saints Ptolemaeus and Lucius*
Magn.:	Ignatius, *Epistle to the Magnesians*
NTS:	*New Testament Studies*
SJT:	*Scottish Journal of Theology*
Trall.:	Ignatius, *Epistle to the Trallians*
Valentinians:	Tertullian, *Against the Valentinians*
W.A.:	Martin Luther, *Werke: kritsche Gesamtausgabe* (Weimar: H. Böhlau, 1883–1993)
War:	Josephus, *The Jewish War*

CHAPTER 1

MAKING MARTYRS

1 THE PROBLEM OF MARTYRDOM

At 0843 (Eastern Daylight Time) on 11 September 2001, a Boeing 767, which had been hijacked 18 minutes earlier, crashed into the North Tower of the World Trade Center, New York. Exactly 20 minutes later, while the world watched, a second hijacked plane flew into the South Tower. Two other aircraft were hijacked that morning: one crashing into the Pentagon; and the other crashing into a field in Pennsylvania after its passengers attempted to retake the plane. Within a little over an hour of the strike on the World Trade Center, the iconic Twin Towers had collapsed, and more than 3,000 people, including the 19 hijackers, were dead. This attack, the most significant terrorist assault on American soil, led directly to then President George W. Bush declaring a 'War on Terror'. Ten years on, following invasions of Iraq and Afghanistan, it is a 'war' which shows little sign of reaching any kind of conclusion.

The events of 9/11 also brought to world-wide prominence a mode of attack which had been employed by a number of groups over the past decades: the suicide mission. While many in the world united in condemning the hijackers, others proclaimed them to be martyrs; heroes who had given their lives in Holy War – *jihad* – against the enemies of Allah. The use of airplanes by the 9/11 hijackers was as spectacular as it was deadly, and brought the issue of 'martyrdom', death for a cause, to worldwide attention. It can be said with little exaggeration that martyrdom has become one of the most pressing theological and religious issues facing the contemporary world.

1

1.1 Suicide Attacks

Suicide bombing is a relatively recent phenomenon, possible only with the advent of explosives. Associated today mainly with Islamicist groups, the technique was first used in the opening decade of the twentieth century by Russian anarchists.[1] This group targeted not only police and other state officials, but also businessmen, factory owners, and bystanders. The first known modern suicide bomber was Nisan Farber, an anarchist of Jewish origin. He threw dynamite at a police station, killing himself and many others in October 1904. Within four years of this attack, anarchist groups in Russia had killed more than 9,000 people, half of which were state officials, but the other half private individuals. By any account, this constituted large scale terrorism.

The attackers of 9/11 were not the first to fly aeroplanes into enemy targets. Japanese pilots of the Second World War were the next group to resort to suicide bombing. Kamikaze pilots deliberately crashed their aircraft into Allied planes and ships. In the final year of the war more than three thousand Japanese pilots died in suicide missions. They succeeded in sinking dozens of ships and damaging nearly 300 more, killing more than 1,000 Allied forces, and maiming many others. Earlier in the war, Japanese soldiers had attempted to prevent the advance of American tanks in New Guinea by suicidal means. However, this practice was largely ineffective, and quickly discontinued. Also relatively unsuccessful was the sea dragon (*kairyu*), a small two-man submarine packed with explosives. These human torpedoes sank only two ships during the course of the war.

Given the association in the popular imagination between martyrdom and religion, it is worth noting that both the Russian anarchists and Japanese kamikaze pilots died for secular causes. To be sure, there was a quasi-religious context for Japanese actions. The term *kamikaze* means 'divine wind', invoking the story of the storms which suddenly blew up and repelled the invasion forces of the thirteenth-century Mongol Emperor Kublai Khan. Japanese pilots were principally taking on the role of that ancient storm, defending the homeland from enemy invasion; the strikes were for essentially defensive military ends.

In a culture heavily constructed around honour/shame codes, death in the face of defeat was preferable to life with dishonour.

Indeed, many Japanese generals committed *hari-kiri* after the country's surrender. In many respects, as we will see, the Japanese attitudes to life and death find significant parallels in the ancient world. However, in the case of the earlier Russian anarchists, there is no ambiguity; their cause was entirely secular. Even into the modern era, many suicide missions of the early 1980s were carried out by secular groups, such as the Tamil Tigers, the Kurdish Workers Party, and the Syrian Social Nationalist Party. Prior to the Second Gulf War, the majority of suicide missions were either of secular or unknown motivation.

Nonetheless, in the early 1980s, suicide bombing as a mode of expression crossed decisively into the religious realm. In 1982, Hezbollah (Party of God) was formed and joined the struggle against foreign occupation of Lebanon. Lebanon had already witnessed dozens of secularist suicide missions, culminating in major attacks against the Iraqi embassy (1981) and Israeli headquarters (1982) in Beirut. Hezbollah entered the scene after Israel's second invasion of the Lebanon. Its formation was supported by Iranian Revolutionary Guards, contributing to the political turmoil a potent tradition of Shi'ite martyrdom (see Chapter 6). Iran had already deployed waves of suicide missions in their war against Iraq (1980–1988). Hundreds of thousands of young men were sent to their inevitable death through being instructed to attack Iraqi outposts and clear minefields. Hezbollah, probably through having a far smaller pool of volunteers from which to draw, was more selective in its attacks. Subsequent major operations against American and French international peacekeeping forces in 1983 led to the withdrawal of international forces from Lebanese soil; one of the very few instances where terrorism has so clearly achieved its political aims.

The use of suicide bombing spread throughout the world, notably in Sri-Lanka, Palestine and the Occupied Territories, Turkey, and Kashmir. Al-Qaeda launched its first major campaign in Africa in 1998. The twenty-first century has witnessed incidents in Chechnya and Iraq, and in Britain there have been attacks in London (2005) and Glasgow (2008). As we have seen, suicide bombing is not exclusively rooted within religious tradition. However, where religion provides part of the stated motivation, the religion is invariably Islam. This fact renders discussion of martyrdom, particularly the Islamicist manifestation in the context of jihad politically sensitive.

1.2 Talking about Martyrdom

The language of Holy War is a foreign concept to Westerners. With no contemporary tradition of Holy War on which to draw (in the sense that religion could propel a state to war), Western intellectuals have dismissed religion altogether as a motivational factor for political behaviour. Where religion can be found as a primary influence in a group's actions, whether violent or non-violent, that group tends to be dismissed as irrational or dangerously fanatical. Their actions are judged to be beyond rationality, beyond reason, and beyond understanding.

Such is its sensitivity, political discourse (at least so far) has refused to countenance any attempts to 'explain' the actions of suicide bombers. Such actions are irrational and evil, and attempts to explain or contextualize suicide-martyrdoms are met with hostility. Cherie Booth, the wife of former British Prime Minister Tony Blair, faced widespread condemnation for appearing to condone a Palestinian suicide bomber. Hours after a 22-year-old Palestinian from a refugee camp near Nablus carried out a suicide attack on a bus in Jerusalem in June 2002, killing 19 people and injuring more than 40, she commented, 'As long as young people feel they've got no hope but to blow themselves up, we are never going to make progress'. The responses to her comments focused almost entirely on the perceived attempt to 'understand' or rationalize such attacks. According to a BBC news report, the Israeli Embassy in London 'regretted any public statements that might be interpreted as expressing understanding for Palestinian terrorism on the day of such an attack'. Ned Temko, editor of the *Jewish Chronicle*, accused Booth of 'crossing the dangerously narrow line between suggesting there could be some sort of rational explanation for targeting civilians in such attacks and justifying them'.[2]

Moreover, in the face of rising anti-Islamic sentiment in the West, it has been particularly important for politicians and academics alike to deny, or at least significantly diminish any religious aspect for the attacks. In an important analysis of the 9/11 hijackers, Stephen Holmes carefully distinguishes political from religious motivations and concludes that religion was not enough to propel such action. Holy War ideology, he concludes, was essentially a religious smokescreen to cover political ends. Suicide bombing was chosen because it is a more effective military means than other forms of terrorism. The motivation was secular, protesting against perceived political injustice perpetrated by the United States.

Similarly, Cherie Booth's 'explanation' for the Palestinian attack was cast in solely secular and political terms; despair in the face of a hopeless political situation. The problem for those who wish to downplay the role of religion is that such acts are self-consciously cast within a religious narrative. There is no evidence a Palestinian or any other Islamic suicide attacker does so out of despair. Indeed, the average Palestinian attacker tends to be in work and of above average education. Furthermore, the distinction between secular and religious can be overplayed; it is not clear injustice would be regarded principally as a secular concern within either Islam or Christianity. Often martyrdom is cast in terms of righting wrongs in the world. Such deaths take on significance far greater than that of a tragic individual. If justice is the cause, the death may contribute to a cosmic righting of wrongs. Indeed, the War on Terror was not without religious overtones!

1.3   The Problem of Definition

If the question of how we speak of martyrdom is a minefield, then so too is the far more obvious question of 'what is martyrdom?' Martyrdom is a contested term. Does a suicide bomber count as a martyr? The hijackers of the planes which crashed into the Twin Towers of the World Trade Center were lauded as martyrs by the Al-Qaeda organization, while the same event was described as the worst instance of terrorism in America's history. Similarly, in the Occupied Territories of Palestine, those who kill Israeli soldiers and often civilians are regarded as martyrs by some Palestinian communities, yet for others, they are terrorists.

Dictionary definitions are of little help. *The Shorter Oxford English Dictionary* defines a martyr as 'one who undergoes death (or great suffering) on behalf of any belief or cause, or through devotion to some object'. Not only does this cast the net impossibly wide to encompass those for whom the term is used metaphorically, it does not help in the martyr/terrorist question. It cannot be denied that those regarded as terrorists do undergo death for a cause.

The word 'martyr' comes from the Greek term *martus*, which had the original sense of witnessing, often in a judicial setting. However, it eventually took on the additional meaning of dying for faith. The first unambiguous use of the term in this way is found with reference to the martyrdom of Polycarp (c. 155 CE).

> We are writing to you, dear brothers, the story of the martyrs (*tous marturēsantas*) and of blessed Polycarp, who put a stop to the persecution by his own martyrdom (*marturias*) as though he were putting a seal upon it. (*M. Polycarp* 1.1)

The Martyrdom of Polycarp was a new genre: the martyr act. However, it is important to stress that the author of *Polycarp*, while he may use the term *martus* in a new way, does not radically develop or advance early Christian understanding of dying for Jesus. The relationship between death and witnessing for Jesus is already present more than half a century earlier in the book of Revelation. In his vision, John sees souls under the heavenly altar cry out for justice. They had been slain for the witness (*marturian*) they had borne (Rev. 6.9). Similarly, in Chapter 20, those who had been beheaded for their testimony (*marturian*) to Jesus come back to life and reign for a thousand years (20.4). The term comes closest to having its later sense in describing Antipas as the faithful witness/ martyr (*martus*) of Jesus, who was killed (2.13). Witnessing is also at the root of Islamic understanding of martyrdom. Those who die in Holy War are martyrs (*shahid*), a word which, like *martus*, has as its other primary meaning 'witnessing'.

Defining martyrdom is not a new problem. Finding a definition to cover all instances of even early Christians, let alone Jews and Muslims, is illusive. Van Henten and Avemarie define a martyr as 'a person who in an extremely hostile situation prefers a violent death to compliance with a demand of the (usually pagan) authorities'.[3] However, this definition excludes a great many instances of death that would be recognized as martyrdom, most notably, the iconic mass suicides of Masada (see Chapter 5). Similar kinds of death can also be found within early Christianity, such as that of Agathonicê, who, after witnessing the execution of Christians in the arena, abandoned her son, and inexplicably leapt to her death.

> She raised her voice at once, 'Here is a meal that has been prepared for me. I must partake of this glorious feast!'
>
> The mob shouted, 'Have pity on your son!'

And the blessed Agathonicê said, 'He has God who can take pity on him . . . '

And taking off her cloak, she threw herself joyfully upon the stake . . .

And thus she gave up her spirit and died together with the saints. And the Christians secretly collected their remains and protected them for the glory of Christ and the praise of his martyrs. (*M. Carpus*, 42–44, 47)

The question of who is and is not a martyr is not clear cut. Even within early Christianity, the term is contested. Clement of Alexandria excludes a group who call themselves Christians, appear to make a faithful witness, and are executed. Yet he denies they are true martyrs.

We say that these men take themselves off without witness, even if they are officially executed. For they do not preserve the characteristic mark of faithful witness, because they do not know the real God, but give themselves up to a futile death. (*Stromaties* 4.16.3–17.3)

We will meet this group again in Chapter 2, but for the time being, we note that the ambiguous nature of who is and is not a martyr is a very early concern, and one of strong contention.

The main points of contention in assessing contemporary suicide bombing cluster around two main issues, both of which are thought to disqualify this type of death from being counted as genuine martyrdom: suicide and killing. However, we have already noted the suicide-martyrdom of Agathonicê, and hers is by no means the only example of a Christian taking his or her own life (see Chapter 2).

2 SUICIDE AND NOBLE DEATH IN ANTIQUITY

Any sharp distinction made between suicide and martyrdom was not as obvious to the Graeco-Roman mind as it is to readers today. There was no word in either Latin or Greek corresponding to our word 'suicide' with its negative connotations. Indeed, in the ancient mind, self-killing in the correct circumstances was considered to be an honourable practice. In general terms, the circumstances of one's suicide, rather than the act itself, determined whether or not it counted as a 'Noble Death'.

2.1 Socrates and the Philosophers

Perhaps the most famous example of Noble Death is that of Socrates (469–399 BCE).[4] As with Jesus, nothing remains of anything Socrates might have written. All our information about his life is second-hand, the main sources being Aristophanes, Xenophon, and especially Plato. Socrates was convicted of impiety (*asebia*) and corrupting the young. As a result, he was sentenced to death by an Athenian court. Despite having the opportunity to go into voluntary exile, he chose to die by drinking hemlock. Epictetus enthusiastically approves of Socrates' refusal to avoid death by exile: 'He saves himself by dying, not by flight' (*Discourses* 4.1.165). Similarly, Plato has Socrates say that the philosopher should welcome death, since through it one attains the greatest blessings (*Phaedo* 64a). Plato portrays the death of Socrates as a voluntary act, and commends the practice; others are urged to come after him as quickly as they could (*Phaedo* 61bc).

However, the Platonic Socrates does not approve of self-killing in all circumstances. Individuals belong to the gods; one should not destroy what is not one's own to destroy. However, he reasons, when the gods place a necessity (*anangke*) upon an individual, then self-killing is permitted. For Socrates, death is no tragedy: 'So long as we have the body, and the soul is contaminated by such an evil, we shall never attain completely what we desire, that is, the truth' (*Phaedo* 66b).

Other philosophical schools echoed Socrates' ambivalence towards death. For Epictetus (*Discourses* 2.19.13), neither life nor death contribute to the good life; they are adiaphorous. The dead are simply as they were before they were born (*Cic Fin* 1.49). The Stoics displayed a similar ambivalence towards death. Death is inevitable, and according to the most famous of the Stoics, Seneca (c. 4 BCE–65 CE), to be alive is to be in the process of dying (*Epistle* 1.2). For the Stoics, the decision to take one's own life should be rational: 'the wise man will for reasonable cause make his own exit from life, on his country's behalf or for the sake of friends, or if he suffer intolerable pain, mutilation, or incurable disease' (Diogenes Laertius 7.130; see also Aristotle, *Eth. Nic.* 1169a). One grizzly out-working of death being for the benefit of others is found where the Emperor Gaius was ill. In order to persuade the gods to look with favour on the ailing emperor, two men made what proved to be rash promises. One promised his life in *devotio* for the emperor's health, while the other pledged to become a gladiator. When the emperor recovered, he held both to the promises they had made (Seutonius, *Caligula* 27.2).

Plato added three further instances to the philosophers' judge-ments of when a person should take his or her own life: when ordered to do so by the State; in the face of devastating misfortune; or when faced with intolerable shame. Shame was one of the more common reasons for Noble Death in the ancient world. In Anton van Hooff's major study on self-killing in the ancient world, more than one third of the total of suicides catalogued is motivated by shame.[5] This is as true of women as of men, and one of the most cel-ebrated cases of female Noble Death in antiquity fits this category. Lucretia, having been raped by the king's son, Tarquinius, killed herself with a sword. According to Livy, the response to her death brought an end to the Etruscan dynasty and ushered in the Roman Republic (Livy 1.58.11).

If the Stoics were positive or at least indifferent towards death, the Cynics were in some cases very enthusiastic, and many killed themselves for what appear to be rather trivial reasons. Two elderly Cynics, Diogenes and Demonax, killed themselves apparently on the grounds of age.[6] However, one of the most notorious Cynics was Peregrinus, a former Christian, who underwent self-immolation at the Olympic games of 165 CE for reasons not entirely clear. His act was dismissed as a publicity stunt by Lucian (*Death of Perigrinus* 20–25, 38–39), and also failed Marcus Aurelius' test on Noble Death, that death should be without dramatics if it is to impress anyone (*Meditations* 11.3).

However, not all philosophical schools were positive about self-killing. The Neo-platonists and the Pythagoreans both condemned the practice, the latter on account that the number of souls in this and the next world were in careful balance, so one ought not upset that balance. Nonetheless, for most schools, so long as there was good reason, suicide could constitute Noble Death.

2.2 Devotio

The most glorious form of Noble Death was that achieved hero-ically in battle for the homeland. Euripides writes of the Trojans, 'in the first place [they] died for their fatherland – the noblest glory of all' (*Troades* 386–387). A similar form of Noble Death is *devotio*, a voluntary death where life was deliberately surrendered to ensure victory, usually through a form of contract with the gods. So, in the Samnite Wars (340 BCE), the Roman general Publius Decius Mus devoted himself to the gods of the underworld, then rushed head-long towards a violent death against the opposing army to secure victory for his depleted army (Livy 8.9.6–10). Similarly Menoeceus (Euripidies, *Phoenissae* 930–959) and Polyvena (*Hecuba* 38–41) also volunteered for death in order to save their respective cities.

These factors combine with the motivation through shame when generals were faced with defeat on the battlefield. After his defeat by Caesar, Cato the Younger stabbed himself rather than being forced to ask his enemy to spare his life. By so doing he remained his own master (Plutarch, *Cato* 69–71). Similarly, having been defeated by the Parthians in 53 BCE, Crassus, the commander of the Roman army, and the rest of his soldiers killed themselves to avoid falling into enemy hands.

> Now there were with Publius two Greeks . . . These joined in trying to persuade him to slip away with them and make their escape . . . But Publius, declaring that no death could have such terrors for him as to make him desert those who were perishing on his account, ordered them to save their own lives, bade them farewell, and dismissed them. Then he himself, being unable to use his hand, which had been pierced through with an arrow, presented his side to his shield-bearer and ordered him to strike home with his sword. (Plutarch, *Crassus* 25.11)

A very similar pattern is found in the Old Testament account of Saul's death. Having been wounded in battle by Philistine archers, Saul asked his armour-bearer to kill him rather than allow him to fall into the hands of the Philistines who would certainly have humiliated him. Whereas in the account of the king's death in 2 Samuel, it appears the young man did as the king asked (2 Sam.

1.8–10), in 1 Samuel, he refuses, and Saul has to fall on his own sword.

> Now the Philistines fought against Israel . . . The battle pressed hard upon Saul; the archers found him, and he was badly wounded by them. Then Saul said to his armour-bearer, 'Draw your sword and thrust me through with it, so that these uncircumcised may not come and thrust me through, and make sport of me'. But his armour-bearer was unwilling; for he was terrified. So Saul took his own sword and fell upon it. When his armourbearer saw that Saul was dead, he also fell upon his sword and died with him. (1 Sam. 31.1–5)

Although the similarity is striking, both texts probably pick up a common fear among those engaging in battle of falling into enemy hands rather than there being any literary dependence between the two stories. Other examples of such deaths include Cleopatra and Mark Anthony, Brutus, Cassius, and from the Old Testament, Abimelech, who similarly instructs his armour bearer to kill him after being hit on the head by a millstone thrown by a woman, so that it could not be said he was killed by a woman (Judg. 9.50–57). Death in the face of defeat is usually portrayed by the narrators as a positive and appropriate noble option.

Often early Christians set their own understanding of martyrdom within this tradition of Noble Death. There is little hint of criticism at voluntary death or what we would term suicide. Chrysostom even argues the deaths of the Christian martyrs are superior to that of Socrates (*Homily IV on 1 Cor. 1.18–20*). Chrysostom, against Plato's view of Socrates, compares the involuntary nature of Socrates drinking the hemlock with the martyrs who die willingly, suggesting the violent and brave deaths of martyrs, often in the prime of life, compare favourably with Socrates' gentle and aged end.

Similarly, Tertullian offers his readers examples of the Noble Deaths of Lucretia, Empedocles (jumped into Mount Etna), Heraclitus (smeared himself with dung and set himself alight) and Cleopatra, but calls on Christians to exceed these actions (*Ad Martyras* 4). Early Christians had little difficulty accepting pagan suicide as patterns for Christian martyrdom. Therefore, we cannot easily rule suicide to be a disqualifier for martyrdom.

3 CONFLICT STORIES

3.1 Murder and Martyrdom

Even if suicide does not rule out a person from being acclaimed a martyr, for many, the line is crossed decisively where so-called martyrs kill others. Larry Hurtado points to the dangers of 'a very different kind of "martyr" whose victory consists, not in his/her own death, but in killing as many others as possible!' He goes on to warn that 'it would be a failure of nerve for Christian and Jewish scholars not to complain about the "high-jacking" or the terms "martyr" and "martyrdom" by some violent groups today'.[7] For Hurtado, as for many, the fact that these 'martyrs' kill others is the criterion by which suicide bombers should be excluded from the category of martyrdom. When George W. Bush denounced suicide bombers as not martyrs but murderers, he declared that one could not be both a martyr and a killer.

This line is pressed most vociferously in a collection of essays edited by Brian Wicker.[8] His laudable concerns are twofold: first, he is concerned to divorce suicide bombing from Islam, and secondly, he believes interfaith dialogue can be promoted between Christianity and Islam, where each could recognize the other's martyrs as heroes and saints. Therefore, he quite self-consciously sets out to 'counteract a false ideology of martyrdom wherever it rears its head',[9] and in his view, suicide bombing is an example of false martyrdom.

However, using violence as the main criterion by which to distinguish false from true martyrdom is not unproblematic. Violence against others, as we will see, has a long tradition in the martyrological discourse of each of the three main religions. Even the earliest Christian martyr narratives, where actual physical violence against the persecutors was not an option, nonetheless display a potent threat of eschatological violence against bystanders and witnesses. God would revisit those who participated or observed the Christians' torment with far worse. In the book of Revelation, this violence is particularly graphic. During the Crusades, this violence against others present in the Apocalypse becomes actualized (Chapter 4). Similarly, Jewish martyr history begins in the Deuteronomistic tradition of Holy War. The Maccabean martyr stories take place in the midst of battle and appear to affect the outcome of that war (see Chapter 5).

Although most readers will readily agree there is a difference between murder and martyrdom, the distinction can be problematic. Soldiers killed in battle have often attracted martyrological language. Most recently, the deaths of soldiers killed in the conflicts relating to the War on Terror have been placed in a martyrological framework (although the term 'martyr' is only rarely employed). Combatants have died for larger universal values of freedom, justice, and democracy. This is not new. The martyr-soldier emerges most clearly from the First World War. Sermons and memorials promoted the strong sense that soldiers who died in that conflict were martyrs. The Bishop of London Winnington-Ingram explicitly attributed the epithet to those killed in the Great War, but implicitly, the language of sacrifice and common parallels to the sacrifice of Jesus on war memorials reinforce the martyrological significance of these deaths.[10]

The idea of martyr-soldiers imitating Christ on the battlefield is found most explicitly in the Christian tradition of the Crusades. Officially, the Church was slow to recognize combatants as martyrs on the ground. However, the popular idea was permitted to grow widely that all who fell in battle in the fight against the Muslims would be granted the crown of martyrdom. Designed to boost recruitment, sermons and songs promised the martyrs' reward for those who joined the Crusades.

3.2 Samson

Problematic for the murderer/martyr distinction is the Old Testament character of Samson. Samson, who had been terrorizing the Philistines with destructive raids, was tricked by Delilah into revealing that the secret of his great strength lay in the Nazorite vow not to cut his hair. The Philistines captured Samson, gouged out his eyes, and made him grind the mill in Gaza. To celebrate the capture of their nemesis, the Philistines held a banquet to celebrate and offer sacrifices to their god, Dagon. 'Our god has given our enemy into our hand the ravager of our country, who has slain many of us' (Judges 16.24). During the celebrations, they called for Samson to make sport of him, precisely the fate Saul, Crassus, and Cato were anxious to avoid.

They made him stand between the pillars; and Samson said to the attendant who held him by the hand, 'Let me feel the pillars on which the house rests, so that I may lean against them'. Now the house was full of men and women; all the lords of the Philistines were there, and on the roof there were about three thousand men and women, who looked on while Samson performed. Then Samson called to the LORD and said, 'Lord GOD, remember me and strengthen me only this once, O God, so that with this one act of revenge I may pay back the Philistines for my two eyes'. And Samson grasped the two middle pillars on which the house rested, and he leaned his weight against them, his right hand on the one and his left hand on the other. Then Samson said, 'Let me die with the Philistines'. He strained with all his might; and the house fell on the lords and all the people who were in it. So those he killed at his death were more than those he had killed during his life. (Judges 16.25–30)

Noteworthy is the way the narrator lingers over the body count, noting the detail that as well as the house being full, the roof held 3,000 women and men. The narrator clearly approves of Samson's self-killing and indiscriminate massacre of the Philistines. Since the Philistines had put the capture of Samson within a cosmic context – it was their god, Dagon, who had captured Samson – the story becomes a contest between their respective gods' prowess. Therefore, that Samson killed more Philistines in his death than in his life is reckoned to be a vindication of Israel's god.

Earlier assaults against the Philistines are narrated positively, even as actions of God. So, for example, after a violent slaughter of the Philistines (Judges 15.8), the people of Judah, in response to threats made by the Philistines, agreed to bind Samson and to deliver him to them.

When he came to Lehi, the Philistines came shouting to meet him; *and the Spirit of the Lord came mightily upon him*, and the ropes which were on his arms . . . melted off his hands. And he found a fresh jawbone of an ass . . . and with it he slew a thousand men. (Judges 15.14–15)

Samson's strength and subsequent killing of 1,000 men is inspired by the Spirit of God. Furthermore, after the slaughter, God miraculously provided water from a rock for Samson to drink (15.19; cf. Num. 20.8); there is no hint of divine disapproval of Samson's killing sprees. Indeed, when Samson desires a Philistine wife, the incident that sparks enmity between him and the Philistines, his parents disapprove, for

> his father and mother did not know that it was from the Lord; for he was seeking an occasion against the Philistines. At that time the Philistines had dominion over Israel. (Judg. 14.4)

Even Samson's desire of a foreign wife is put down to God's initiative so he can move against the Philistines.

Samson also wins approval in Christian tradition. The author of the Epistle to the Hebrews lists him as one of the heroes of faith.

> And what more shall I say? For time would fail me to tell of Gideon, Barak, Samson, Jephthah, of David and Samuel and the prophets – who through faith conquered kingdoms, enforced justice, received promises, stopped the mouths of lions . . . won strength our of weakness, became mighty in war, put foreign armies to flight . . . suffered mocking and scourging, and even chains and imprisonment. (Heb. 11.32–36)

Despite the entirety of his biblical story being one of killing, culminating in his suicidal mass slaughter, Samson is commended as one of the great crowd of witnesses which inspires Christians on their own race of faith (Heb. 12.1). The Samson narrative provides the sensitive reader with an uncomfortable story of suicide-killing at the heart of the Judea-Christian tradition, undermining any easy dismissal of such actions as sub-religious.

3.3 Conflicting Narratives

Martyr stories are often set in a context of war, even if that war is metaphorical or metaphysical. Martyrologies are essentially conflict stories operating on many levels. Martyrdom has a long history; as long as individuals have been dying for their faith or cause, others have been telling and, more importantly, interpreting their stories. Usually there is some form of personal confrontation, which may be between a believer and an official. However, whether or not this element is present, the death is normally interpreted within the framework of a far wider conflict, which may itself be external to the narrative or report. This conflict may be regional, global, or even cosmic. The martyr becomes a symbol of a community's desires and hopes, or for that matter, their terrors and fears, but in either case, the martyr is representative of a larger struggle. This struggle might be political, spiritual, or often both. Usually some form of final outcome is envisaged and the martyr contributes in some way to that larger end.

The way the aftermath of 9/11 has been narrated demonstrates these conflicting narratives quite clearly. For the Islamicist, a terrorist's death is in reality that of a martyr who has contributed to a Holy War in defence of Islam. Bin Laden gives this contemporary battle a particularly apocalyptic spin:

> The world has been divided into two camps: one under the banner of the cross (as the head of the infidels, Bush, has said), and one under the banner of Islam . . . Adherents of Islam, this is your day to make Islam victorious.[11]

In the apocalyptic Holy War in which bin Laden believes he and all adherents of Islam are engaged, we find a radically polarized dualism. There is the language of war, a call to take a committed position in that battle, and importantly, the expectation they will be victorious in the end. However, the War on Terror, in the way it has been narrated, also contains elements of Holy War. George W. Bush, whether intentionally or not, struck an unmistakably religious apocalyptic note.

> Our war on terror begins with Al-Qaeda, but it does not end there. It will not end until every terrorist group of global reach has been found, stopped and defeated . . . Every nation, in every region, now has a decision to make. Either you are with us, or you are with the terrorists.[12]

These words of the former American president are full of the same apocalyptic resonances as those of Osama bin Laden. Within a call to battle there is a clear radical dualism with the warning that every nation has to make an urgent eschatological decision, with an implicit threat of judgement for those who choose incorrectly. This battle, in which the participants are called to serve – almost divinely – will be won decisively in the end.

Again, any attempt to draw distinctions between secular and religious motivation is found wanting, for the initial aims of Bush's war (the capture of bin Laden) broadened to the defence (and expansion) of an American (Christian) way of life: freedom, democracy, justice. Indeed, in its early days, Bush made this religious backdrop to the war explicit: 'This crusade, this war on terrorism, is going to take a long time'.[13] Crusading language set the conflict within the context of Christianity's earlier conflicts with Islam.

All who are killed in this war fit into one of two grand conflict narratives. As we saw with Clement's rejection of a group of Christian 'martyrs', one community's martyrologies may be resisted by another. Wicker's claim that the definition of a martyr is a matter of fact rather than opinion is simply wrong. Martyrs are not defined; martyrs are made. While one community may 'make' martyrs by their narratives, other communities can equally vociferously 'unmake' them. Martyr narratives – whether textual, oral, a poster, or even a CNN news report – do more than simply report a death; they contain the interpretative framework by which that death should be understood – either 'making' or 'unmaking' martyrs.

Martyr narratives or anti-narratives contain the key to their own interpretation, an interpretation which can, of course, be accepted or rejected. Whether a Christian confessing her faith before a bemused Roman governor, or a suicide bomber blowing himself up in a crowded café in Jerusalem, the way these death stories are recounted – positively or negatively – reflects a wider conflict in which the narrator and his community find themselves.

Counter-intuitively, in this understanding of martyrdom, the individual martyr becomes a secondary concern. What 'makes' martyrdom is not principally a martyr but a narrative. Most martyrs would not know how they would be remembered, and although they may deliberately die for a cause, they have little control over how their story will be told. In most cases, a martyr's understanding of what they thought they were doing is unknown, and ultimately beside the point. Even where we do possess the video testimony of suicide bombers, the narratives fit a predetermined form, placing their deaths in a larger religio-political context. The elements usually include a statement that what they are doing demonstrates faithfulness to Allah, a condemnation of atrocities the West has inflicted on Muslims, often Palestinians more specifically, and the belief that what they are doing forms part of a scheme of divine judgement for that treatment. This is essentially the repetition of a public and corporate grand narrative. Video testimonies tend to add nothing to our understanding of these deaths. It is this predetermined discourse which motivates, radicalizes, and contextualizes actions which appear to the West incomprehensible, and gives their deaths purpose and meaning.

Crucially, this discourse is by no means restricted to contemporary Islamic manifestations of martyrdom. In every age, across all religions which have valourized death in some way, martyrs' deaths fit into larger narrative frameworks so that they somehow contribute to the winning of a wider conflict, whether it be the early Christians' cosmic battle against Satan, the Maccabean martyrs' contribution to the war against the Seleucid Empire, or the self-immolation in 1963 of the Tibetan monk, Thich Quang Duc, in protest against religious suppression by the Vietnamese authorities. Duc, with the help of others, set light to himself and burned to death while sitting in the lotus position. In Duc's case, the 'martyr narrative' was Malcolm Browne's iconic Pulitzer Prize-winning photograph. Without that image and the significant political aftermath provoked by it, no one would have heard of Thich Quang Duc, and even though he would still have killed himself in this way, he would not be remembered as a martyr. Martyrs require martyr narratives.

4 MAKING MODERN MARTYRS

We now turn to five contemporary 'martyr' narratives to demonstrate how such narratives are constructed. These accounts describe very different kinds of deaths in various ways, yet each illustrate many of the points made thus far.

4.1 Dietrich Bonhoeffer

Much of the ambiguity in the creation of martyrs is found in the portrayal of Dietrich Bonhoeffer after his death. Bonhoeffer, a theologian and Lutheran Pastor, belonged to a group which helped Jews to escape from Germany to Switzerland. Prominent in the ecumenical movement and Confessing Church, he was arrested in 1943 for his part in the conspiracy to kill Adolf Hitler. He was executed when, by chance, papers were discovered proving his link with the plot. His execution and those of his co-conspirators were ordered by Hitler himself. Bonheoffer was hanged on 9 April 1945, fewer than two weeks before the end of the war in Europe.

Although many regard Bonhoeffer as a martyr, his political and conspiratorial involvement in the plot to assassinate Hitler have made this accolade controversial. His own Lutheran Church did not recognize him as such, and in 1953 the Lutheran Bishop Hans Meiser refused to attend a memorial service for him in Flossenbürg. Even though he was involved in efforts to help Jews escape Germany, he is not remembered at *Yad Vashem* as one of the 'Righteous among the Nations' as his stance against the Nazis is judged to have been motivated more by Church politics than concern for the Jews. However, as I hope I have already demonstrated, all these objections are beside the point. Bonhoeffer *is* a Christian martyr because that is precisely how he is remembered.

This 'memory' began at the memorial service held for Bonhoeffer on 27 July 1945 at Holy Trinity Church in Kingsway, London. In his sermon, Bishop Bell of Chichester said of his friend:

His death, like his life, marks a fact of the deepest value in the witness of the Confessing Church. As one of a noble company of martyrs of differing traditions, he represents both the resistance of the believing soul, in the name of God, to the assault of evil, and also the moral and political revolt of the human conscience against injustice and cruelty.[14]

Bell anticipates some of the religious objection to Bonhoeffer being regarded as a martyr by referring to both the resistance of the believing soul, but also the moral and political revolt against injustice. Bell could, of course, have cast resistance to injustice in a purely religious framework. However, he also attributes to those outside the Church something of Bonhoeffer's religious motivation.

He and his fellows are indeed built upon the foundation of the Apostles and the Prophets. And it was this passion for justice that brought him, and so many others . . . into close partnership with other resisters, who, though outside the Church, shared the same humanitarian and liberal ideals.

Bell, perhaps as a conscious apologia for Bonhoeffer against the charge that his involvement in the political plot contaminated any claims to make him a pure Christian martyr, suggests rather that Bonhoeffer's involvement in the plot hallows the actions of the political resistance, bringing the conspirators' actions into consort with the values of the apostles and prophets.

Similarly, Reinhold Niebuhr and members of the Ecumenical Movement quickly proclaimed him to be a martyr. Today, most books and articles on Bonhoeffer simply assume his martyr status. Any resistance to this assessment of his death as martyrdom is surely futile, given he is now remembered in the 'Chapel of Saints and Martyrs of Our Own Time' in Canterbury Cathedral, and also listed as one of the Ten Modern Martyrs in Westminster Abbey.[15] However, his place among the martyrs has spawned a disturbing contemporary 'copycat' martyrology.

4.2   Paul Hill

The second example was also a clergyman, Presbyterian pastor Paul Hill. Unlike Bonhoeffer, Hill succeeded in killing those he regarded as the enemy, including a doctor who carried out abortions. He was sentenced to death and executed on 3 September 2003. The BBC reported his execution.

> Paul Hill, 49, died at 1808 local time (2208 GMT) in northern Florida, following his conviction for the murder of two people outside an abortion clinic in 1994 . . .
>
> . . . He gave no resistance as the lethal injection was administered, a Florida department of corrections spokesman said . . . In a last statement before his execution, Hill thanked God for his family and urged anyone against abortion to do what they could to prevent it.
>
> 'Two of the last things that I would like to say – You have a responsibility to protect your neighbour's life, and to use force if necessary to do so. In an effort to suppress this truth, you may mix my blood with the blood of the unborn, and those who have fought to defend the oppressed. However, truth and righteousness will prevail. May God help you to protect the unborn as you would want to be protected'.

Before the execution, Hill said he would kill again to save the unborn and was looking forward to dying for his cause.[16]

On the face of it, this simply looks like a news report on the execution of a dangerous murderer. However, by reporting the last words of Hill, the BBC's impartial report can now be read in other ways. Hill, by employing religious rhetoric to justify his actions, interprets his impending death as martyrdom. He told a news conference, 'I believe the state, by executing me, will be making me a martyr'. Hill's self-understanding may be judged delusional, and his justification of murder on Christian grounds, perverse. However, he is not alone in that perspective. In the highly charged American 'culture wars' on the question of abortion, many professing Christians see no contradiction in saving the lives of the unborn through killing. At the time of his execution, supporters outside the prison held placards affirming their belief that Hill was a martyr. Fundamentalist Christian magazines and websites celebrate Hill's actions and support his claim to martyrdom. One website, which may be considered a martyrology, justifies his act of murder by drawing parallels between Hill and Dietrich Bonhoeffer.

> Bonhoeffer and Hill were clergymen who were at odds with the passivity and cowardice of their fellow Christians to resist a holocaust . . . Paul Hill witnessed the abortion holocaust . . . and determined to resist it. Both men spoke out for years at a cost to themselves and their careers as clergymen – but were determined to defend the defenceless . . . Bonhoeffer joined the plot to assassinate Hitler . . . Paul Hill took up arms to end the baby killing of abortionist John Britten . . . To the very end of their lives, Bonhoeffer and Hill refused to recant their beliefs that their actions were justified . . . With their lives at stake, they bravely upheld the principle of active resistance to evil and evil governments. The Nazi holocaust and the American murder of 45 million unborn children did not conquer the spirit of these men. They followed Christ in life and in death and challenge us to do the same today.[17]

The narrative does have internal logic. If Bonhoeffer can be regarded as a martyr despite his involvement in the (albeit failed) plot to murder, then murder in itself is not a disqualification to the title 'martyr'. Both men's struggles are set in the context of standing up against a 'weak Church' (so attempting to counter any Christian objections) and evil States, the latter advocating and the former colluding with the Holocaust.

Crucially, the narrative which sets the martyr against the State self-consciously models the death of Hill on the struggle, witness, and deaths of the early Christians. To make this connection explicit the narrative stresses that Hill refused to recant, even though the state of Florida did not ask him to, made a confession of faith, and was killed. The act of murder is explained by the edict from the government allowing the slaughter of unborn children. This led to crisis, where in 'defending the defenceless' the potential martyr took the action of 'justifiable homicide', just as Bonhoeffer had joined the plot to kill Hitler. The act was subsequently accompanied by confession of faith and a refusal to recant, and as a result, he underwent martyrdom.

It was not the United States judiciary who made Paul Hill a martyr; they executed a criminal. Rather, those who approved of Hill's actions *created* a martyr. By retelling his story in a certain way, they constructed a narrative utilizing unmistakably Christian martyrological language, and reinforced their own (Christian) understanding of how the world works. To reinforce (and perhaps justify) their world view, the example of ancient Christian martyrs is used as a template. Like Hill, the early Christians did not recant under pressure and were finally executed by the State. The discrepancy over what the State believed it was doing and the reinterpretation of Hill's supporters is caused by a clash of narratives. However, though mutually inconsistent, each narrative reinforced quite different views of the world; one where Hill's actions were evil and unjustified, and the other where his actions were a legitimate, indeed God-inspired response to a heinous situation.

4.3 Cassie Bernall

The clash of narratives occurs in a different form in the case of Cassie Bernall, one of the victims of the Columbine Massacre. On 20 April 1999, two students at Columbine High School, Littleton, Colorado went on a shooting spree with shotguns, killing 12 students and one teacher, as well as injuring a further 21, before shooting themselves. The twentieth casualty of the gunmen was Cassie

Bernall, who along with 51 other students and four school staff, was hiding in the library. In a now famous exchange, one of the gunmen on finding her under a desk reportedly asked if she believed in God. When she said, 'Yes', she was shot dead. Very soon afterwards, Cassie was acclaimed as a martyr in newspapers and websites. Her mother, Misty Bernall, released a book, *She Said Yes: The Unlikely Martyrdom of Cassie Bernall*, recounting how her daughter had been a troubled teenager struggling with drugs and alcohol until she was dramatically converted to Christianity. The story resulted in an upsurge of membership of religious youth groups inspired by Cassie's example. In the retelling of Cassie's story, we also see the development of a limited hagiography also present in the Hill narratives. However, in distinction to 'Lives of Saints', hagiography is not a necessary part of a martryology, as we will see.

A few weeks after the massacre, doubt was cast on the veracity of the account of the exchange between Cassie and the gunman. The story had originally come from one survivor, Craig Scott, but two other accounts soon emerged. In one version, Cassie was saying, 'Dear God. Dear God. Why is this happening? I just want to go home'. The gunman, Dylan Klebold, then slammed his hand on the table, yelling 'Peekaboo' and shot her without any further words being exchanged. The third version has another student, Valeen Schnurr, interacting with Klebold:

Schnurr was down on her hands and knees bleeding, already hit by 34 shotgun pellets, when one of the killers approached her. She was saying, 'Oh, my God, oh, my God, don't let me die', and he asked her if she believed in God. She said yes; he asked why. 'Because I believe and my parents brought me up that way', she said. He reloaded, but didn't shoot again. She crawled away.[18]

The investigators believe this latter account to be the most likely 'historical reconstruction'. However, the first, with Cassie saying, 'Yes', is the dominant narrative. Many accounts frame Cassie's death in terms of American 'culture wars' between Christianity and secularism, and it is secular websites which are often found to vigorously challenge the 'official' martyr record. These claims and counter-claims (martyr and anti-martyr narratives) reinforce the conflicted context in which the story is told. The actual historical situation really no longer matters. Cassie Bernall did not choose to become a martyr; martyrs do not control their own stories. Indeed, a potential martyr cannot guarantee he or she will be remembered as such. Much of the fear that the execution of Saddam Hussein would transform him into a martyr has not come to pass.

Many people have been killed for a cause, but not all become martyrs. Nineteen other students were murdered in Columbine, yet only one is remembered as a martyr. Four other members of Bonhoeffer's family were murdered, yet he alone is commemorated as a martyr. To become a martyr, a particular death needs to be recounted in a certain way; it requires a martyr narrative. In many ways, the central character becomes relatively unimportant.

Martyrology requires conflict – real or perceived. Martyr stories are told in order to make a difference, to advance a cause, or provoke a reaction, either in the minds, attitudes or behaviours of the 'persecutors' or 'persecuted'. This conflict may be the culture wars into which the stories of the deaths of Cassie Bernall and Paul Hill are located. Although Hill did consciously see himself in that conflict, Bernall did not. The dislocation of the martyr hero from the conflict their story addresses is taken a stage further in the retelling of the brutal murder of 21-year-old Matthew Shepard. In this case, there is no religious contribution to the actual death, but the narratives of his death take on religious significance, creating a powerful and significant gay martyr act.

4.4 Matthew Shepard

Matthew Shepard was a gay 21-year-old political science student at the University of Wyoming. In the early hours of 7 October 1998, Shepard met two other men in a bar in Laramie, Wyoming. After offering him a ride in a car, they robbed Shepard, tied him to a fence in a remote area, brutally beat him causing horrific injuries, and left him bleeding profusely in freezing temperatures. He was found by chance some 18 hours later by a passing cyclist, and rushed to hospital in Fort Collins. His injuries were too severe to treat, and he never regained consciousness. Matthew died on 12 October 1998.

Shepard's brutal murder was one of several gay murders in the States that year, and there have been many more since. Yet something about the retelling of this particular story has caused Matthew to be remembered in a way in which others have not. The reasons for this are not particularly clear, and reporters have speculated that it may have been the particular brutality of the attack, the fact it took place in such a small town, or the innocent features of his profile. In any case, while Shepard lay in a coma on life support, President Bill Clinton condemned the attack and promised hate crime legislation, while churches held candlelight vigils. His death coincided with the first day of National Gay Awareness Week, which placed the story of his death within the struggle (or conflict) to stop violence and discrimination against lesbian and gay people.

However, it is perhaps the fact he was left to die on a wooden fence which chimed with a graphic and instantly recognizable image on the American mind, and has caused his story to find particular resonance worldwide. The cyclist who found him remarked that he mistook him for a scarecrow, and connections with the crucifixion naturally followed. At his funeral his godfather made the parallel explicit:

> There is an image seared upon my mind when I reflect upon Matt on that wooden crossrail fence.. However, I have found a different image to replace that with and that is the image of another man, almost 2,000 years ago . . . When I concentrate on the Son of God being crucified, only then can I be released from the bitterness and anger I feel.[19]

Clinton introduced hate crime legislation named after Matthew, and though it stalled under George W. Bush, it has recently been passed under Barak Obama. Film makers, playwrights, artists, and songwriters have all taken up Shepherd's story, many taking up the image of the crucifixion imagery, such as iconographer, William Hart McNichols, whose icon is accompanied by the words:

Covered with blood,
save where the tears ran down,
that's how the officer who found him
described him.
More scarecrow than human.
Hung on a cross.
Left to die.
Despised.
Rejected.
The object of ridicule, oppression and hate.

The Passion of Matthew.
Another echo from the book of Isaiah.
Another victim of hate.
Dear Lord, how long?

In many reports, websites, and memorials, there is a noticeable lack of detail about Matthew's life. His iconic death overshadows everything else. However, Shepard's mother, disturbed by the comparison to Jesus, gave a frank interview with *Vanity Fair* in which she stated,

> You must understand, it's like putting him on a pedestal that just won't work. I'm concerned that if people find out he wasn't a saint, they'll be disappointed or angry or hate him.

Melanie Thernstrom, the author of the piece, perceptively noted that

> The mythologizing of Matthew – his overnight transformation into a national and international symbol – has left him oddly faceless. No one has seemed interested in publishing the details of his life – as if they would detract from his martyrdom.

Her article seeks to reveal something of the 'real' Matthew Shepard. However, as we have seen, martyr narratives tend to dispense with such details. Nothing about Matthew's life will alter the significance of his death. To put it bluntly, the Matthew Shepard of the martyr act is not the Matthew Shepard his parents buried. While saints require a 'life', martyrs simply need a death.

Shepard was not a gay rights activist, and never intended to die for a gay cause, but the narratives of his death have created Matthew Shepard, the martyr. His depression, the details of his life, his HIV positive status are simply not important in these narratives. Contrary to his mother's fears, the fact that Matthew was not a saint makes no difference to the way people think about him. Rather, the fact he was gay and murdered, and that his death has provoked and inspired change, makes him a gay martyr and a gay Christ figure. Matthew's death has become a death *for* others.

4.5 Neda Solton

A similarly unintended but significant death for a movement is found in the recent accidental shooting of Neda Solton. In the pro-democracy protests in Iran of June 2009, a 26-year-old philosophy student was shot in the chest. Neda Salehi Agha Solton became the face of the struggle as a short video of her final moments was posted on YouTube and watched by millions. The footage of her death is a mere 40 seconds long and shows her being helped to the ground after she was shot in the chest by a stray bullet. A man's voice is heard to comfort her, gently telling her not to be afraid. Her eyes are clearly seen to roll sideways as she loses consciousness. As blood begins to stream from her nose and mouth the scene becomes frantic. Agitated voices are heard in vain urging her not to die. Despite Iranian state media not mentioning her death, the mobile phone footage quickly spread around the world, transforming an ordinary woman into a martyr for freedom.

The following day, crowds marched bearing placards, 'I am Neda', in response to the pictures, while others proclaimed her 'the Angel of Iran'. Joe Joseph of *The Times* called it an iconic image like the nameless student standing before a tank in Tiananmen Square or the young girl running naked down a road burnt by a napalm bomb in Vietnam,[20] to which could be added the self-immolation of Thich Quang Duc. Recognizing the potency of this 'martytrdom', the Iranian authorities instructed the family to remove posters of Nada, and even the black mourning flags from their house, and denied her a public funeral. Stories suggesting the video was a forgery began to circulate immediately. However as reporter Martin Fletcher wrote the day after the shooting:

> The authenticity of the video, and the source of the bullet, cannot be verified independently but that hardly matters anymore because millions of Iranians and hundreds of millions of others around the world firmly believe the story to be true.[21]

By all accounts, Neda was not part of the protest, but became caught up in the traffic chaos caused by the demonstration. Nonetheless, in her martyrology, she is subsumed into the struggle between the State and the pro-democracy cause. Similarly the State appears to promote or at least sanction an anti-martyr narrative by refusing any public displays of mourning for Neda. Although under government security, her grave has been vandalized twice, demonstrating a concerted effort to attack her story. Although essentially a secular martyr, like Shepard, some of the language and imagery of her martyrdom stands within a rich religious tradition. Again, were it not for someone capturing the death of Neda, she would have died anonymously, and Iran would be looking for another martyr.

4.6 Independence Day

For our final example of martyrdom we turn to film. There are many examples of Noble Death in films: Spock in the *Wrath of Khan*; the astronauts in *Deep Impact*; Fox in *Wanted* to name a few. Although fictitious, films reflect the values of the intended audience. Like all drama, they depend on the audience fastening their sympathies on particular characters. My final example, Roland Emmerich's *Independence Day* (1996) contains an example of a redemptive Noble Death. This death is also an example not only of a suicide, but a suicide killer, but one whose actions presume the sympathy of a Western audience.

In the film, an alien mother ship enters the earth's orbit on 2 July from which begins an invasion of the earth with devastating destructive consequences. Over the next two days, various attempts to repel the attack, including the use of nuclear missiles, fail. On Independence Day (4 July), two pilots fly a captured alien craft back to the mother ship in order to plant a nuclear device on board, as well as upload a computer virus to disable the shields of the other alien ships attacking the earth. The upload is successful, but even with disabled shields the aliens appear to have enough fire power to repel the defence aircraft. A crop duster, Russell Casse, who has volunteered to take part in the mission, possesses the final missile, but his firing mechanism jams at the critical moment. Casse has been thus far presented as a failed father with an alcohol addiction, whose life had fallen apart after an alleged alien abduction. His children had effectively disowned him, but in his death he finds redemption. He deliberately flies his aircraft into the schism at the bottom of the alien ship from which it was about to unleash its own attack on the earth.

RUSSELL
Do me one favor . . .
OFFICER
Who is that guy?
MIGUEL
Russell!
Miguel races over to the microphone, attempts to grab it.
RUSSELL
. . . tell my children I love them very much.
Russell nears the schism, a hail of alien firepower erupting around him.
MIGUEL
Dad! No!
Russell smiles at being called 'Dad'.
RUSSELL
I've got to, kid. You were always better at taking care of them than I was anyways.
Russell turns off his radio as he banks upward towards the open schism. The climb is steep, and the bi-wing nearly stalls out.
Suddenly the bright lights vanish and the beam begins to form.
Russell's bi-wing just makes it inside the open schism and disappears from view.

Russell detonates his bomb inside the alien craft and it is destroyed. In his final act, he redeems his failure as a father, and saves the world by destroying the enemy. His death also demonstrates the Western mind does not disapprove of suicide killers per se; we simply have to buy the particular martyrological conflict narrative, which turns a shared enemy into a legitimate target.

5 CONCLUSION

We have examined martyr narratives, observing they interpret not only the death of an individual, but also place that death within a larger conflict, whether real or imagined. This conflict can be political, religious, local, or cosmic (or even intergalactic). We have located some of the martyr tradition within the locus of ancient Noble Death tradition, particularly death *for* others. More controversially, we have seen that the one who dies at his own hand is not necessarily debarred from the accolade of martyr; neither is the one who kills others in dying, so long as the narrators of the martyrology agree the target is a legitimate enemy. Above all, I have argued that martyrdom is not a category that can be defined. Martyrdom is essentially created when a narrative about a death is told in a particular way. The central character is not the most important element in the creation of martyrdom; it is the narrator.

We now turn to the world's three main religious traditions: Christianity, Judaism, and Islam, to examine ways in which they have understood and narrated death for their religions. First, we will examine various attitudes to death in early Christianity, arguing that even in the earliest church it was a contested term, and that later reflection on Christian martyrdom has covered a wide variety of practice, particularly an enthusiasm for death. Next, we look to ways in which early Christian martyrdom was interpreted. The first three chapters taken together provide a framework for examining martyrologies in later Christianity (Chapter 4), Judaism (Chapter 5), and Islam (Chapter 6).

CHAPTER 2

PERSECUTION AND MARTYRDOM IN EARLY CHRISTIANITY

1 PERSECUTION

From its beginning, Christianity was a religion that had to contend with the experience of suffering, persecution, and martyrdom. Indeed, William Bramley-Moore in his introduction to Foxe's *Book of Martyrs*, goes so far as to make the claim that 'the history of Christian martyrdom is, in fact, the history of Christianity itself'. Whilst this is somewhat overstated, early Christian religion developed in a time of political turbulence in Palestine. It experienced a traumatic split from Judaism, and its adherents faced suspicion from pagan neighbours. Christianity was a religion with no natural allies. Their worship of an executed criminal, novel rites, and exclusivity of worship, combined with their scorning state, city, and familial gods made Christians unpopular, so much so that Luke can write of Christianity, 'We know that everywhere it is spoken against' (Acts 28.22).[1]

1.1 Persecution in the New Testament

Persecution and the possibility of death form a backdrop to virtually the whole of the New Testament. Paul warns that believers will face persecution, which they must endure for the sake of the gospel. Paul describes his own suffering, often in graphic terms: he endures imprisonment; he has been beaten, lashed, and stoned.[2] It is the lot of apostles and messengers of Jesus to suffer hardship:

We are afflicted in every way, but not crushed; perplexed, but not driven to despair; persecuted, but not forsaken; struck down, but not destroyed; always carrying in the body the death of Jesus, so that the life of Jesus may also be manifested in our bodies. For while we live we are always being given up to death for Jesus' sake, so that the life of Jesus be manifested in our mortal flesh. So death is at work in us, but life in you. (2 Cor. 4.7–12)

Paul reflects a situation of suffering throughout many of his letters. He tells the young church at Thessalonica that they received the Word with both affliction and joy (1 Thess. 1.6), and that in their suffering, they have become imitators of the churches in Judea (2.14–16). He goes on to reflect in his writings that suffering can be beneficial: it makes one worthy (2 Thess. 1.5), produces endurance, character and hope (Rom. 5.3–5), inspires boldness (Phil. 1.14), and can bring others to repentance (2 Cor. 7.7–9). Paul expects his converts to suffer if they are faithful (Rom. 8.17; Phil. 1.29–30; 1 Cor. 4.9–13; 2 Cor. 6.4–10), for suffering demonstrates the legitimacy of the Church (Gal. 4.12–15; Phil. 1.3–7, 4.14–15; 1 Thess. 1.6, 3.1–5; cf. 2 Tim. 1.8). For Paul, the experience of suffering was something in which he could boast (2 Cor. 11.21–30, 12.10; Phil. 1.19–26), and when suffering came, the appropriate response was joyfulness (Rom. 12.2; 2 Cor. 6.10, 8.2, 13.9; Phil. 2.17, 4.4–6; Col 1.11, 24). After all, Jesus had said:

Blessed are you when people revile you and persecute you and utter all kinds of evil against you falsely, on my account. Rejoice and be exceedingly glad for your reward is great in the kingdom of heaven. (Matt. 5.11–12)

Similarly, the first Petrine epistle assumes a high level of background trouble for the Church. Peter's addressees, he tells them, suffer for righteousness (1 Pet. 3.13), and like the Church in Thessalonica, they share in the sufferings of the wider Church (5.9). He tells his readers that though they must suffer various trials, these trials will test the genuineness of their faith (1.6–7), but that this experience of suffering will lead to subsequent glory (1.10–11). He addresses converts who appear to be experiencing mistreatment (2.18–25), and urges that they do not retaliate (3.8–11). As we found in Paul and in the final beatitude, the appropriate response to such suffering is joy (1.6, 4.13–14).

The gospels too reflect experiences of suffering.

But take heed to yourselves; for they will deliver you up to councils; and you will be beaten in synagogues; and you will stand before governors and kings for my sake, to bear testimony before them. And the gospel must first be preached to all nations. And when they bring you to trial and deliver you up, do not be anxious beforehand what you are to say; but say whatever is given you in that hour, for it is not you who speak, but the Holy Spirit. And brother will deliver up brother to death. And the father his child, and children will rise against parents and have them put to death; and you will be hated by all for my name's sake. But the one who endures to the end will be saved. (Mk 13.9–13)

These words have probably been shaped to reflect the experiences of some early Christians. They indicate suffering coming from both Jews and Gentiles. In addition, pressure also appears to come from family members, and indeed, there is an unmistakable anti-familial strand within the Gospels.[3] If taken at face value, these words appear to indicate that hatred of Christians will be universal, and may result in capital punishment.

In the Parable of the Sower, Jesus warns that in the face of persecution, many will fall away and desert (Mk 4.17//Mt. 13.20–21). So, in order to be a true disciple, believers will have to 'take up the cross' and follow behind him (Mk 8.34). It is not clear how literally this statement is to be taken, neither is it apparent whether or not Jesus expected his immediate followers to suffer and die with him. Nonetheless, the call to lose one's life is well attested in the tradition, and is found in the synoptic tradition, the Q tradition (Lk. 14.27), John (12.25), and Thomas (*Gospel of Thomas* 55), increasing the possibility this was a genuine word of Jesus directed at his immediate followers to join him in dying in Jerusalem. That physical death was originally envisaged is perhaps strengthened by Luke's alteration to the text giving it a less literal and more spiritual meaning: 'take up the cross *daily*' (Lk. 9.27). The expectation that believers may be martyred is also reflected in Jesus' warning that disciples should not fear those who can kill the body, but instead the one who can destroy the body and soul (Mt. 10.26//Lk. 12.2). Of course, if it was Jesus' expectation that his followers would join in him dying in Jerusalem, then it was one his immediate disciples failed to meet. However, as we shall see, it was a call which others would take up enthusiastically.

Despite much of the New Testament reflecting a fairly constant level of persecution that believers will suffer or are already experiencing, there are very few actual instances of martyrdom. Despite the list of martyrs in Hebrews 11, and the injunction to go and suffer like Jesus (13.12–13), the author says of his current readers, 'In your struggle against sin you have not yet resisted to the point of shedding your blood' (12.4). Only in Acts and Revelation do we find examples of Christian martyrs in the New Testament. In Acts, Stephen is killed by a Jewish mob (7.54–8.1) while James is executed by Herod (12.1–5).

When we turn to the book of Revelation, the language of martyrdom is found throughout. Christians are called to be faithful to death (2.10); there are already martyrs under the altar (6.9); there is a vast crowd of martyrs (7.9–17, 14.1–5); two witnesses will be slain (11.1–14); the saints conquered the dragon by not loving their lives to death (12.10–11); the Beast slays faithful Christians (13.15); so that all who die in the Lord are blessed (14.13); those who have slain Christians are punished (16.4–6), the harlot is drunk with the blood of the saints and martyrs of Jesus (17.6); and those beheaded for Jesus will reign for 1,000 years (20.4). The author of the Apocalypse creates a narrative that appears to expect the deaths of all its readers. However, when it comes to those who have actually died for the faith, John has only a single name, Antipas, 'who was killed among you, where Satan dwells' (2.13). Therefore, although there is a strong backdrop of persecution throughout the New Testament, the body count at that point was low. However, documents like the Apocalypse rightly predicted this would not be the case for long.

1.2 Pressure from the Synagogue

The earliest persecutions of the Church came from the synagogue, which regarded the Jesus movement as a heretical group.[4]

And on that day [of Stephen's death] a great persecution arose against the church in Jerusalem; and they were all scattered throughout the region of Judea and Samaria, except the apostles . . .

. . . Saul, still breathing threats and murder against the disciples of the Lord, went to the high priest and asked him for letters to the synagogues at Damascus, so that if he found any belonging to the Way, men or women, he might bring them bound to Jerusalem. (Acts 8.1, 9.1–2)

Luke's account of Paul's persecution of the Church is corroborated by Paul's own testimony (1 Cor. 15.9; Gal. 1.13). But Paul, himself, would later find opposition in the synagogue, where he claims to have been lashed no fewer than five times at the hands of the Jews (2 Cor. 11.24). Opposition to the Christ movement from the synagogue is highly schematized throughout Acts, generally taking the pattern of Paul visiting the synagogue, meeting hostility, and then preaching to the Gentiles with more success. The ordered pattern of Jewish behaviour renders it historically suspicious, especially the unlikely Jewish complaint made by representatives of the Thessalonian synagogue, that Paul is preaching an alternative king to Caesar (Acts 17.7).

Nonetheless, it is clear there was a good deal of trauma experienced by Christ-believing Jews, who found themselves in some cases expelled from the synagogue. John's story of the healing of the blind man almost certainly reflects the current or past experiences of the Johannine Christians at the hands of synagogue communities. After questioning the man, the Jews do not believe he had been blind from birth, so interrogate his parents, but his parents refused to testify 'because they feared the Jews, for the Jews had already agreed that if anyone should confess him to be Christ, he was to be put out of the synagogue' (Jn 9.22). The interrogation of the blind man continues with the accusation put that the man is one of Jesus' disciples, contrasting with their discipleship of Moses (9.28), until finally, the Jews pass judgement: 'You were born in utter sin . . . ' and they cast him out (9.34). In its historical context, the punishment makes no sense, but instead reflects a period after the Temple's destruction when Jews were asking the question of what it meant to be Jewish, and this, for at least some synagogues, excluded those who confessed Jesus. Although disputed, the twelfth of the first-century Jewish benedictions, the curse on the heretics (*Birkat ha-minim*), may have been specifically directed against Jewish Christians, and resulted in their exclusion from the synagogue.

For the apostates let there be no hope. And let the arrogant government be speedily uprooted in our days. Let the *Nazarenes* and the *heretics* be destroyed in a moment. And let them be blotted out of the Book of Life and not be inscribed together with the righteous. Blessed art thou, O Lord, who humblest the arrogant.

Ominously, the gospel also anticipates the rivalry between Jew and Christian will result in bloodshed: 'They will put you out of the synagogues; indeed, the hour is coming when whoever kills you will think he is offering a service to God' (Jn 16.2).

Later texts do indeed accuse the Jews of being involved with the State in the persecution of Christians, notably in the *Martyrdom of Polycarp*, where the Jews not only help build the fire which will burn the saint (13.1), but instigate the total destruction of the corpse, so there would be nothing for the Christians to collect and bury (17.2). The portrayal of the Jews collaborating with the Romans to kill Polycarp is an echo of the way in which the New Testament incriminates the Jews in the death of Jesus.

Again, we must be wary of the historicity of such accounts. The split between Church and Synagogue is not clear cut, and Jewish Christians are found well beyond the fourth century. There is no doubt Christ-believing Jews did face hostility and even death at the hands of fellow Jews. But however traumatic the effect of the tension and eventual split between Church and Synagogue, it is persecution at the hands of Rome that is most significant in the developing experience and Christian theologies of martyrdom.[5]

1.3 Roman Persecutions

When we consider Christian experiences of persecution at the hands of Rome, we are immediately confronted with a question. Just why did Rome persecute the Christians? For the Christians, the answer was clear: they suffered for the name of Jesus. As they had been forewarned, loyalty to Jesus meant hostility from the world; they would be hated by all. Experiences of persecution therefore confirmed this worldview. However, the legal basis on which Christians were challenged is not clear. There is no evidence of Christianity being explicitly proscribed in any way until well into the third century. Yet unless the New Testament is entirely divorced from the experience of the early Church, there was a fear and expectation among Christians that they would be brought before governors and kings.

Yet, despite fears of a hostile world, we find in the New Testament conflicting attitudes to the State. In the Gospels, there are positive views of Romans (e.g. Lk. 7.1–10, 20.19–26), and the role they play in the death of Jesus is downplayed. Paul's famous and problematic assertion that the State is the servant of God (Rom. 13.1–7) is hardly hostile, and later epistles urges Christians to 'honour the emperor' (1 Pet. 2.17), and to pray for all kings (1 Tim. 2.1). Yet at the same time, the State could be the Beast and the Whore of Babylon, bent on the persecution and destruction of the Christians (Rev. passim). Even Paul, who is so positive in Romans, does confront the claims made for the emperor, and attacks the main achievement of the empire, the *pax et securitas*: 'When people say peace and security, sudden destruction will come upon them' (1 Thess. 5.2–3). Despite some obvious conceptual confrontation, there does appear to be a conscious effort on the part of some Christians to live peaceably with the State. For much of the first few centuries, Christians were fairly successful in this aim, but from time to time, persecution flared up.

The first bout of severe persecution came under Nero (54–68) from 64 to 68 CE. Although restricted to Rome, these few years set the context for future thinking about persecution and martyrdom. However, this affliction had little to do with Christian beliefs and practices. After the great fire of Rome, Nero, in order to remove the suspicion that he had himself started the fire, sought to pin the blame on the Christians. Tacitus, writing around half a century after the event, describes the events.

But all human efforts, all the lavish gifts of the emperor and propitiations of the gods did not banish the sinister belief that the conflagration was the result of an order. Consequently, to get rid of the report, Nero fastened the guilt and inflicted the most exquisite tortures on a class hated for their abominations, called Christians by the populace. Christus, from whom the name had its origin, suffered the extreme penalty during the reign of Tiberius at the hands of one of our procurators, Pontius Pilate, and a deadly superstition, thus checked for the moment, again broke out not only in Judea, the first source of the evil, but also in the City, where all things hideous and shameful from every part of the world meet and become popular. Accordingly, an arrest was first made of all who confessed,

then, upon their information, an immense multitude was convicted, not so much for the crime of arson as of their hatred
of the human race. Mockery of every sort was added to their
deaths. Covered with the skins of beasts, they were torn by dogs
and perished, or were nailed to crosses, or were doomed to the
flames and burnt, to serve as a nightly illumination when daylight had expired. Nero had offered his gardens for the spectacle, and put on a show in the circus, mingling with the people
in the dress of a charioteer or standing up in a chariot. Hence,
even for criminals who deserved extreme and exemplary punishment, there arose a feeling of compassion, for it was not, as it
seemed, for the public good, but to glut one man's cruelty, that
they were being destroyed. (Tacitus, *Annals* 15.44)

Assuming the accuracy of at least the main points of Tacitus'
account, it is noteworthy just how easily the populace was willing
to believe the Christians' guilt. It is clear from Tacitus' description of the Christians that he held them in some contempt. He says
Christians are 'hated for their abominations' and practice 'deadly
superstition'. This, he maintains, is a popular view, and although
he appears to know very little of the practices of Christianity, and
openly doubts any Christian involvement in the conflagration, he
still believes they deserve 'extreme and exemplary punishment' for
their 'hatred of the human race'.

It is this final charge of misanthropy which will become a recurring theme in persecution literature. We will see that pagan critics of
Christianity are almost always ignorant of its beliefs and practices,
yet hatred of the human race, disloyalty to Rome, and atheism are
frequent motifs. Many of these accusations were also made against
Jews; their exclusivity of religious practice, disregard of the state
gods, and refusal to eat with non-Jews rendered them suspicious.
Such idiosyncrasies could be just about tolerated in a religion with
a long pedigree, and Judaism was a *religio licita* (a licensed religion).
However, the novelty of Christianity made Christians vulnerable to
attack, particularly when their founder was a criminal executed by
a Roman procurator.

Some of these themes are also found in Pliny the Younger's
famous letter to the Emperor Trajan. Pliny, who was governor of
Pontus 111–113 CE, wrote to Trajan for guidance on a case where
individuals had been denounced to him as Christians.

Meanwhile, in the case of those who were denounced to me as Christians, I have observed the following procedure: I interrogated these as to whether they were Christians; those who confessed I interrogated a second and a third time, threatening them with punishment; those who persisted I ordered executed. For I had no doubt that whatever the nature of their creed, stubbornness and inflexible obstinacy surely deserve to be punished . . . Those who denied that they were or had been Christians, when they invoked the gods in words dictated by me, offered prayer with incense and wine to your image which I had ordered to be brought for this purpose together with statues of the gods, and moreover cursed Christ – none of which those who are really Christians it is said can be forced to do – these I thought should be discharged. Others named by the informer declared that they were Christians, but then denied it, asserting that they had been but had ceased to be some three years before, others many years, some as much as twenty-five years. They all worshipped your image and the statutes of the gods, and cursed Christ. (Pliny, *Epistles* 10.96)

As with Tacitus, Pliny does not know what the Christians do, nor is he sure whether being a Christian is an offence. He goes on to explain he has been 'not a little hesitant as to . . . whether the name itself, even without offences, or only the offences associated with the name is to be punished'. Even without detailed knowledge of their practices, Pliny finds their inflexible obstinacy objectionable, and has no doubt this alone deserves to be punished. He later goes on to describe the religion as a 'depraved excessive superstition', categorizing Christianity with the notorious Bachanalia cult, which had been outlawed in 186 BCE. Again, as with Tacitus, Pliny is not sure for what Christians should be punished, but he is nonetheless convinced that they ought to be punished for something.

The principle reason for writing to the emperor is to confirm his preference for 'rehabilitation'; he is unsure what to do about those who claim no longer to be Christians. His practice had been to test whether or not they are telling the truth by making them pass a series of tests: sacrificing to the gods, worshipping the image of the emperor, and cursing Christ, since he has heard that those who remain Christians cannot be forced to do such things. If they passed the test, he freed them. Trajan agrees with Pliny's practice.

You observed proper procedure, my dear Pliny, in sifting the cases of those who had been denounced to you as Christians. For it is not possible to lay down any general rule to serve as a kind of fixed standard. They are not to be sought out; if they are denounced and proved guilty, they are to be punished, with this reservation, that whoever denies that he is a Christian and really proves it – that is, by worshiping our gods – even though he was under suspicion in the past, shall obtain pardon through repentance. But anonymously posted accusations ought to have no place in any prosecution. For this is both a dangerous kind of precedent and out of keeping with the spirit of our age.

It has been incorrectly inferred from Pliny and Trajan's correspondence that Christianity was an illegal religion at this point, and that sacrifice to the emperor was enforced. Nor is it correct to conclude that Christians were persecuted simply for being Christians. It is clear there is a series of assumed, though unspecified crimes, behind the name. The new religion looked very much like secret societies that had been banned under Trajan. Had Christianity really been specifically outlawed, then Trajan's relaxed attitude, to the point of refusing the legitimacy of anonymous accusations, would be inexplicable.

Nonetheless, it is clear there is deep mistrust and suspicion over the activities of the Christians. Their secret meetings at daybreak, and perhaps misunderstandings of 'love feasts' or 'eating the flesh of the Son', led to accusations of immorality and cannibalism. Some of the claims of what Christians did at their meetings are hysterically extravagant, such as is contained in a second-century novel:

At that moment another naked man arrived . . . He threw the boy's body on its back, struck it, opened it, removed the heart and placed it over the fire . . . When it was sufficiently prepared, he distributed portions of it to the initiates.[6]

Other stories of cannibalism and incest abound, but as well as charges of immorality, Christians were also accused of atheism. This was a more serious charge which could also lead to accusations of destabilizing the empire. For the Romans, the 'crime' so far as the early Christians were guilty of one, was not so much religious but political, although in the context of the Graeco-Roman world, such a distinction is difficult to make.

In many regards, the Roman Empire was a multicultural achievement. To be sure, this achievement was backed up by an impressive army, but conquered peoples were encouraged to maintain their own social and religious identities. The Roman pantheon was flexible enough to absorb any number of family, city, or national deities, and so new peoples to the empire would add Roman deities to their own, and indeed contribute their local gods to the Roman panoply. There was no reason to resist this arrangement since Rome's superior forces demonstrated the prowess of their gods. In a diverse empire with many strange peoples and gods, the state religions, together with the figurehead of the emperor, were the glue that bound the empire together.

State religions and the emperor cult became a means by which cities and the wealthy could win themselves recognition and prestige. Cities could build temples and statues, or compete to win the Imperial Games to outdo their neighbours and win kudos from Rome, rather in the same way that today much effort and money is spent to win the right to host events such as the Olympic Games. The emperor cult, despite the impression given in the Apocalypse, was not universally enforced throughout the empire in the first century. Even the requirement to offer sacrifice to the emperor in Pliny's letter is not because it is a compulsory activity, but because it is something Pliny has heard Christians will not do. The emperor cult was a way in which the central power in Rome could be represented to a vast empire, and so statues, temples, and coins – the 'hardware' of the cult – reminded the people of the peace and stability Rome offered, as well as its power to those tempted to revolt.

However, this is not to say that the populace did not gain in other ways from the cults. The wealthy could advance socially through sponsoring building projects or buying priesthoods. The poor could participate in festivals, which offered a rare opportunity for eating meat. Slaves could claim sanctuary from cruel masters both in temples and at the statues of the emperor. Therefore, all people, at least to some extent, had a stake in the local and state cults. The Christians threatened a system in which all had at least some benefit, and this was unpopular.

At the centre of the empire was the emperor, who existed in a world between humans and the gods. He in some way represented the people to the gods, and also the gods to the people. The peoples of the East who, since Alexander the Great, had been used to a ruler cult, where a strong leader was accorded divine honours, enthusiastically embraced the emperor cult. The West was rather more cautious, and many emperors had to write to curb enthusiastic excessive honours. Nevertheless, much of the language used to speak of the emperor overlapped with Christian acclamations for God and Christ, which in addition to an inherited antipathy of idolatry from Judaism, caused Christians to withdraw from participating in State religion.

For the Romans, the emperor was lord, saviour, and even God. Although it was generally accepted emperors became divine on death, citizens to the East often accorded the emperors divine honours while they were still living. Some emperors were ambivalent towards these divine honours, although others were less reticent in accepting them.

> On being reminded that he [Caligula] had surpassed the heights of both princes and of kings, he began . . . to lay claim to divine majesty for himself . . . He made it his business to have statues of the gods . . . including the Olympian Zeus brought from Greece, so as to remove their heads and replace them with his own . . . He also set up a separate temple to his own godhead with priests and sacrificial victims . . . In this temple stood a golden life-sized statue, and it was dressed each day in clothing such as he himself wore. Very rich persons obtained in turn the office of master of the priesthood . . . by offering the highest bids. (Seutonius, *Life of Caligula*, 22)

For the Christians, God was the supreme ruler, and Jesus, the king of kings and lord of lords. Christian theology and language competed with Roman ideology, although it is unclear the extent to which Romans would have been aware of the details of Christians' beliefs. All they saw was a suspicious secret sect whose members refused to take part in honouring the emperor and participating in State religion. This was no small matter; social cohesion, civic order, art, sport, and the safety of the empire depended on the worship of the god. The *pax romana* depended on the *pax deorum*. To upset the gods was to invite potential disaster upon the empire. At moments of crisis, emperors such as Decius and Valerian tried to enforce a return to traditional Roman values, with severe consequences for the Christians.

Since the gods were generally recognized to offer protection to all from family to State, to denounce them was effectively to wish ill on their neighbours, city, and state. Tertullian reflects the perceived danger alienating the gods could bring on the lives of the populous:

> [Pagans] suppose that the Christians are the cause of every public disaster, every misfortune that happens to the people. If the Tiber overflows or the Nile does not, if there is a drought or an earthquake, a famine or a pestilence, at once the cry goes up, 'The Christians to the lions'. (Tertullian, *Apology* 40)

Romans simply could not understand why Christians refused to take part in cultic activities. Rejection of the gods was absurd and threatened the fabric of society and the heavens. This is why Christians were viewed with suspicion. Though the violence against them was local and sporadic, it was nonetheless real, and could be deadly, such as in Lyons in 177 CE and Scillitia around 188 CE. However, for the most part, the Church enjoyed relative peace and grew rapidly throughout the empire. However, as we move into the third and fourth centuries, persecution becomes more organized and systematic.

1.4 Later Persecutions

The relative peace Christianity enjoyed in the empire came to an end when Decius (249–251) became emperor. A few decades earlier, Septimius Severus (193–211) outlawed conversion to either Judaism or Christianity. It was at this time Origen's father, encouraged by his son, was martyred. Origen was spared because his mother hid his clothes, concerned that he would hand himself over for arrest. In North Africa, two of the most prominent Christian women martyrs, Perpetua and Felicitas, met their deaths.

By the mid third century, the empire was facing instability with its borders at the Rhone, Danube, and Euphrates, all threatened with breach. Origen describes how a mob took this fear of instability out on the Christians of Alexandria in 248 CE, blaming the atheist Christians for the threat posed by the Goths (Origen, *Celsus* 3.15). A year later, the Emperor, Philip (244–249), died in a disastrous defeat at the Rhine at the hands of Decius. Decius sought to return the empire to traditional Roman values, including the worship of the old gods, and so ordered all citizens of the empire to sacrifice. Whilst this edict had a profound effect on the Church, this was not designed to be a specific attack on Christianity. There was no requirement that citizens should abandon worship of their own gods. Sacrificing to the gods was simply regarded as the base-line gesture any loyal citizen of the empire could make. The sacrifice was enforced by the issuing of a certificate (*libellus*) to all who participated.

By the time of the Decian edict, Christianity had become widespread, and even in some places was a means of social advancement. However, the resolve which had characterized the Church during periods of sporadic persecution evaporated against a sustained campaign to force religious conformity. Faced with a choice between loyalty to the empire and loyalty to their religion, many Christians offered sacrifice. From Cyprian's account, it appears that many Christians not only lapsed, but did so eagerly even before being forced. To make matters worse, he laments that the official had to turn Christians away such was the number of those who wished to sacrifice.

From some – ah, misery! – all these things have fallen away, and have passed from memory. They indeed did not wait to be apprehended before they ascended, or to be interrogated before they denied. Many were conquered before the battle, prostrated before the attack. Nor did they even leave it to be said for them, that they seemed to sacrifice to idols unwillingly. They ran to the market-place of their own accord; freely they hastened to death, as if they had formerly wished it, as if they would embrace an opportunity now given which they had always desired. How many were put off by the magistrates at that time, when evening was coming on; how many even asked that their destruction might not be delayed! (*On the Lapsed*, 8)

While there were prominent martyrs-bishops – notably Fabian of Rome, Babylas of Antioch, and Alexander of Jerusalem (who died in prison) – other bishops and clergy, most notoriously Euctemon of Smyrna, not only sacrificed, but also encouraged others to do likewise (*M. Pionius* 15).

The effect of mass defection had a devastating effect on the morale of the Church. It had happened previously, as Pliny's letter indicates, and also at Lyons in 177 CE when, in the face of persecution instigated by a mob, many turned cowardly; those, the writer describes as being untrained and unready for combat. However, this text goes on to describe how not only were such cowards shamed, but some of them, when they saw the resolve of the martyrs, changed their minds and offered renewed confession (*M. Lyons* 45). The historicity of this account may be doubted, but it is noteworthy that in the accounts from the Decian persecution of desertion, there is no such positive spin put on these events. In *The Martyrdom of Pionius*, the fact of the desertion by what appears to be the majority is simply acknowledged.

[You ask] why was it that some, without any pressure, came to sacrifice of their own accord? But would you condemn all Christians because of these? Consider the present life as though it were a threshing-floor. Which pile is the larger, the chaff or the wheat? For when the farmer comes to clear the threshing-floor with his winnowing-fan, the chaff, being lighter, is easily carried off by the wind. (*M. Pionius* 14)

Pionuis simply argues that Christianity is not invalidated by the actions of the deniers. He puts the failure down to sinfulness in the community, and regards the persecutions as a test of faith which many simply failed (*M. Pionius* 12).

The persecution lost momentum when Decian again turned his attention to the northern frontier, where he died in 251. However, the peace the Church was to enjoy for a short time from the outside was in marked contrast to turmoil within. Thousands of Christians had sacrificed to the gods and were excommunicated. The lapsed lost social as well as spiritual benefits of Church membership, not least provision for the poor and burial, and so a great many presented themselves for restoration. Those who had fled were criticized, and Cyprian had to defend himself from those who accused him of abandoning his flock. Whereas Tertullian had taught that those who fled persecution were cowards and apostates, Cyprian, who would later be martyred, defended those, like himself, who had fled, justifying his own absence as the 'exile' of a confessor (*Ep.* 8.1). Cyprian argued against easy restoration, not only of those who had sacrificed, but also those who had obtained a *libellus* through fraud or bribery. When the next bout of persecution broke out, Cyprian softened his stance, believing the lapsed Christians would do better inside than outside the Church.

Though initially well disposed to the Christians, Valerian (253–260) later became hostile to the Church, and in several edicts ordered the confiscation of goods and places of worship, and prohibited Christian gatherings. In the edict of 257, Christians were ordered to the mines; the next, in 258, prescribed death. This time Cyprian did not flee, and having first been exiled, he was martyred.

> The proconsul . . . said, 'the most reverend emperors have ordered you to perform the religious rites.' The Bishop Cyprian said: 'I will not' . . .
>
> Galerius Maximus . . . spoke as follows: 'You have long persisted in your sacrilegious views, and you have joined to yourself many other vicious men in a conspiracy. You have set yourself up as an enemy of the gods of Rome and of our religious practices; and the pious and venerable emperors Valerian and Gallienus Augisti and Valerian the most noble of Caesars have not been able to bring you back to the observance of their sacred rites . . . Cyprian is sentenced to die by the sword'.
>
> The Bishop Cyprian said: 'Thanks be to God!' (*Acts of Cyprian* 4.3–5.1)

As before, the charge was that Christianity was a destructive force in the empire. The Christians were enemies of the gods and the emperors. In short, their refusal to sacrifice to the gods and demonstrate sufficient loyalty to the emperors made them self-confessed enemies of the State.

The persecution came to an end when Valerian was captured and killed by the Persians at Edessa in 260. His son Gallienus (260–68) ended the persecution and restored confiscated property. Aside from soldier martyrs, such as Maximilian and Marcellus, from the end of the third century when Maximian (286–308) restored strict discipline among the ranks of the army, the next and most brutal repression of Christians occurred under Diocletian (284–305).

In February 303, the Christian sanctuary opposite the imperial palace at Numidia was razed. The next day, Diocletian issued an edict, specifically aimed at the Church, that all scriptures should be handed over and burnt, churches should be destroyed, Christians in the upper classes were to lose their status, and Christian freedmen returned to slavery. The impetus for the persecution is not clear. However, Diocletian had instigated religious reform in promoting the worship of the old Roman gods, and had ordered the burning of Manichean sacred writings a year earlier in Egypt. According to Lactantius, Diocletian, in contrast to Galerius, stopped short of the death penalty (*On the Death of the Persecutors* 11.8), although such restraint was probably ignored in some places, while in others, the edicts against the Christians may have been ignored altogether. Further edicts ordered the imprisonment of clergy, but also the release of those who were prepared to offer sacrifice. *The Martyrdom of Felix* reflects the popular punishment of burning, although he was eventually beheaded:

Magnilianus the Magistrate said to him, 'Are you Felix the Bishop?

Felix the Bishop said, 'I am'.

Magnilianus the Magistrate said, 'Hand over whatever books or parchments you have'.

Felix the Bishop said, 'I have some, but I will not hand them over.'

Magnilianus the Magistrate said, 'Hand over the books so they can be burned.'

Felix the Bishop said, 'It would be better for me to be burned than the holy writings.'

In 304, the fourth edict, issued by Diocletian's second, Galerius, ordered universal sacrifice, and many Christians, including large numbers of lay folk, lost their lives, beginning with the Martyrs of Caesarea, the sisters Agape, Chioné and Eirene, and Crispina. *The Martyrdom of Crispina* again reveals the incredulity at Christian refusal to sacrifice:

'Revere the religion of Rome, which is observed by our lords the unconquerable Caesars as well as ourselves.'

'I have told you again and again', replied Crispina, 'I am prepared to undergo any tortures that you wish to subject me to, rather than defile my soul with idols which are stones and the creations of men's hands'.

'You utter blasphemy', said Anullinus, 'in not honouring what is conducive to your safety'. (2.4)

Again we find pagan mystification at the Christians' refusal to sacrifice. Anullinus tries to explain to the martyr that the gods also protect her safety. A comment made by Celsus neatly captures this sense of credulity: 'If everyone followed the Christians' example and opposed the emperor, the result would be anarchy and everything would be destroyed – including Christian worship!' (*Contra Celsum* 8.68). For the pagans, Christian refusal to join in the cults was threatening not only to the empire, but also to the Christians themselves.

Nonetheless, as with previous persecutions, much of the leadership of the Church lapsed, which is noted in the same *Act*.

'I will have you beheaded', said the proconsul, 'if you will not obey the edicts of our lords the emperors. You will be forced to yield and obey them: *all the province of Africa has offered sacrifice* as you are well aware'. (1.7)

Another example of the laity outperforming their leadership occurs in the *Martyrdom of the Abitinians*. Despite the defection of their bishop, the Church in Abitina continued to hold services until they came to the notice of the authorities and the whole congregation was arrested and sent to Carthage for trial, and executed.

After the abdication of Diocletian and Maximian in May 305, persecution ended in the West, and although there were further persecutions in the East by 311, Galerius came to realize his attempts to move the Christians back to traditional religion had failed, and on his deathbed granted them toleration. In return he asked them to pray for his health and the State. Within two years, Constantine was emperor and Christianity was the favoured religion of the empire.

2 CHRISTIAN APPROACHES TO MARTYRDOM

We now turn to the way in which Christians responded to persecution. We have noted that until Decius, there was little in the way of official state-sponsored persecution. Nonetheless, the texts produced by Christians seem to imply the opposite. The State was the Beast of Revelation, the Whore of Babylon, who was drunk on the blood of the saints (Rev. 17.6). Even if, as appears to the case, relatively few Christians actually lost their lives before the Decian and Diocletian persecutions, so much were the martyrs celebrated, there exists the impression that martyrdom was waiting around the corner for just about every Christian.

Attitudes to and interpretations of martyrdom varied among the early Church from enthusiastic embrace to outright denial of its value. On one hand, there were groups who eschewed martyrdom completely, who saw no value in giving oneself over to death. Tertullian complains that when 'the faith is greatly agitated and the church on fire . . . then the Gnostics break out; then the Valentinians creep forth; then all the opponents of martyrdom bubble up'. Elaine Pagels has convincingly drawn a connection between attitudes to the death of Christ and attitudes to martyrdom. So the more 'Gnostic' Christian, who believed that Jesus did not in fact die on the cross, would be less likely to seek out martyrdom.[7] These groups argued that those who sought martyrdom were ignorant, witnessing only to themselves, and wrongfully believing God desired human sacrifice.

> The foolish – thinking [in] their heart if they confess, 'We are Christians', in word only, not with power, while giving themselves over to ignorance, to a human death, not knowing where they are going to, nor who Christ is, thinking that they will live, when really they are in error – hasten towards the authorities. They fall into their clutches because of the ignorance that is in them. (*Testament of Truth* 31.21–32.21)

There has been a long consensus that the correct attitude to martyrdom in the early Church was that Christians should not seek out martyrdom, but accept death when the opportunity presented itself. Although a more radical form of martyrdom has been noticed, where some Christians intentionally sought out or provoked their own death, it is criticized. Summing up the dominant scholarly position, Reasoner writes, 'It is an established tradition within *the Christianity which became identified as orthodox* that those who intentionally sought martyrdom would not be recognised as martyrs'.[8]

Indeed, we have already seen the way in which Clement criticizes those he believes too eager for death, dismissing their 'martyrdom' as futile, in strikingly similar language to the Gnostic criticism of 'orthdox' martyrdom (see above p. 7)! Similarly, in the *Martyrdom of Polycarp*, there is criticism of a certain Quintus, who after handing himself over to arrest, denied at the crucial moment.

There was a Phrygian named Quintus who had only recently come from Phrygia, and when he saw the wild animals he turned cowardly. Now he was the one who had given himself up and had forced some others to give themselves up voluntarily. With him the governor used many arguments and persuaded him to swear by the gods and offer sacrifice. This is the reason, brothers, that we do not approve of those who come forward of themselves: this is not the teaching of the gospel (4).

Here then are two influential Christian voices from the second and third centuries criticizing the practice of intentionally seeking out arrest, and this is the position which is taken by most commentators to be normative.

However, as we will see, many voices contemporary with Clement demonstrate some resistance to the direction he takes. Whereas Clement accuses the radicals by not attempting to avoid persecution and death and of hatred towards the Creator, Tertullian urges Christians to do nothing to avoid death, including flight in the face of persecution, as both Clement and Cyprian would do. For Tertullian, 'Flight was fearfulness not faithfulness' (*De Fuga* 9).

Many early Christians sided with Tertullian, and were similarly more enthusiastic about death than Clement and the author of the Quintus pericope, and in fact, it is difficult to draw any clear distinction in Christian martyr acts between an eager seeking after death, and the so-called 'orthodox' position. Within the spectrum of belief that made up early Christianity, some Christians embraced the significant phenomenon of 'voluntary death', or radical martyrdom, and may even be said to have demonstrated a lust for death in intentionally seeking out opportunities for martyrdom.

The earliest example of such desire is Ignatius, bishop of Antioch, who on his way to Rome to be martyred wrote letters to local Christian communities. The letters speak of his enthusiasm for death, as well as a concern that his fellow Christians do nothing to prevent his death. He may have been trying to avoid Christians bribing his captors to have him released, which was common at the time.

> Allow me to be eaten by the beasts, through which I can attain God. I am God's wheat, and I am ground by the teeth of wild beasts, so that I may become pure bread of Christ. (*Romans* 4.1–5.3)

Ignatius' desire, has been dismissed by many as a morbid obsession, but chimes with Tertullian, who, although not himself martyred, urged Christians to take control of their own death.

> Desire not to die on bridal beds, nor in miscarriages, nor in soft fevers, but to die the martyr's death, that He may be glorified who has suffered for you. (*De Fuga* 9)

Many Christians did just that, and we have many stories positively told of Christians presenting themselves for arrest without condemnation. As late as the early fourth century, 100 years after Clement's statement of supposed normative practice, we find the story of Euplus: 'Outside the veil in front of the prefect's council chamber, a man named Euplus shouted out to them and said, "I want to die; I am a Christian"' (*Acts of Euplus* 1.1).

In the *Act*, Euplus' course of action is never condemned. He is tried and tortured in an attempt to force him to sacrifice to the gods. Euplus resists, and finally 'endured the contest of martyrdom, and received the crown of orthodox belief' (2.2). For enduring the torture, Euplus, despite his voluntary arrest, is counted among the ranks of the blessed martyrs, and received the unfading crown (2.4). Clearly, the difference between Euplus' story and the Quintus pericope is that while both handed themselves over of their own accord, Euplus maintained his testimony whereas Quintus denied.

There are many other examples of such behaviour including actions taken not merely by individuals, but by crowds of Christians. Tertullian recounts an occasion the 'Euplus phenomenon' affected a whole town, when they all presented themselves to a bemused proconsul of Asia, demanding to be martyred. The official's response betrays a connection in the pagan mind between martyrdom and suicide; he tells them to go jump off a cliff if they really want to die.

Tertullian, writing to the hostile proconsul Scapula, threatens him with the same action.

Your cruelty is our glory. Only see you to it, that in having such things as these to endure, we do not feel ourselves constrained to rush forth to the combat, if only to prove that we have no dread of them, but on the contrary, even invite their infliction. When Arrius Antoninus was driving things hard in Asia, the whole Christians of the province, in one united band, presented themselves before his judgment-seat; on which, ordering a few to be led forth to execution, he said to the rest, 'O miserable men, if you wish to die, you have precipices or ropes.' If we should take it into our heads to do the same thing here, what will you make of so many thousands, of such a multitude of men and women, persons of every sex and every age and every rank, when they present themselves before you? How many fires, how many swords will be required? (*Ad Scapulam* 5.1)

A similar incident is found in the *Martyrs of Palestine*, set in the year 305. Eusebius recounts that a rumour spread that Christians were going to be thrown to the lions as part of a festival in Caesarea. On the way to the amphitheatre, the Roman governor was met by six young men with their hands bound who demanded to be thrown to the lions, 'evidencing great zeal for martyrdom'. The governor had them arrested, but instead of sending them to the lions, put them in prison, where they were later beheaded (3.2–4).

Even where the more conservative position is found, it is not always followed. In *The Acts of Cyprian*, Clement's position is restated: 'Our discipline forbids anyone to surrender voluntarily' (1.5). However, when Cyprian is asked where the rest of the Christians are, he replies that though they may not give themselves up, if they are sought they will be found. It may be that even here, the words put into the mouth of the bishop are equivocal. He appears to say that the Christians will not hide themselves particularly enthusiastically. In the end, there is no need for the official to launch a search, for at the moment of sentence, the Christians appear:

Then he read from a tablet, 'Thanscius Cyprian is sentenced to die by the sword'.

The Bishop Cyprian said, 'Thanks be to God!'

After the sentence, the crowd of his fellow Christians said, 'Let us also be beheaded with him!' (4.3–5.1)

Despite Cyprian repeating the line that Christians are not to hand themselves over, the missing Christians all voluntarily present themselves to the authorities wishing to die with their bishop.

Other examples of Christians volunteering for arrest are mentioned in passing without comment, indicating that for the authors there was no controversy attached to the practice. So in the *Passion of Perpetua and Felicitas*, the Church leader, Saturus, is said to have given himself up of his own accord (4–5). Saturus is described as the builder of the Church's strength, and although he was not present when the group were arrested, he later gives himself up. In Perpetua's dream, he ascends the ladder of martyrdom and calls Perpetua to follow suit.

In addition to voluntary arrests described with approval in the martyr acts, we also find suicides described as martyrdom. Agathonicê is a young mother attending the games with her young son. After the martyrdom of Carpus and Papylus, she receives a vision and throws herself on the pyre (see above pp. 6-7). Agathonicê, to the horror of the crowd, simply leaves her place and kills herself, without any explicit profession of faith, without arrest, trial, and condemnation. Yet, she is still recognized as a martyr.

And she thus gave up her spirit and died together with the saints. And the Christians secretly collected their remains and protected them for the glory of Christ and the praise of his martyrs. (47)

The text undergoes subsequent revision, and in a later version the story is changed to make it more like a traditional martyrdom. After the death of Carpus, Agathonicê is given a trial before the proconsul, but refuses to offer sacrifice, even for the sake of her children, answering, as in the Greek recension, 'My children have God who watches over them' (*Carpus* [Latin] 6.3). She is hung on a stake and burned. A later hand, perhaps squeamish at the self-killing martyr, has transformed Agathonicê's suicide into a more traditional martyrdom.

Agathonicê is not the only self-killing martyr. The elderly Apollonia was threatened with burning unless she recited what

Eusebius calls 'blasphemous sayings'. She asked for some time to think about the matter, but then threw herself onto the flames (*H. E.* 6.41.7). Similarly, during the Diocletian persecution many Christians eagerly rushed to death:

At this time Anthimus, who then presided over the church in Nicomedia, was beheaded for his testimony to Christ. A great multitude of martyrs were added to him, a conflagration having broken out in those very days in the palace at Nicomedia . . . Entire families of the pious in that place were put to death in masses at the royal command, some by the sword, and others by fire. It is reported that with a certain divine and indescribable eagerness men and women rushed into the fire. (*H.E.* 8.6.6)

Where martyrs neither kill themselves nor hand themselves over, the voluntary nature of the martyr's death is often stressed. Even in the arena when facing execution, in many cases, it is the martyrs who bring about or choose their moment death.

Perpetua . . . had yet to taste more pain. She screamed as she was struck on the bone; then she took the hand of the young gladiator and guided it to her throat. It was as though so great a woman, feared as she was by the unclean spirit, could not be killed unless she was willing. (*M. Perpetua* 21.8–10)

This is a common theme throughout the martyr acts. Carpus, Papylus, and Agathonicê are said to have 'given up' their lives, (*M. Carpus* 37, 41, 47). Clear parallels can be drawn with the voluntary nature of Jesus' death (see especially Jn 10.18), who similarly gives up his spirit (Jn 19.30; cf. Lk. 23.46).

After their sentence of death, Carpus and Papylus rushed to the amphitheatre 'that they might all the more quickly depart from the world' (*M. Carpus*, 36). Similarly, Polycarp also rushes 'eagerly and quickly' towards the place of execution (*M. Polycarp*, 8) and Germanicus drags the wild beasts upon himself to effect his death (*M. Polycarp*, 3). Added to the examples above, we see that the Christian martyrs not only welcomed death to the point of seeking it out, but that in many instances, even at the point of death, the martyrs were very much in control.

When we turn to critics of Christianity, it is the more radical form of death which is corroborated by pagan perceptions of Christians. Though these are hostile witnesses, we must remember that death and suicide had a noble tradition in the Graeco-Roman mind. Pagans would therefore have not thought strange a desire for martyrdom. However, what the pagans seem to react to is an over-enthusiastic desire that appears to them excessive. Lucian, writing in the second century, says about the Christians:

The poor wretches have convinced themselves, first and foremost, that they are going to be immortal and live forever, in consequence of which they despise death and even willingly give themselves over to arrest. (*Death of Peregrinus* 13)

For Lucian to associate voluntary arrest suggests this was a practice widely associated with the Christians. Similarly, Marcus Cornelius Fronto (c. 100–166) reflects the observation that Christians have no fear of death:

They despise torments . . . while they fear to die after death, they do not fear to die for the present: so does their deceitful hope soothe their fear with the solace of a revival. (*Octavius* 8–9)

Epictetus (*Discourses* 4.7.1–6) regarded this lack of fear and drive for death as madness. Christians were so associated with contempt for death, that their preparedness for death appeared to be unreflective.

Therefore, the way in which Christianity presented itself to the outside world was as a group who were ready to face death. If the Romans knew little about their theology, worship, and practice, they knew the Christians were prepared to die, even to the point of handing themselves over to arrest. The view that there was somehow a 'normal' attitude to Christian martyrdom that excludes radical enthusiasm cannot be maintained. To be sure, when it came to periods of persecution, the majority chose to live. However, the texts, the narratives, and the ideals promoted by Christian communities prized martyrdom, often in its radical form, even if many failed to live up to it.

It is important to correct the established notion of martyrdom in early Christianity. Even if it makes the early martyrs appear more distant, and even if readers find their desire uncomfortable, they belong to the mainstream of early Christian attitudes to death. Having described the phenomenon of early Christian martyrdom, we now turn to its explanation. We have seen that early Christians idealized martyrdom even to the extent of voluntarily seeking it out. How, we now ask, was this position maintained theologically? What did early Christians believe in order to sustain this radical embrace of death?

CHAPTER 3

THE THEOLOGY OF MARTYRDOM
IN EARLY CHRISTIANITY

In their martyr texts, the early Christians promoted a radicalized form of volitional martyrdom. Despite a general lack of State persecution, Christians nonetheless 'imperialized' their experiences, so that even where violence was local, sporadic, or mob driven, the Christians interpreted it as having a more centralized origin. It is, of course, possible that such radical death could be valourized in the early years, because most Christians would not be called upon to give their lives. However, living with a general atmosphere of suspicion, life in the empire could be unpredictable, and although the Neronic persecution was restricted to Rome, it would have imprinted a scar on the Christian psyche. In addition, their scriptures were replete with experiences and images of suffering. And so there was a twin evangelical call to share in the sufferings, not only of those early communities, but of Christ. We now turn to theologies of suffering and martyrdom that sustained the Christians in their promotion of martyrdom, and in particular, the symbolic world they created that made radicalized death a preferred option for Christians who might be called to give their lives for their faith.

1 MARTYRDOM AS SPECTACLE

Language used to describe the struggles of the martyrs is varied; yet, imagery associated with the Roman games was frequently employed. In texts produced by the Christians, martyrs are often described as athletes or gladiators locked in combat as they head towards their deaths, which are, of course, interpreted as victory. Paul had already employed imagery from the games to interpret the Christian struggle (Phil. 2.16, 3.12–14; Col. 1.29; cf. 1 Tim. 6.12), with a later author summing up Paul's own life as a race to the finishing line:

For I am already on the point of being sacrificed; the time of my departure has come, I have fought the good fight, I have finished the race, I have kept the faith. Henceforth there is laid up for me the crown of righteousness, which the Lord, the righteous judge, will award to me on that Day, and not only to me but also to all who have loved his appearing. (2 Tim. 4.6–8)

The author speaks of Paul being awarded the victor's crown from the judge of the contest, adding that it is available to all who follow Paul in the Christian race. Similarly, an imperishable crown waited for the martyrs who endured to the end.[1] Indeed, there is a suggestion that the messier the death, the greater the crown.

Saturnus indeed insisted that he wanted to be exposed to all the different beasts, that his crown be all the more glorious. (*M. Perpetua* 19.2)

1.1 Earthly Spectacle

Virtually every one of the early Christian martyr acts, recording the death of the heroes, reach their climax in the public arena of the games.[2] The games, put on to bring honour to a city, a wealthy patron, or the emperor, not only entertained but also held together a complex mix of political, religious, and social elements of the empire. In the stadium, the power, justice, and glory of the empire were celebrated amid the spectacle of gladiator duels, wild beasts, and the execution of criminals.

Christian reflection on these deaths appropriated the image of the combatant at the games not only literally, but also symbolically. The trials, the fight with beasts, and the tortures inflicted upon the followers of Christ were almost always portrayed as a contest;[3] Christians were described as athletes or combatants, whether or not they ended up facing wild animals.[4] Tertullian (*Ad Martyras* 3; *On Modesty* 22) explicitly employed athletic or military metaphors in his writing on martyrdom; Christians were soldiers serving under God's oath not to commit idolatry. Trials or interrogations of Christians, with the pressure placed on the believer to recant, marked the fulcrum of battle.

> I am challenged by the enemy. If I surrender to them, I am as they are. In maintaining this oath, I fight furiously in battle, am wounded, hewn in pieces, slain. Who wished this fatal issue to his soldier, but he who sealed him by such an oath. (*Scorpiace* 4.4)

A wealth of contest imagery was available to those who reflected upon Christian martyrdom, which no doubt influenced the way death for the religion was narrated. Within the acts themselves, athletic imagery is liberally used. Blandina, considered doubly weak, being both a slave and a girl, defeats the torturers through her power, and is cast in the role of a 'noble athlete' (*M. Lyons* 16–19).

Similarly, the new catechumen, Martus, also displayed the characteristics of a 'noble contestant' in his struggle (*M. Lyons* 17). In contrast, within the Christian community at Lyons, there were those who were not yet ready to undergo martyrdom. They are described as untrained, unprepared, and weak, being unable to bear the strain of a 'great contest' (*M. Lyons* 11). They had not undergone the training and self-discipline required to produce endurance, the necessary quality to become a successful athlete and martyr. But even their lack of preparedness to face death was still cast in athletic language; they had not trained sufficiently to attain the appropriate level of endurance.

Endurance (*hupomonē*) was identified as the key element in Ignatius' strategy to confront suffering (*Magn.* 1.1; *Trall.* 4.1). It is the same quality that an athlete develops in self-training for the contest,[5] as it was for gladiators in training for the games. For Paul, endurance was perfected by suffering (Rom. 5.3–5). Training in endurance was required for those who desired to follow the martyrs' example.

> Gathering here . . . we celebrate the anniversary of his [Polycarp's] martyrdom, both as memorial for those who have already fought the contest and for the training and preparation of those who will do so one day. (*M. Polycarp* 18.3)

Athletic imagery and endurance are quite explicitly linked in the *Martyrdom of Carpus, Papylus, and Agathonicê*. During his torture,

Papylus endured being scraped with iron combs by three pairs of torturers. By not uttering a sound, he was said, like Blandina and Martus before him, to have 'received the angry onslaught of the adversary like a noble athlete' (*M. Carpus*, 35). Endurance of pain was a notable virtue in antiquity, with Seneca speaking of the nobility of enduring pain. In addition to the athletes, he holds up those tortured in the arena as an example of courage to be emulated.

What blows do athletes receive on their faces and all over their bodies! Nevertheless, through their desire for fame, they endure every torture, and they undergo these things not only because they are fighting but in order to be able to fight. Their very training means torture . . . Think of all the brave men who have conquered pain . . . of him who did not cease to smile, though that very smile so enraged his torturers that they tried upon him every instrument of their cruelty. If pain can be conquered by a smile, will it not be conquered by reason? You may tell me now of whatever you like – of colds, hard coughing-spells . . . yet worse than these are the stake, the rack, the red-hot plates, the instrument that reopens wounds while the wounds themselves are still swollen and that drives their imprint still deeper. Nevertheless, there have been men who have not uttered a moan amid these tortures. 'More yet!' says the torturer; but the victim has not begged for release. 'More yet!' he says again; but no answer has come. 'More yet!' the victim has smiled, and heartily, too. Can you not bring yourself, after an example like this, to make a mock at pain? (*Epistle* 78.15–19)

Insensibility to pain is an important feature in the martyr acts. Papylus' silence under torture, points to another element, borrowed from the games, that is crucial in the description of martyrdom; the importance of public witness.

Martyrdom was a public spectacle for the Roman and Christian. For the Romans, it was important that lawbreakers be punished as publicly as possible to act as a deterrent for other would-be deviants. The games were public entertainment that reinforced the social, moral, and religious order of the empire. The Christians, as a threat to that order, had to be publicly executed in the arena. For the Romans, this did not constitute persecution of Christians, rather as prosecution of individuals deemed to be a threat to the State. However, the Christians did not play the part of the criminal:

You find that criminals are eager to conceal themselves, avoid appearing in public, are in trepidation when they are caught, deny their guilt, when they are accused; even when they are put to the rack, they do not easily or always confess; when there is no doubt about their condemnation, they grieve for what they have done. In their self-communings they admit their being impelled by sinful dispositions, but they lay the blame either on fate or on the stars. They are unwilling to acknowledge that the thing is theirs, because they own that it is wicked. But what is there like this in the Christian's case? The only shame or regret he feels, is at not having been a Christian earlier. If he is pointed out, he glories in it; if he is accused, he offers no defence; interrogated, he makes voluntary confession; condemned he renders thanks. What sort of evil thing is this, which wants all the ordinary peculiarities of evil – fear, shame, subterfuge, penitence, lamenting? What! Is that a crime in which the criminal rejoices; to be accused of which is his ardent wish, to be punished for which is his felicity? (Tertullian, *Apology* 1.10–13)

Whereas it was usual for guilty condemned parties to lower their eyes, the Christian texts stress a more aggressive attitude taken by the martyrs. Polycarp looks straight at the crowd and shaking his fist at it, denounces them as atheists (*M. Polycarp* 9.2). Perpetua, it is also noted, stares at the crowd as she enters the arena (*M. Perpetua* 18.2). Indeed, when she and Felicitas are stripped naked in the arena, it is the crowd that flinch.

It is difficult to overstate the perceived importance of directly gazing at one's accusers. Pliny the Elder (*Historia Naturalis* 11.54.144) recounts that of Caligula's twenty thousand gladiators, only two were able to stand unflinching when threatened, and were therefore considered to be invincible. Tertullian therefore argues that by refusing to play the part of the criminal, the Christian does not fit the role of lawbreaker. In these simple acts of defiance, some scholars have seen subtle acts of resistance to Roman power.[6] In any case, for the Romans as for the Christians, the drama took place in public. There were no private martyrdoms. Tertullian urged Christians to 'be exposed to the public; it is for your own good; for he who is not publicly exposed by humans is publicly exposed by God' (*De Fuga* 9.4).

One consequence of the acts taking place in public is that the crowd take on an important role in the martyrological drama. Sometimes they are recorded as being extremely hostile:[7] they demand the martyrs' arrest or appearance;[8] they call for certain punishments;[9] even on occasion taking part in the execution or mob violence;[10] or they desecrate the remains of the martyr.[11] Seneca also notes with some distaste the bloodthirsty nature of audiences at executions. Whilst the games were noble, he regarded the execution of criminals as a somewhat savage activity, during which the upper classes went for lunch. Such was the reputation for barbarity of the crowd, he pointedly notes, 'In the morning, men are thrown to the lions and bears. At midday, they are thrown to the spectators themselves' (*Letters* 7.2). However, on other occasions, the courage of the martyrs provokes amazement in the crowds. So the soldiers who come to arrest Polycarp are amazed at his piety, and are sorry to have to arrest such an old man (*M. Polycarp* 7.3), the governor is amazed at Polycarp's joyful courage and gracious countenance as he is questioned (12.1), and as Polycarp dies, 'even the crowd marvelled that there should be such a difference between the unbelievers and the elect' (16.1).

The significance of their deaths on the pagan crowds was not lost on the Christians, and they urge one another to die well. Putting on a good show, not reacting to the pain, and keeping the soul tranquil were all important and explicit elements in the making of a good death for the sake of the unbelievers (Origen, *Exhortation to Martyrdom* 2, 36). On many occasions, the fact that the martyr is able to undergo the tortures without cries of pains is especially noted. On occasions, the Christians are said to have been able to keep miraculous tranquillity *for the purpose of* impressing the crowd.[12]

Consequently, a recurring theme on the potency of martyrdom is the resolve of the Christians in the face of death, which brought admiration from onlookers, and also strengthened the resolve of those about to undergo martyrdom.[13] It has been suggested that it was in fact through martyrdom that pagans became aware of the existence of Christianity in the second and third centuries.[14] The deaths of the Christians were a public testimony to unbelievers.

1.2 Cosmic Spectacle

Paul writes of his own experience of suffering in terms of humiliation at the games. God has 'exhibited us apostles as last of all, like men sentenced to death; because we have become a spectacle to the world, to angels and to men' (1 Cor. 4.9). The early Christians depicted their arrests, trials, and in particular the moment where they faced their interrogator and were urged to recant, as a contest. In both a literal and metaphorical sense, they were athletes or gladiators at the games. But this was no localized contest; as Paul suggests martyrdom has a crucial apocalyptic dimension. Martyrdom was a cosmic contest.

If the Christians' struggle was often played out in the arena before the crowds of onlookers, and if the battle was against the forces of the Roman Empire, on a more fundamental level, their struggle was cosmic in scale. Standing in the centre of the arena, the beasts before them and the crowds around them, Christians were depicted as standing beneath the heavens – where the angels waited to receive those who walked through the gate of life – and above the fires of hell – where the devil was waiting to devour those whom he successfully snared. Ultimately, the contest fought by the Christians was against the devil, and it was primarily because of his activity that they endured persecution, trial, and danger. The Christians were not only athletes in the games; they were soldiers in a cosmic war.[15] The *Martyrdom of Lyons* has an apocalyptic opening (1.3–6), where the scene is set with Satan about to manifest his final appearance. The combatants are God's servants armed with God's grace, prepared to charge into battle against the slaves of Satan (1.5).

Everything that happened to the young Church communities was played out on the cosmic stage. Torture, persecution, arrest, and death all fitted within the world view with which the Christians operated. Their enemies were not so much wild beasts and governors; the adversary was Satan. After one of her prison visions, Perpetua realizes 'that it was not with the wild animals that I would fight but with the Devil, but I knew that I would win the victory' (*M. Perpetua* 10.14).[16]

In this battle, Satan plans the skirmishes with Christians; he has a battle strategy.

They [the martyrs] stood in battle formation, steadfast and brave. Their steadfastness in the Lord beat back the blows of the raging devil. But when the fury of the devil could not prevail over all the soldiers of Christ together, he demanded them in combat one by one. (*Abitinian Martyrs*, 4)[17]

Satan did not desire the physical death of the martyrs; his purpose was to cause denial. The Romans were not primarily interested in killing the Christians but in dissuading them from their illogical defiance.[18]

For the Romans, of course, each successful recantation was a victory of common sense, and each execution reinforced the power of Rome. Pagans believed that the Christians slighted the gods of the ancient world. In some way, some of the persecution and punishment is seen as the revenge of the gods (*M. Lyons* 1.60). The pagans themselves felt that they had to restore the honour of their traditional gods against the *atheoi* Christians (*M. Lyons* 1.31). The charge made against Polycarp is that he was 'the father of the Christians and the destroyer of our gods – the one that teaches the multitude not to sacrifice and do reverence.'[19] In this context, to offer sacrifice to the emperor was to become a denier, and align oneself with demons, with all the attendant consequences. The call to martyrdom, therefore, takes place within the context of lining up with God or Satan; it is a battle between God's soldiers and Satan's servants (*ministri diaboli*).[20] Therefore, just as the Christians were combatants and athletes training in endurance for God, so too Satan trained his legions in preparation for the final apocalyptic battle.[21] The opening of the *Martyrs of Lyons* is loaded with apocalyptic overtones, including the eschatological 'troubles' (*thlispis*) God's saints had to endure.

The intensity of our afflictions here, the deep hatred of the pagans for the saints, and the magnitude of the blessed martyrs' sufferings, we are incapable of describing in detail . . . The Adversary swooped down in full force, in this way anticipating his final coming which is sure to come. He went to all lengths to train and prepare his minions against God's servants: the result was that we were not only shut out of our houses, the baths and the public square, but they forbade any of us to be seen in any place whatsoever. (*M. Lyons* 1.4–5; cf. 1 Thess. 1.6)

The witness and deaths of Christians affected the cosmic order; they were God's foot soldiers in the final eschatological battle. It is a battle that they won, and we now turn to the mechanism by which the Christians could interpret the deaths of those executed by the State as nothing less than cosmic victory. This was achieved by a theology of participation in Christ – his suffering, his death, and his victory.

2 FOLLOWING JESUS THE MARTYR

2.1 Dying and Rising with Christ

At the centre of the early Christian communities was the devotion of a martyr crucified by the Roman State; behind every martyrdom was the death of Jesus. Early martyrological reflection portrayed the martyrs as imitators of Christ. Indeed, at times, it appears that in order to *become* a disciple of Christ, one had to imitate his death:

> For even though I am in chains for the sake of the Name, I have not yet been perfected in Jesus Christ. For now I am only beginning to be a disciple, and I speak to you as my fellow students.[22]

In the New Testament, discipleship often involves imitating the example of Jesus' suffering and death. So baptism is the dying and rising (Rom. 6.3–10) of those who have been crucified with Christ (Gal. 2.20). Believers are called to suffer with Christ (Rom. 8.16–17), and follow after him on the road of suffering (Mk 8.35), imitating the true witness of Jesus (Rev. 1.5).

The authors or redactors of the martyr texts often made explicit the connection between their heroes and Christ. Of Ponthius, bishop of Lyons, it is written:

> He was brought to the tribunal by the soldiers, accompanied by some of the civil magistrates and the entire mob, who raised all kinds of shouts at him as though he were Christ himself.[23]

Often, the way the deaths of the martyrs are narrated are modelled on the Passion of Jesus. This can be seen quite clearly in the deaths of Stephen and Polycarp.

Luke's account of Stephen's death is the first recorded martyrdom for Jesus. His death is preceded by the instigation of persecution against the Christians by the high priest and the Sadducees, apparently jealous at the success of the Church (Acts 5.17). The apostles are arrested and imprisoned, although miraculously freed (5.18–19). The apostles are later brought before the council and questioned by the high priest, after which the council wants to kill them (5.33), until the Pharisee Gamaliel intervenes (5.34). After being beaten by the council, the apostles leave rejoicing 'that they were counted worthy to suffer dishonour for the name' (5.41).

Stephen then appears, full of the Holy Spirit, working wonders and speaking wisdom, but is falsely accused before the council of blasphemy and speaking against the temple (6.8–13). After a very long speech recounting the unfaithfulness of the Jews (7.2–53), and after having a vision of the Son of Man standing in the heavens (7.56), he is cast out of the city and stoned (7.58).

As they were stoning Stephen, he prayed, 'Lord Jesus, receive my spirit.' And he knelt down and cried with a loud voice, 'Lord, do not hold this sin against them'. And when he had said this, he fell asleep (7.59–60).

The death of Stephen is self-consciously modelled on the Passion of Jesus, and has many elements in common:[24] He refutes his opponents (Acts 6.10; cf. Mk 12.34); he is seized by officials (6.12; cf. Mk 14.43, 46); tried by the Sanhedrin (6.12, 7.1 cf. Mk 14.53); false witnesses make charges against him (6.13; cf. Mk 14.56–57); he is accused of threatening the temple (6.14; cf. Mk 14.58); there is a saying about the Son of Man (7.56; cf. Mk 14.62); he is accused of blasphemy (Acts 6.11; cf. Mk 14.64); questioned by the High Priest (7.1; cf. Mk 14.61); commits his spirit to Jesus (7.59; cf. Lk. 23.46 where Jesus commits his spirit to God); issues a loud cry (7.60; cf. Mk 15.34); and prays for his executors (7.60; cf. Lk. 23.34).[25]

The parallels in the Polycarp story are even more striking (see Table). The composite picture stresses that Polycarp was a 'sharer of Christ (*Christou koinōnos*; *M. Polycarp* 6.2)'. Polycarp and all the martyrs do not simply imitate Christ (17.3); their bodies are completely given over to Christ. Christ, it is said, is the 'pilot', or the 'helmsman of the bodies' of the faithful (19.2). Therefore, identification with Christ formed a crucial element in the self-understanding

The parallels in the Polycarp story are even more striking.	*M. Polycarp*[26]	The Passion
'Just as the Lord did', Polycarp waits to be delivered for arrest.	1.2	
There are prominent names from Jesus' passion, such as Herod and Judas.	6.2	
Polycarp has betrayers in his own household.	6.2	Mk 14.18
The police come out to him 'as though against a brigand'.	7.1	Mk 14.48
Polycarp rides into the city on a donkey.	8.2	Mk 11.7–11
Polycarp is said to drink the cup of Christ.	14.2	Mk 14.36
Polycarp predicts his own death and its manner.	4.2	Mk 8.31
He offers a prayer for the Church before his arrest.	7.3–8.1	Jn 17
He affirms that the will of God be done.	7.1	Mt. 26.42
A dagger is plunged into Polycarp's side.	16.1	Jn 19.34
The Jews make trouble concerning his remains.	17.1–2	Mt. 27.62–64
A centurion stands by witnessing the death.	18.1	Mk 15.39

of the martyrs, and dramatically influenced the way their stories were told. The martyrs were portrayed as being eager to deliberately mimic the suffering of Jesus. For example, in another incident, martyrs demand to be scourged before a line of gladiators that they may 'obtain a share in the Lord's suffering' (*M. Perpetua* 18.17). Blandina, the heroine of *Lyons*, is said to be insensitive to the pain because of her 'intimacy with Christ'.[27] Hung on a post as bait for the wild animals, she seemed as though she were hanging on a cross. Therefore, those who were facing torture in the arena

saw in their sister him who was crucified for them, that he might convince all who believe in him that all who suffer for Christ's glory will have eternal fellowship in the living God. (*M. Lyons* 1.41)

This theme of sharing intimacy with Christ through mimetic suffering develops into the idea that Christ actually suffers within the martyrs. Felicitas in the pains of childbirth is mocked when it is observed how much more she will suffer in the arena. She replies: 'What I suffer now, I suffer by myself. But then another will be inside me who will suffer for me, just as I will be suffering for him'

MARTYRDOM: A GUIDE FOR THE PERPLEXED

(*M. Perpetua* 15.6). Felicitas suffers in childbirth *for* the one inside her. At the day of her death, Christ will be inside her, suffering for *her*, just as she will suffer for Christ. For the martyr there is a mutuality of suffering through, with, and for Christ, and the suffering of Christ with the martyr brings comfort, strength, and release.

2.2 Confessing Christ

This theme of identification with Christ is presented most obviously, and most powerfully, in the words of confession on the lips of the martyrs themselves. Confessing Christ together with warnings of denial is an important theme throughout the New Testament. Many sayings could plausibly fit within the setting anticipated by Mk 13.9, where Christians will be brought before governors and kings to testify for Jesus. Not least the warning earlier in the gospel:

> Whoever would save his life will lose it; and whoever loses his life for my sake and the gospel's will save it . . . For whoever is ashamed of me and of my words in this adulterous and sinful generation, of him will the Son of Man also be ashamed, when he comes in the glory of his Father with the holy angels. (Mk 8.35–38)

A similar death or life situation is assumed by the warning to fear not the one who can kill the body, but the soul (Mt. 10.26–27). So with the writer to the Hebrews, who warns that once a believer has been saved, if he commits apostasy, he cannot be restored (Heb. 6.4–6; cf. 10.26–31 and 12.15–17), a theme that is important in the controversy over the lapsed. One further possible example of an anticipated trial where Christians are called to confess Christ is in 2 Timothy:

> The saying is sure: If we have died with him, we shall also live with him; if we endure, we shall also reign with him; if we deny him, he will also deny us. (2.11–12)

The confessional formula is of great importance in many of the martyrological texts. During their tortures Carpus and Papylus repeatedly claim the name 'Christian'. So on being asked his name, Carpus replies, 'My first and most distinctive name is that of Christian' (*M. Carpus* 3). Both he and Carpus persistently make only the response 'I am a Christian' to all other questioning, torture, or demands to sacrifice (5, 23, 34). In the *Martyrs of Lyons*, Saturnus repeats over and over 'I am a Christian' in response to every question instead of his name, birthplace, or nationality, 'and the pagan crowd heard not another word from him' (1.20). Christians like their New Testament predecessors, suffer for the name. In the *Martyrdom of Saint Justin and his Companions*, the trial scene is constructed in such a way that each of the accused can make their confession, 'I am a Christian'.[28] Recension B of the text adds the communal confession 'We are all Christians' (5.7), while Recension C has the more emphatic, and slightly melodramatic: 'I have always been a Christian, I currently am a Christian, and I will always be a Christian' (3.5).[29] Similarly, the confessions of Polycarp are given prominence by the proconsul sending a herald to announce 'three times, Polycarp has confessed himself to be a "Christian"' (*M. Polycarp* 12). These confessions are the central element of the story, the frame on which the narrative hangs. The moment of confession or denial is the point on which everything else depends. It is the moment where the Christian openly affirms his or her relationship with Christ, making themselves a sacrifice to God.[30] The martyr Perpetua, under pressure from her father to recant, instead confesses, 'I am a Christian'. In doing so, she renounces every other mark of her identity: daughter, mother, and wife.

Confessing the name of Jesus, and publicly identifying with his suffering had several effects. First, it bound the suffering communities to the one they followed, giving additional rationale, not only for their experience of suffering, but for their choosing death in the face of it. It also connected one Christian community to another, creating a language for uniting themselves with a much larger group than their insecure status would suggest. Finally, it created a powerful identity marker for the Christians as those who suffer.[31]

Furthermore, remembering the martyrs' stories, gave each community a connection with their own past, and provided a model to help when they too would face the ultimate trial. In the *Acts of the*

Martyrs, a desire is often expressed to follow their example and give as good witness as they had done:

We love the martyrs as the disciples and imitators of the Lord, and rightly so because of their unsurpassed loyalty towards their king and master. May we too share with them as fellow disciples. (*M. Polycarp* 17)

'Following in the footsteps' of the martyrs is a recurrent theme in the *Acts*,[32] and is one of the primary reasons why the stories were told; to strengthen, and to provide a pattern and example for future believers.

The model offered to prospective martyrs was not miraculous deliverance, such as is found in the book of Daniel, which similarly called Jews to stand fast to their religion. Christians were offered ideal literary types who were tortured and killed. Miraculous deliverance would be the strength to die well, and the grace to withstand the pain of torture. Most of all, the martyrs knew that they were imitating the example of Jesus, following the Lamb wherever he goes (Rev. 14.4), and therefore sharing in the 'life' of Christ.

However, there was also a disincentive to deny. By the time a Christian came to trial, that trial would take place before the cosmic archons. Whereas a good confession and death led to life, so to become a denier was to become prey to the devil. In the midst of the battle in which the Christians were engaged, there could be no neutrality. In a dualistic cosmos, one could align oneself with God or Satan. Identifying with Jesus through confession, suffering, and death resulted in a successful martyrdom and faithful struggle. The alternative was to deny either through torture, or even refusal to take part in the contest, as other groups of Christians advocated. Within the apocalyptic framework with which the advocates of martyrdom operated, this was disaster; both for the denier, but also for the cosmos. The suffering of the Christians signalled that the end was near; their deaths were strikes against Satan:

Arrayed against him [Satan] was God's grace, which protected the weak, and raised up sturdy pillars that could by their endurance take on themselves all the attacks of the Evil One. These then charged into battle, holding up under every sort of abuse and torment; indeed they made light of their great burden as they sped on to Christ, proving without question that the sufferings of this present time are not to be compared with the glory that shall be revealed in us. (*M. Lyons* 1.6)

The martyrs were the foot soldiers of God. They were involved not just in an earthly battle against their persecutors, but a cosmic one against Satan and his legions. Persecution, trials, and fighting with the beasts in the arena constituted the battlefield on which this war was to be fought. Faithfulness and endurance were the weapons with which the Christians were armed. 'Charging into battle' was giving themselves over to torture. 'Making light of their burden' was the way in which victory was to be achieved. Accepting pain and torture with grace was to deny the gods of the world victory over the Christians' god. The Christians could advance the war in Christ's favour by holding fast to their confession and swelling the ranks of martyrs. The opportunity for martyrdom, for Justin, testified to the truth of Christianity and that the 'new covenant has come' (*Trypho*, 11).

The contest motif with its elements of struggle, combat, and war, set an impressive backdrop to the experiences of the Christians. In order to compete successfully in this contest, the Christian had to participate in Christ, and become a sharer in his suffering. Ultimately, sharing in Christ's suffering resulted in participating in Christ's victory.

2.3 Martyrdom as Victory

If the martyrs were contestants at the games and soldiers in a battle, the ultimate result was victory. In death, they are described as victors and conquerors.[33] Participation in Christ meant not only sharing in his suffering; through suffering and death, the faithful martyrs participated in Christ's victory over death and Satan. Through the weapon of confession and sharing in Christ's suffering, the martyrs were victors and conquerors.

The Christian is snatched by faith from the jaws of the devil, but by martyrdom he fells to the ground the enemy of his salvation. By faith the Christian is delivered from the devil, by martyrdom he merits the crown of perfect glory over him. (Tertullian, *Scorpiace* 6)

They win life and the crown; they gain the wreath of immortality.[34] Over them Satan has not prevailed.

Those who were condemned to the beasts endure[d] terrifying torments . . . the purpose was that, if possible, the tyrant might persuade them to deny the faith by constant torment. For many were the stratagems the Devil used against them. But thanks be to God, he did not prevail over them. (*M. Polycarp* 2.4–3.1)

The tortures and deaths of the martyrs are set not only against the backdrop of Christ's suffering and death, but also his resurrection, and promise of the Second Coming. This context of martyrdom signals Satan's total defeat. Their experiences were signs of end-time suffering, reinforcing the apocalyptic dimension to their struggle. In the meantime, holding fast to their confession, the martyrs won their skirmishes with the devil before his final overthrow. Sanctus, by withstanding torture and sticking to his confession, brought glory to Christ, '*overwhelming* the Adversary', and gave an example to the Christians (*M. Lyons* 1.23). Sanctus' victory over Satan was achieved because through his suffering, 'Christ suffered in him', so completing an important triad of themes in the death of martyrs: confession, participating in the suffering of Christ, and winning the victory over Satan.

Furthermore, Satan could also be overcome by rescuing of the souls of deniers. Sanctus, through his successful witness, caused one of those who had previously denied to 'awake from sleep'. His torture was the catalyst that brought Biblis to her senses:

There was a woman named Biblis among those who had denied Christ, and the Devil thought that he had already devoured her; hoping further to convict her as a slanderer, he brought her to the rack and tried to force her to say impious things about us, thinking she was a coward and easily broken. But once on the rack she came to her senses and awoke as it were from a deep sleep, reminded by that temporal torment of the eternal punishment in Gehenna. Instead she contradicted the blasphemers, saying, 'How could such people devour children when they are not even allowed to drink the blood of brute beasts?' And from then on she insisted she was a Christian, and so was counted among the number of the martyrs. (1.25–26)

Satan is so utterly defeated he cannot hold even those he had devoured. The devil is humiliated as he is forced to disgorge his prey. The martyr has redeemed those who were lost and strengthened the resolve of others who will wield the sword of confession at Satan. In the *Martyrdom of Perpetua and Felicitas*, this victory is described as 'trampling on Satan's head'. In the first of her four prison visions, Perpetua sees a ladder ascending to heaven with a dragon at its base. The dragon sought to dissuade her from climbing the ladder of martyrdom, but she ascends, first standing on his head (4.7). In a further vision the dragon is transformed into an Egyptian, whom Perpetua also defeats by standing on his head. However, the true moment of victory is when the martyrs make confession and die. It is through death that Perpetua finally stands on the head of her adversary (18.7).

Christ had already defeated Satan, and the martyrs not only participated in, but contributed to, that victory. On account of their treatment of the martyrs, the persecutors stored up wrath for themselves. Though they seemed weak, vulnerable, and helpless in the throes of torture, the cosmos turned on the potential martyrs' decisions to remain faithful or deny. Holding fast to their confession through tortures and trials was a great victory, where they would attain a martyr's reward and defeat the enemy. The 'noble athletes after sustaining a brilliant contest and a noble victory . . . [won] the great crown of immortality' (*M. Lyons* 1.36). Satan's kingdom crumbled with each martyr's death. Perpetua was already conquering – treading on the head of the Egyptian – as she entered the arena (18.7). In the cosmic war in which they were engaged, the Christians claimed victory by their deaths; they were wounded soldiers.[35] Martyrs participated and contributed to Christ's victory over Satan, but they also won for themselves a glorious reward. As victors at the games, the martyrs were rewarded by Christ. To those who had pursued the contest to death, there was an immortal treasure. Like successful athletes, they won a crown, only theirs was eternal.

The martyrs are also involved in the judgement of their persecutors come the final judgement.[36] Satan will be defeated totally and his legions will suffer with him. The blood of the martyr contributes to their judgement,[37] for just as the Christians belong to their god, so too, the persecutors are following their master, Satan. The Christians share in Christ and not in the sins and judgement of the world. For the others, the reverse is true; those who are not in Christ belong to Satan and share in his destruction.

The fire you threaten me with burns merely for a time and is soon extinguished. It is clear you are ignorant of the fire of everlasting punishment and of the judgement that is to come, which awaits the impious. (*M. Polycarp* 11.2)

Carpus warns that those who worship demons will share in their eschatological punishment. Just as the Christians who participate in Christ's suffering will share in his triumph, so too will the worshippers of demons share in their gods' fate; they will perish in Gehenna (*M. Carpus* 7–8). The actions and the fate of the Christians are inexorably linked with the fate of the cosmos. Martyrs are not passive in this drama; they are active combatants. Seeking death brings judgement upon their persecutors, and this judgement is not an unimportant component of the martyrological schema. Martyrdom was a potent weapon in the eschatological war that inexorably led to ultimate victory.

2.4 Life and Death

The martyrs' deaths were interpreted through the life, death, resurrection, and ultimate eschatological victory of Jesus. The martyrs followed his footsteps, and in so doing, laid a path that other Christians desired to follow. The struggle of the Christians was set in the midst of a cosmic arena, where they engaged in combat against Satan and his legions, and won the victor's crown by holding to their confession and dying well. It is to this moment of victory we now turn and examine more closely.

The Christians created a symbolic world where the normal categories of life and death lost their meaning. To live was to die; to die was to live (2 Cor. 6.9). Consistently, dying and facing torture is portrayed as the better choice. Crucially, it is not better because embracing suffering was more noble, rather if one inhabited the symbolic world of the Christians, it was to any rational person, the better, even the obvious choice. For Perpetua, her day of suffering and death was in actuality her day of triumph (5.5).

One of the most striking and consistent interpretative manoeuvres used by the Christians was the reinterpretation, or perhaps more accurately, redefining of the categories of life and death. Through the breaking down of temporal and spatial boundaries, taken together with a radical conviction of the part they were playing in the cosmic scheme of things, the early Christians were able to sustain a belief not only that those who died were alive, but that those who were currently alive were dead. The temporal movement for human beings was not life leading to inevitable death; paradoxically, they believed that death – that is, life in the world – could potentially lead to life for the faithful, or continued death for the unfaithful. The commands of God bring life; to follow the commands of the emperor was to court death even though one's earthly life might be spared.

In creating new social symbols, they could challenge and reinterpret the situation of persecution and death positively. Therefore, Christians could have contempt for their earthly bodies,[38] for it is through death that they live and reach perfection.[39] Death was not to be feared but welcomed; charging towards death was in reality 'rushing towards life',[40] so much so that the martyr could even be found to express thanks to his persecutor, who speeds him on to life.[41]

[The proconsul] Dion said, 'I shall send you to your Christ directly'.

'I only wish you would', he [Maximilian] replied, 'that would be my glory'. (*Acts of Maximilian* 2.5)

So well did this imagery of life and death work that martyrs could be said to be born at the point of their death, and those who succumbed to torture and denied their faith at the moment of trial, could be said to be stillborn. They had begun the process of birth, only to be snatched from the womb, dead, by Satan. In the *Martyrs of Lyons*, deniers are still born, but are restored or even saved or redeemed through the deaths of others. When the writer observes, 'the dead were restored to life through the living' (1.45), a remarkable transformation has occurred. Each category used to understand life has been reversed. Death equals life; life equals death. Death equals victory; life constitutes defeat and failure. Death means reward; life means judgement. So in the *Acts of Thomas* (160), execution is not death but deliverance.

Language reversal is found in the death of Blandina, who rejoices and glories in her death, and is said to be partaking of a bridal banquet while being food for the wild beasts (1.55). Similarly, comparisons were often made contrasting the temporal fire with which the martyrs were threatened with the far more impressive eternal fire from which they are escaping and with which they can threaten their persecutors. Saturnus warns those sharing in his final meal to note what the martyrs look like, as they will recognize them again come the Day of Judgement, where those who will be martyred will be involved in judging the onlookers and scoffers (*M. Perpetua* 17.2).

The world of the Christians was highly dualistic, offering each potential martyr a series of profound and stark choices. Life and death; confession and denial; heaven and hell; reward and punishment; Christ and Satan; these were all binary oppositions with no middle way. In the Christian's cosmos, normal spatial and temporal barriers were dismantled, and the fundamental categories of life and death were deconstructed. The martyrs would win a reward, while deniers and persecutors would face God's judgement in the presence of the martyrs.

3   THE DEMISE OF RADICAL MARTYRDOM

Despite there being relatively early criticisms of radical martyrdom in early Christianity, we have observed a high level of enthusiasm for death amongst the early Christians to the point where believers would seek out opportunities for death, or even take their own life in order to win martyrdom. This behaviour was sustained by the belief that Christians were taking part in a cosmic struggle against Satan, where dying not only contributed to that victory, but was in fact winning life. This belief sustained many Christians as they withstood pressure to conform to Roman religious practices. However, opposition to the value of martyrdom had always existed, first among more 'Gnostic' Christians, but later among those who came to be orthodox. We now turn to some of the reasons for the decline of martyrdom.

At first, one's willingness to undergo martyrdom was a sign of one's orthodoxy. So, for example, Justin Martyr makes the claim that the followers of Marcion and other 'heretical' leaders are demonstrably not truly Christian because they are not persecuted or killed by the Roman officials (*Apol.* 1.26). Suffering, as it had been for many New Testament writers, was a sign of true devotion and right belief. Tertullian also links the lack of persecution to heresy:

> Now we are in the midst of . . . persecution . . . the fire and the sword have tired some Christians, and the beasts have tired others; others are in prison, longing for martyrdom which they have tasted already . . . and the heretics go about as usual. (*Scorpiace*, 1, 5, 7)

However, martyrdom was not simply reserved for those regarded as orthodox, and so-called heretical groups did contribute to the ranks of the martyrs. We have already noted Clement's criticism of a group who had been arrested and, he concedes, officially executed. However, his belief that they did not know the real God, rendered their martyrdom futile.

3.1 The Problem of the Lapsed

The second issue accounting for the declining enthusiasm for martyrdom was pragmatic. During times of sporadic persecution, the examples of those who had been faithful were remembered and recalled, whereas those who had denied under pressure were shamed. As we have seen in the three persecutions of Decius, Valerian, and Diocletian, the numbers of those who had deserted the Church and sought restitution were so great that the importance of martyrdom was bound to be downplayed. Both Clement and Cyprian, who began the dampening down of enthusiasm for radical martyrdom, fled during periods of persecution. Nonetheless, the martyrs were still very much honoured, and held to have special powers because of their witness. This power was also shared by the confessors, who as we have seen were instrumental in restoring the lapsed to the Church. Constantine's Edict of Toleration was issued before the problem of the lapsed had been resolved after the Great Persecution, and the numbers of bishops who had cooperated with the authorities in handing over scriptures for burning again reduced the value of martyrdom in the life of the Church in more favourable times.

3.2 Martyrdom, Authority, and Episcopacy

This ecclesiological issue is my third explanation for the demise of martyrdom. A rudimentary cult of the martyrs had been in existence since the second century, with relics of martyrs being collected, and meetings taking place near their graves.[42] Martyrs were revered, and by extension so were those who had faithfully witnessed and were awaiting execution in prison. It was believed they could forgive sins and heal sickness. In the *Passion of Perpetua*, the eponymous heroine possesses spiritual authority, and is able to alter the postmortem state of her deceased brother (7–8). Moreover, she appears to possess ecclesiastical authority when she is asked to intervene in a squabble between a bishop and presbyter.

> Then we went out and before the gates we saw the bishop Optatus on the right and Aspasius the presbyter and teacher on the left, each of them far apart and in sorrow. They threw themselves at our feet and said: 'Make peace between us'. (13)

The authority of the martyrs threatened the developing episcopal authority of the Church. Cyprian, in his treatise, *On the Lapsed*, skilfully defends his own decision to go into hiding rather than face persecution, but is very careful not to criticize either the martyrs or the confessors. Yet, he limits their authority. Confessors, as we have seen, were asked to pardon the lapsed, and appeared to do so almost indiscriminately. However, Cyprian argues they have no right to forgive sins easily, and may in fact be doing the lapsed a disservice.

> But if any one, by an overhurried haste, rashly thinks that he can give remission of sins to all, or dares to rescind the Lord's precepts, not only does it in no respect advantage the lapsed, but it does them harm . . . Under the altar of God the souls of the slain martyrs cry with a loud voice, saying, "How long, O Lord, holy and true, dost Thou not judge and avenge our blood upon those who dwell on the earth?" And they are bidden to rest, and still to keep patience . . . The martyrs order something to be done; but only if this thing be just and lawful, if it can be done without opposing the Lord Himself by God's priest. (18)

Even the martyrs cannot forgive sins without God first doing so.

The martyrs can either do nothing if the Gospel may be broken; or if the Gospel cannot be broken, they can do nothing against the Gospel, since they become martyrs on account of the Gospel. (20)

Even then, only the bishop, he argues, can pronounce God's forgiveness. The confessors are made clergy without ordination on account of their deeds, but of course, simultaneously putting them under the authority of the bishop. A century earlier, the Montanists had contributed their share of martyrs, but again, on account of their disruption of episcopal authority were branded heretics. Despite the honour and power accorded the martyrs, when it came to authority, they were always going to take second place to the developing episcopacy. The final incident which signalled the end of an enthusiasm for martyrdom combines all three of the previous factors, and that is the Donatist Controversy.

3.3 The Donatist Controversy

In 304 a riot broke out outside a prison in Carthage when a group of prisoners tried to bring food and comfort to confessors who had been arrested for refusing to comply with the fourth edict of the Great Persecution, ordering all citizens to offer sacrifice. When they arrived, they were set upon:

The cups for the thirsty inside in chains were broken. At the entrance to the prison food was scattered only to be torn apart by the dogs. Before the doors of the prison the fathers of the martyrs fell and the most holy mothers. Shut out from the sight of their children. They kept their vigil day and night at the entrance of the prison. There was the dreadful weeping and the bitter lamentation of all who were there. (*Abitinian Martyrs* 20)

What marks this incident out from all previous martyr stories is that the violence was perpetrated by other Christians. The Deacon Caecilian had been sent by Mensurius, the bishop of Carthage, to prevent the confessors being visited in prison. The reasons for the bishop's actions are unclear, although Tilley speculates that it may have been to save other Christians from falling foul of a ban on visiting Christian prisoners, the penalty for which was starvation.[43] Whatever the reason, it is said that Caecilian set about his task with enthusiasm, being 'more ruthless than the tyrant, more bloody than the executioner' (20).

As with the previous persecutions under Decius and Valerian, although many Christians, such as Felix, had remained resolute against the demands to hand over the scriptures, others, including bishops and clergy, had succumbed. These were dubbed the *tradiatores*, and after the persecution had ended, there was a severe division between the tolerant and rigorist parties. The Donatists held that anyone who had been guilty of cooperating with the persecution could not hold office, and anyone ordained by them had dubious orders. Schism occurred in 311 when the bishop, Mensurius of Carthage, who had ordered the blockade of the prison, died. Before any bishops from the rigorist stronghold of Numidia arrived, the Carthaginians elected one of their own. The rigorists retaliated by electing their own rival bishop, Majorinus, who was succeeded by Donatus.

In 313 the Donatists appealed to Constantine to arbitrate between the two bishops. As well as the bishopric, funds and recognition by other cities and the imperial court were at stake. Two commissions in Rome (313) and Arles (314) ruled in favour of Caecilian, and the Donatists were ordered to submit to his authority. When the Donatists refused to back down, Constantine responded with repression, confiscating Donatists' goods and churches and sending the bishops into exile in actions reminiscent of Diocletian's first edict. Intense persecution followed in 317–321 and the *Donatist Martyr Acts* were produced. For the first, although certainly not the last time, Christians created other Christian martyrs. The *Acts of the Abitinian Martyrs*, although recounting events from the Diocletian persecutions, was an important piece of propaganda for the contemporary battle the Donatists now endured.

He [the devil] sought to burn the most holy testaments of the Lord, the divine scriptures, to destroy the basilicas of the Lord, and to prohibit the sacred rites and the most holy assemblies from celebrating in the Lord. But the army of the Lord did not accept such a monstrous order . . . Quickly it seized the arms of faith and descended into battle. This battle was to be fought not so much against human beings as against the devil. Some fell from faith at the critical moment by handing over to unbelievers the scriptures of the Lord and the divine testaments so they could be burned in unholy fires. But . . . many more . . . bravely resisted by freely shedding their blood for them. When the devil had been completely defeated and ruined and all the martyrs were filled with God's presence, bearing the palm of victory over suffering, they sealed with their own blood the verdict against the traitors and their associates, rejecting them from the communion of the Church. (*Abitinian Martyrs* 2)

The writer affirms the standard belief that persecuted Christians are engaged in a cosmic battle against the devil, in which some of the Christian army fall. The martyrs become the judges of those who failed, and testify on the Donatists' behalf against their Catholic opponents, recording their treachery, while preparing the *Acts'* readers for martyrdom. The Donatists claim the legacy of the martyrs and employ them to justify their current stance.

Constantine abandoned the persecution of the Donatists in 321, and for the next 25 years, the two churches coexisted. But in 346, after the Donatists again appealed to the emperor to confirm the Donatist bishop as the primate of Carthage, Constans ruled in favour of the Catholics and instigated the second of the persecutions. If the *Acts of the Abitinian Martyrs* implied the Donatists' Christian opponents were in league with Satan, the martyr acts from this period do not hold back:

The rage of the Gentiles [the Catholics] who were obeying the Devil chose the martyrs for the heavenly kingdom; and so the savagery of the traitors who were serving the Antichrist sent them to heaven. (*M. Marcellus* 1)

Just as the pagan Roman State had been transformed into the anti-Christ in the Apocalypse so now the Christian State is found to take on this mantle.

Christianity in North Africa had a history of commitment and martyrdom. As well as the Scillitan martyrs (c. 188), and Perpetua and Felicity (203), there had been strong rigorist tendencies led by Tertullian in that region. Therefore, it was not difficult for the Donatists to claim the martyrs' legacy. However, even after the end of the persecutions of Constans in 348, the Donatists' enthusiasm for martyrdom did not end. The movement spawned a radical fringe group, the Circumcellions, with a stronghold in Numidia. Frustrated by the lack of persecution, they created their own opportunities for martyrdom by attacking Catholics on the road, hoping to be killed. Others were more direct, and simply killed themselves. Augustine, who was the principal Catholic voice against the Donatists, complained:

If they could not find anyone whom they could terrify into slaying them with his sword, they threw themselves over the rocks or committed themselves to the fire or eddying pool. (*The Correction of the Donatists* 3.12)

In 411 Augustine had preached a sermon urging peace between the Catholics and Donatists. However, in the face of this provocation, he changed his position to advocate coercion to bring the Donatists back to the fold:

It is indeed better (as no one ever could deny) that men should be led to worship God by teaching, than that they should be driven to it by fear of punishment or pain; but it does not follow that because the former course produces the better men, therefore those who do not yield to it should be neglected. For many have found advantage (as we have proved, and are daily proving by actual experiment), in being first compelled by fear or pain, so that they might afterwards be influenced by teaching, or might follow out in act what they had already learned in word. (6.21)

Violence against the Donatists escalated, instigated by other Christians and enforced by the State, so that the Donatist Petilian could with some justification accuse the Catholics of acting like the persecutors of old:

The Lord Jesus Christ commands us, saying, 'When they persecute you in this city, flee ye into another . . . ' If He gives us this warning in the case of Jews and pagans, you who call yourself a Christian ought not to imitate the dreadful deeds of the Gentiles.

Or do you serve God in such wise that we should be murdered at your hands? You do err . . . if you are wretched enough to entertain such a belief as this. For God does not have butchers for his priests. (Augustine, *Answers to Petilian the Donatist*, II. 42)

Augustine's answer is since the Donatists are heretics, they cannot be persecuted. This is an important move by Augustine. Not only did he seek to restrict who could and could not be called martyrs as Clement had attempted two centuries earlier, he denies that it is possible to persecute those with whom he disagrees over doctrine. It is the cause not the death which makes a martyr, argued Augustine. His advocacy of violence against erring Christians together with a sharp redefinition of martyrdom, effectively 'unmaking' the martyrs of another tradition, would play itself out throughout the following centuries. However, whereas Tertullian had urged Christians to desire martyrdom rather than dying in bed, Augustine draws back from earlier Christian enthusiasm:

If we loved death it would be nothing to bear it for the faith . . . We praise the martyrs precisely because they bear what they do not love: suffering. By nature, not only humans but all living things fear death and protest against it. (s. 299.8)

Augustine effectively rewrites three centuries of Christian martyrdom with these words, and when he went further, insisting that one could die in bed and still be a martyr, the rhetoric of martyrdom became totally spiritualized. When martyrological language was claimed by the radical ascetics, the age of radical martyrdom was over.

CHAPTER 4

CHRISTIAN MARTYRDOM IN
AN ERA OF CHRISTENDOM

1 MARTYRDOM AND HOLY WAR

1.1 Spiritual Martyrdom

With the end of persecution came the end of martyrdom. However, the language of martyrdom was recycled. Whereas Christians of the past had to fight wild beasts in the arena, those who lived after the Christianization of the empire would face down and conquer spiritual foes through the renunciation of worldly temptation. This interpretation of martyrdom received a significant boost with Augustine emphasizing the witnessing aspect of the martyrs rather than their tortures and death. The torture that a martyr in the past might have had to undergo in order to demonstrate ultimate loyalty to and identification with Jesus in an age of persecution gave way to the voluntary self-denial of asceticism.

The crucial martyrological text in the gospels where followers of Jesus were called to deny themselves, take up the cross, and follow after Jesus, with its dramatic application to a judicial situation where a Christian could deny self and live or confess Christ and die, was totally spiritualized. This move had, of course, begun with Luke's rendering of the saying, where the taking up of cross was to be done daily (9.27), removing any possibility of a literal interpretation. So Athanasius can speak of Anthony's life of one where he is 'martyred daily' (*Life of St Anthony* 48).

Importantly, with martyrological language now applied to a life of spiritual discipline rather than death in the arena, 'martyrdom' could become democratized. Everyone could participate. So John Chrysostom urges all Christians to mortify your body, and crucify it, and you will yourself receive the crown of martyrdom. For what in the other case the sword accomplishes, then in this case, let a willing mind. (*Homily on Hebrews* 11.6)

Similarly, Augustine chides his congregation, 'Let no-one say "I cannot be a martyr because there is now no persecution." Trials are never lacking' (*Sermon on Martyrdom*). Martyrdom without persecution, as Basil put it, was clearly a more palatable prospect for the faithful. Everyone could battle against the forces of evil in their lives; against lust, temptation, envy, pride, and so on. The Christian's life was to be refashioned as a daily struggle in order to witness to Christ. To be sure, asceticism predates the end of persecution, and Cyprian, who was a promoter of martyrdom, lays the foundation for 'bloodless martyrdom'.

Let us be occupied at all times in spiritual works, that as often as the enemy approaches, as often as he tries to come near, he may find our heart closed and armed against him. Actually, for the Christian there is not only one crown which is obtained in time of persecution. The time of peace, too, has its own crowns, with which we are crowned as victors . . . after the adversary is laid low and overcome. To have conquered lust is the palm of continence. To have struggled victoriously against anger and insult is the crown of patience. To spurn money is to triumph over avarice. To bear the adversities of the world by hope in the things to come is the praise of faith . . . In this arena of the virtues we run daily, and to these palms and crowns of justice we attain without intermission. (*De zelo et livore* 16)

For Cyprian, one could win both a crown of martyrdom and a crown in times of peace, depending on where and when one lived.

Nonetheless, just as martyrdom had produced heroes who had displayed acts of extreme courage and endurance, so asceticism could be taken to an extraordinary level. Where once the martyrs had been the objects of pious reflection and devotion, now the desert ascetics became the Christian superstars. On his homily on the rich man and Lazarus, Jerome taught that living a life of extreme poverty carried the same rewards as martyrdom had centuries before (*Homily* 86). Relics of saints and holy hermits became as sought after as had the remains of the martyrs. Ascetics became the new spiritual elite, the combatants and athletes, who demonstrated *in extremis* what all Christians could now do: win the martyrs' crown. The language of martyrdom was simply too ingrained, to potent, to simply disappear in an age when persecution had ended. Martyrdom became spiritualized, though represented in outward displays of self-deprivation or even self-harm, through the mortification of the flesh. However, it would not be long before a new enemy at the door of Christendom would demand a new way of conceiving martyrdom.

1.2   The Crusades

If martyr language had been entirely spiritualized in the minds of the ascetics, with the rise of Islam in the East, Christians would have cause to almost completely despiritualize the war with Satan in their confrontation with the new threat. If, for the author of the epistle to the Ephesians, the fight was against principalities and powers (6.12), the battle into which his spiritual ancestors charged would be against flesh and blood, as Christians took up arms in ecclesially sanctioned wars against pagans and infidels.

Augustine had already laid out the conditions in which Christians could take up the sword. In the early formulation of the Just War, later refined by Aquinas, Augustine reasoned that so long as the cause was just, sanctioned by a legitimate authority, and was carried out with correct intent, violence could be inflicted by Christians. In addition, the Old Testament provided examples of Holy War demanded by God. This Holy War imagery had already been invoked in relation to Charlemagne's wars against the Saxons. In the face of Muslim threats to Rome, both Leo IV (r. 847–855) and John VIII (r. 872–882) offered indulgences to those who took up arms to defend the city. Once killing in battle was theologically justified as participation in Christian Holy War, it was only a small step before the dead in such conflicts were viewed as martyrs.

Although rare, some Christians who had died in battles against pagans, even by the ninth century, had been accorded the accolade of martyr. St Oswald, king of Northumbria died in battle against the Mercians in 642. Bede composed a martyr narrative for Oswald by describing in his account how he died in the act of praying, suggesting that the king died for God after the fashion of early martyrs. Soon miracles came to be associated with his dismembered remains, confirming his popular martyr status. Another English martyr-king, St Edmund, was venerated as a martyr soon after his death in 869 or 870 against the invading Danes. Similarly, a vision given to the monk Reichenau confirmed the martyr status of yet another warrior noble, Gerold of Bavaria, who had been killed in 799 fighting the Avars. The martyr-warrior tradition continued to develop, and two centuries later, moved from individuals to a whole band of soldiers, who were accorded martyr status in a vision recorded by Ralf Glaber in his *Histories*, written not long after the turn of the first millennium. Glaber recounts a story of the monk Wulferius, who, after celebrating Trinity mass on the altar of St Maurice the Martyr, saw a ghostly army of soldiers who had died in battle against Muslim invaders fill the church. Wearing white robes and purple stoles, signifying their martyr status, they told their story:

We are all men of Christian professions, but while we were fighting for the defence of our country and the Christian people against the Saracens, the sword severed us from this earthly flesh. Because of this divine Providence is now taking us all into the lot of the blessed.[1]

The Christian conception of Holy War developed throughout the eleventh century, so that all who fought in conflicts blessed by the pope were *militia Christi*. Pope Leo IX (r. 1048–1054) granted absolution to those who fought against Norman bandits in Italy. The promise of the abolition of sins continued to be an important factor in the recruitment for battle or the consolation of the fallen, so Leo could claim those who died were 'not to be mourned by funerals and ceremonies, but were joined with the holy martyrs in glory on high'. Similar honours were given to the troops who invaded Sicily in 1060 and England in 1066. However, it was under Gregory VII (r. 1073–1085) that Christian Holy War was most fully developed. He promised salvation to everyone who fought for whatever cause he promoted, especially in his own conflict against the Emperor Henry IV (1050–1106). Fighting in battle was to imitate the trials and suffering of Christ, he argued. When he pronounced that participation in war was an act of penance, he set the ideological and conceptual stage for the First Crusade of 1096.

Although Urban II offered penance for all who engaged in the First Crusade, it is not clear that he promised those who died in battle would become martyrs. However, that did not prevent the dead being proclaimed as such by popular acclamation. Songs that encouraged recruitment described those who had perished as wearing a heavenly crown. As kings and queens would discover in later centuries, even the Church could not dictate to the people who was and who was not a martyr. The first chronicle of the Crusade, the *Gesta Francorum*, is unambiguous about those who died during the siege of Nicaea in 1097:

Many of our men received martyrdom there and gave up their happy souls to God with joy and gladness, and many of the poor died of hunger for the name of Christ. Triumphing in heaven, they wore the stole of the martyrdom they had received, saying with one voice: 'Lord, avenge our blood, which was shed for you'.[2]

Similarly, the chronicler, Fulcher of Chatres, accords martyr status to the fallen in the First Crusade.

As soon as he had been laid to rest on earth, he was already crowned in heaven. Blissful, whom the Lord grants such glory, to be crowned by the laurel of martyrdom and counted among the martyrs'. (Fulcher of Chatres)

As we move into the period of the Second Crusade, the leaders of the Church become less reticent about the war dead. The great Second Crusade preacher, Bernard of Clairvaux, for example, in a recruitment sermon, enumerates the rewards for those who may die in the cause of Christ.

How blessed are the martyrs who die in battle. Rejoice, courageous athlete, if you live and conquer in the Lord, but exult and glory the more if you die and are joined to the Lord. Life is indeed fruitful and victory glorious . . . but death is better than either of these things. For if those are blessed who die in the Lord, how much more blessed are those who die for the Lord.[3]

The first Christian martyrs saw their struggle in terms of a spiritual conflict, not so much against lions and other wild beasts, but against Satan, who sought to remove them from their confession through the instruments of torture inflicted by the Romans. By resisting to death, Christians won that battle, and the crown of martyrdom. In the Crusades, that spiritual battle was actualized. The conception of the martyr-warrior, which itself developed from Jewish Holy War tradition, became associated with those who took up the sword in offensive battle against the infidel. Bernard assures the Crusaders that both killing and dying for Christ makes one worthy. 'The knights of Christ may safely do battle . . . as death for Christ, inflicted or endured, bears no taint of sin, but deserves abundant glory'. Martyrdom was now not only associated with dying, but with the act of killing.

2 MARTYRDOM AT THE REFORMATION

2.1 Martyr Devotion in the Pre-Reformation Era

The Crusades had provided Christians with an opportunity to fight, kill, and die for their religion, and although in the popular mind those who died were martyrs, the patterns of death were quite different from those of the early Christians. Nonetheless, the example of the early martyrs came to be an important devotional tool for medieval Christians as the martyrs took their place among other saints through whom intercessions were offered. In the *Book of the Hours*, martyrs were second only to apostles in the order of holy merit. However, the vast majority of Christians would not expect to follow their example in suffering for their faith. If anything, martyrs were often portrayed in a non-suffering beatific state. By their bravery and endurance of suffering, they had won the right to ask special favours of Christ, and so were often invoked in prayer:

O Virgin glorious hope, certain refuge of sinners, and you my good angel, and you blessed Saint Peter and the glorious ten thousand martyrs of great merit that suffered such martyrdom as Jesus Christ wherefore ye be glorious in paradise, be then unto me help, be ye there for to comfort me.[4]

Similarly, on continental Europe in the fifteenth century, prayers were offered to the 14 holy helpers, all of whom except St Giles were martyrs. This cult originated in Germany around the time of the

Black Death, and prayers were offered to individual saints for cure and protection from particular ailments, from headaches to sudden death.

At the same time there was renewed pietistic interest in the sufferings of Jesus. Throughout the Middle Ages, devotion to the Five Wounds of Christ grew in popularity, and images of the crucifixion were ubiquitous. Although opportunities to literally follow the model of martyrdom laid down by Jesus and the early martyrs were practically non-existent, save for the missionary campaigns of the Franciscans, popular literature emerged urging people to follow their attitude to dying, particularly in affliction. The *Ars moriendi* (the *Art of Dying*) became an influential manual on how to die well. The *Ars* underwent more than 70 printings in the last 30 years of the fifteenth century and was widespread throughout Europe. In its second of six chapters it depicts the time of death as a time of great temptation where the dying would face the attempts of devils to steal the soul to damnation. As with the early martyrs, in the final hour of one's life, the Christian hovered between heaven and hell. In this situation, the example of the martyrs' patient endurance of pain was to be followed. As Christ and his martyrs overcame affliction, so the Christian should not succumb to pride, heresy, or despair at the end. Death was placed in the theatre of cosmic conflict in the same way as the death of the early martyrs had been centuries before. Therefore, even though the actual experience martyrdom was far removed from the populous of Europe, the concepts, the images, and the traditions of martyrdom were very much part of the apparatus of medieval spirituality.

The presence of martyrological concepts probably explains a readiness among the people to proclaim as martyrs heroes who had died in all kinds of circumstances, such as Henry VI (1421–1471) and Archbishop Richard Scrope of York (c. 1350–1405) in England, and St Panacea (1378–1383) in Italy, all of whom enjoyed flourishing popular cults despite a lack of official recognition by the Church. Perhaps the most bizarre of the martyr cults was that of the thirteenth-century St Guinefort of Lyons. Miracles were reported at the grave of the martyr-saint, especially the curing of children from illness. All well and good but for the fact that St Guinefort was a dog! Guinefort had been killed by its master after he mistakenly thought it was attacking his baby, when in fact it had been protecting the child from a snake, and was thus declared a martyr!

Therefore, local martyr cults sprung up throughout the Middle Ages despite the Church's reluctance to canonize martyrs. Indeed no martyr-saints were created between 1280 and 1481. Martyrdom was most contested in this period in the case of the Franciscan followers of Peter John Olivi (1248–1298), who created a shrine to their founder and then sought martyrdom at the hands of the inquisitions at the turn of the fourteenth century. More conventionally, but still controversial, were those Franciscans killed attempting to evangelize Muslims in the early thirteenth century. Seven friars were arrested and executed in Morocco in 1227, but rather than attaining recognition as martyrs, many believed their mission had been suicidal. It would be more than 250 years later before the Church began to recognize the Franciscans killed in mission as martyrs.

2.2 The Proto-Reformation

With the onset of the Reformation, the contested nature of martyrdom would split the Church. What one group saw as the execution of heretics, others proclaimed as the witness of the martyrs. So when in 1429, William Emayne was put on trial for heresy, he proclaimed that William Sawtry, a Lollard who had been burned in 1401, was counted among those worshipped in heaven as martyrs. As well as the Lollards, the other significant proto-Reformation movement which produced martyrs were the Hussites of Bohemia.

Jan Hus (c. 1372–1415), whose work would be a profound influence on Martin Luther, was himself influenced by the teaching of John Wycliffe (c. 1328–1384). As rector of the Czech university, he set about reforming the Bohemian Church, speaking out against restricting communion to one kind, and in particular against the sale of indulgences advocated by the 'anti-pope' John XXIII against his rival, Gregory XII. In July 1412, a mob burned the papal bulls, and in response three men were beheaded. Their corpses were carried through the streets of Prague to Bethlehem chapel, bearing placards reading '*Ita sunt martyres* (these men are martyrs)'. On arrival at the chapel, Hus gave them a 'mass for martyrs' before they were interred in the chapel.[5] Hus was later arrested, and tried. He protested that many views ascribed to him were ones he did not profess. Nonetheless, he refused to recant unless the council could demonstrate his error from scripture. On 6 July 1415, Hus was condemned to death and burned at the stake for heresy. His death flamed Bohemian nationalistic passions, and led to the Hussite wars. As well as the political turmoil in Bohemia caused by Hus's death, Hus shaped what would become a full-blooded Protestant theology of martyrdom in two important ways. First, in his letters, Hus turned Christ's suffering and the experience of martyrdom in the early Church away from tools for devotion towards models faithful Christians would have to literally undergo.

> The creator, the King the Sovereign Master of the world, without being forced to it by his Divine nature, humbled himself . . . he suffered, whilst instructing us, sorrow, and grave affronts from the priests and scribes, to such a point that they called him a blasphemer, and declared him to be possessed of a devil, averring that he was not God, whom they excommunicated as a heretic, whom they drove out of their city, and crucified like one accursed. If, then, Christ supported such things from the priests . . . why should we be astonished that the ministers of the antichrist, who are more avaricious, more debauched, more cruel, and more cunning than the Pharisees, now persecute the servants of God, overwhelm them with insult, excommunicate, imprison, and kill them?[6]

Hus then applied Jesus' warning to the disciples that as the world hated him so it would hate them (Jn 15.20), casting the new proto-Reformation movement in the role of the faithful early Church, while the Catholic Church played not only the Roman State, but the role of the anti-Christ.

Secondly, before his death, he asked that his letters be preserved and his followers remember him (*Letter* 99). Both requests were granted. Printed literature was a potent carrier of the Protestant message of martyrdom. He was venerated as a martyr by his followers and added to litanies of saints, and remembered in songs, much to the annoyance of ecclesiastical authorities. Hus and Jerome of Prague (d. 1416) became models and points of resistance against Catholic pressures. Hussites and Catholics fought over the interpretation of these contested deaths. In 1419, Hussite preacher Jan Želivský (1380–1422) denounced those who had consented to the execution of Hus as murderers, while the Catholics responded by declaring it to be a capital offence to deny the burning of Hus and

Jerome had been just and holy. John Krása, a merchant of Prague (d. 1420) and Matthau Hagen (d. 1458) were both burned, among other things, for holding those convicted by the Catholic Church to be saints. Even when the Hussites were reincorporated back into the Catholic Church, the legacy of Hus and Jerome proved to be controversial as their feast day continued to be celebrated.

Many of Hus's letters looked forward to his impending martyrdom with some trepidation; above all, he was anxious that he die well. There are two conflicting contemporary accounts of his burning; a sympathetic account by Peter of Mladoňovice, and that of the hostile Catholic chronicler, Ulrich von Richental. Peter's more detailed narrative describes Hus praying and singing while he was burning, while Richental suggests he let out a terrible scream and died quickly. The attempt to control the accounts and legacies of such executions would play out time and time again throughout the Reformation period, as both Roman Catholic and Protestant apologists understood the important propaganda potential of the spectacle of martyrdom.

2.3   The First Reformation Martyrs

By the time Martin Luther nailed his 95 theses to the door of All Saints' Church, Wittenburg, in 1517, the Hussite controversy had passed. However, the martyrs the cause had produced, along with the Lollards, and followers of Wycliffe became models for the new Reformation movement. Indeed, in the early years of the Reformation, when it appeared Luther might pay with his life, he announced 'we are all Hussites'. For Luther, the suffering and resolve of the Hussite martyrs demonstrated the credibility of their cause.

In 1523 the Reformation movement gained its first martyrs, when two Augustinian friars, Johann van Esschen and Heinrich Voes, were burned in Brussels. Luther, in a pamphlet about the friars, interpreted these deaths as a confirmation that his vision was of the true Church, since persecution and martyrdom was a sure sign of the apostolic nature of the faith (WA 17.425.15–21). Scriptural texts warning that true disciples of Jesus would face persecution, be hated, and killed just as Jesus had been, gave the Reformers confidence of the authenticity of their cause. William Tyndale (c. 1494–1536) also related the suffering of the Protestants to that of Christ.

Comfort thyself with the hope of the blessing of the inheritance of heaven, there to be glorified with Christ, if thou here suffer with him. For if we be like him in his passions, and bear his image in soul and body, and fight manfully, that Satan blot it not out, and suffer with Christ with bearing record to right-eousness, then shall we be like him in glory. (*Exposicion uppon Matthew* 5–8)

Martyrs signified the rediscovery of the Gospel.

The importance Luther placed on martyrdom in the 1520s, that it was the mark of true faith, sat uneasily with the relative lack of persecution he personally suffered. He wrote of his shame when reading accounts of those known to him succumbing to Catholic persecution: 'How it shames me when I read this story that I had not long ago been found worthy to suffer the same. After all, I was ten times more deserving of it in the world's eyes'.[7] Of course, for the Roman Catholic authorities, the Reformers were heretics who required correction, and if they remained obstinate, death was the appropriate punishment. The difference between a martyr and a heretic was a matter of perspective. However, just as a simple corol-lary between martyrdom and truth caused problems in the early church, so too, when those not considered to be orthodox began suffering martyrs' deaths, Luther had to rethink.

The main problem for Luther was the Anabaptist movement, which produced more martyrs in the early reformation period than other Protestants and Catholics added together. In 1525, Thomas Müntzer was executed for his part in the German Peasants' Revolt. Müntzer was a radical reformer, who not only departed from Luther on many key issues, including his rejection of infant bap-tism, but also criticized Luther for his easy life. Faced with news of Müntzer's good death, and indeed of the Anabaptists in gen-eral, who had begun to be executed for religion from 1527, Luther resorted to Augustine's dictum: *non poena sed causa facit martyrem*. Of course, this is exactly the same reasoning the Roman Catholic Church would use to disqualify all Protestant martyrs.

Anabaptists were particularly vulnerable in the sixteenth century. Whereas Lutheranism and Calvinism gained important and stra-tegic strongholds in Europe, the Anabaptist theology that there was no kingship other than God's meant they were without the security of a civic safe haven, save for the Moravian Huttite communities of the later sixteenth century. In the 1520s, the Anabaptists found themselves squeezed between the Roman Catholic authorities on one side, and the Lutherans and Calvinists on the other. Re-baptism was made a criminal offence in Zurich in 1526, and hundreds of martyrs were made in South Germany, Austria, and Switzerland before 1530. Between 1527 and 1530 around 500 were martyred in the Low Countries and France. The experiences of persecution reinforced the Anabaptists' own sense of radical separation from civic society.

Anabaptists were persecuted/prosecuted for various reasons. Obviously, Roman Catholics pursued them for heresy, while for some Protestants, the issue was their destabilizing influence on the State. Their rejection of infant baptism, anti-clericalism, and radicalized separation from the State, reinforced by the uprisings and revolts of 1524 and 1534, made Anabaptists appear dangerously revolutionary. Anabaptists were not only burned and decapitated, but as a fit punishment for re-baptism, many were drowned. To choose to become Anabaptist was effectively to place oneself in danger of martyrdom, and so the possibility of death defined them. In pamphlets, but more often songs, the bravery and example of the faithful dead were recalled. Many of those songs were collected in the *Swiss Brethren Hymnal*, first printed in 1564, which not only recalled trials, but urged the faithful to stand resolutely against inevitable persecution, and to follow the example of the martyrs. Hundreds of songs were included in Mennonite martyrologies, most famously 'The Martyrs' Mirror', which although published in 1660 had many incarnations through the previous century. In general, persecution, suffering, and martyrdom were given an apocalyptic interpretation; the experience of the faithful was a sign of the End.

Both Catholic and Protestant observers commented favourably on the way in which many Anabaptists met their deaths. So Florimond de Raemond said of the Huguenot martyrs:

[People] see the simple minded little women seek out tortures as a way of proving their faith, and going to death they cry out only 'Christ', 'Saviour', singing some psalm, the young virgins walking more cheerfully to their place of execution than they would have done on the way to the marriage bed. The men rejoice seeing the terrible and frightening preparations and instruments of death that have been readied for them, and half-burned and roasted, they regard from above the executioners the cuts received by the pincers with an unconquered courage.[8]

Catholic and Protestant opponents of Anabaptists are often found to marvel at their happiness to die:

They dance and jump in the fire, view the glistening sword with fearless hearts, speak and preach to the people with smiles on their faces; they sing psalms and other songs until their souls have departed, they die with joy, as if they were in happy company, they remain strong, assured, and steadfast to the point of death.[9]

Although impressed by the manner of the death of the Anabaptists, both Catholic and Protestant were united that ultimately, not only were they in error, but their executions were justified.

2.4   Protestant Martyrs

Protestantism posed a far greater threat to the peace and stability of Medieval Europe because as well as the religious turmoil caused by the movements around Luther and Calvin, Protestantism not only spread quickly, but gained the support of princes, so that in many areas the new version of the faith was supported by the civil authorities. This meant that although Charles V (r. 1519–1556; d. 1558) and his son, Philip II, husband of Mary Tudor, (d. 1598) were zealous in their desire to prosecute heresy throughout the empire – Philip is reported to have said that he would rather lose all his states than be the sovereign of heretics – their desires were often thwarted by there being no sympathetic magistrates to carry out the campaign. Indeed, political alliances often crossed traditional religious lines, such the initial alliances forged with Protestant princes by Francis I of France against the Holy Roman Emperor Charles V. Political instability led to various conflicts, especially the Wars of Religion, the most notorious incident of which is the St Bartholomew's Day Massacre (1572).

Nonetheless, thousands of Protestants were tried for heresy and burned at the stake, particularly in France, Germany, the Low Countries, and Switzerland. However, for the first time heretics were not isolated individuals, but comprised a mass movement of mutual support and encouragement, aided in no small measure by the printing press. Soon after the burning of the Augustinian monks in 1523, no fewer than 16 editions of a martyrological pamphlet were in circulation, explicitly calling the friars both saints and martyrs. Stories of martyrs, letters of exhortation, and sermons created a theology for a new age of martyrdom.

Luther and Calvin both wrote to those in prison urging them to remain steadfast to the true faith, and follow the example laid down by the martyrs before them. So Calvin in his *Brief Treatise* speaks of his expectation of those awaiting martyrdom.

I require nothing of them except to follow as much as what a thousand martyrs before us have done . . . [T]his doctrine . . . is the one that the martyrs of Jesus Christ have pondered in the middle of all the torments that they had to endure. And through this reflection, they were strengthened for conquering the horror and the fear of prisons, furnaces, fire, the gallows, the sword, and every other kind of death . . . [T]heir steadfastness is not recited for us so that we merely praise it, but so that it will be an example for us, and so that we will not renounce the truth which they so powerfully maintained; that we will not deny and will not corrupt the glory of God, which they so esteemed that they shed their blood to seal and confirm it.

Both Calvin and Luther faced criticism that they wrote from relative comfort about the sufferings of others, a point that caused Luther some anguish. Nonetheless, the Protestants saw themselves as faithful followers of Jesus:

We have not only Christ for our example, but also the godly, both prophets and apostles, which in likewise be tempted, persecuted, stoned, killed, and crucified, as Paul of himself witnesseth.[10]

Potential martyrs were also able to send letters to one another in prison, and often met together, which undoubtedly strengthened their resolve to die. Witnessing the martyrdom of those who had gone before provided a spur to faithfulness to others. As the example of the early Christian martyrs, such as Polycarp, were used to inspire similar acts of courage, so too, Protestant martyrs were incorporated into the 'great cloud of witnesses' (Heb. 12.1), and became models of noble warriors to be imitated. George Joye expounds this idea in a reworking of Tertullian's maxim about the blood of the martyrs being the seed of the Church.

> Let us therefore, Christian brethren, be constant in obeying God rather than men, although they slay us for the verity. For our innocent blood shed for the gospel, shall preach it with more fruit . . . than ever did our mouths and pens. Consider the beginning of the Christian religion, and the first fruits of the primitive Church, and we shall see innumerable innocents slain, as it hath been these twenty years past . . . Let us therefore rejoice and thank God that it would please him to use our bodies and blood unto his glory and promoting of his work . . . For the Lord's field when it waxeth dry, lean, and barren, it must be watered, made fat, dunged, and composed with the innocent blood and bodies of his faithful. [11]

The early Church provided models for martyrdom, and those who persecuted the Protestants were cast in the roles of evil Roman emperors, such as Nero or Diocletian, but also Satan.

Of course, it was not only the witness of the early Christians who provided an interpretative framework for the Protestants; the New Testament, with its teaching on suffering and discipleship could have been written for that time. Jesus had demanded that Christians confess him before governors and kings, and warned of dire eschatological punishments for those whose witness wavered. Luther interpreted the experience of the Reformation Church as evidence they were living in the Last Days, while others focused on the threat of damnation in so-called anti-Nicodemite tracts:

> We must never let slip out of our minds those most holy, most true, and healthful words of our Lord Christ . . . 'Everyone that shall knowledge me before me, him will I knowledge also before my Father which is in heaven. But whosoever shall deny me before men, him will I also deny before my father which is in heaven'.[12]

Calvin and Bucer were particularly strenuous in their warnings against prevaricating. However, faced with the reality of persecution in areas where massacres had all but wiped out Protantism, such as France after the St Bartholomew's Day Massacre, many of the small numbers of Protestants either returned to Rome or adopted the appearances of Catholicism. Where Protestants formed at least a significant minority, defiance in the face of death threats was more likely.

2.5 The Marian Martyrs

Martyrdom in England reached its height under Mary Tudor (r. 1553–1558). Her efforts to return England to the Roman Catholic fold, and the zealousness with which she prosecuted Protestant 'heretics', has left her the epitaph Bloody Mary. In her short reign she had more than 300 Protestants burned at the stake, around the same number of Roman Catholics executed in the entire period from Henry VIII (r. 1509–1547) to 1680. However, for the first time in England, martyrdom became a shared activity that defined group identity. Until then, most executions had been carried out for individual acts of treason or disobedience to the king. To be sure, Henry had executed men for heresy, but his targets had been somewhat diverse in belief. Although Thomas More and John Fisher would later be claimed as martyrs for the Roman Catholic faith, the vast majority of executions under Henry were of reformers. Indeed, More, as lord chancellor, had been responsible for carrying out the majority of them. Under Mary, doctrine and faith were centre stage in public execution, replacing the previously common charges of treason.

Many of Mary's victims were not men or women of nobility; most were of the lower classes. Indeed, there was a high proportion of women among those executed. There was also a surprising lack of clergy among those condemned for heresy. When Edward VI (r. 1547–1553) died, most clergy simply returned to Roman Catholicism. However, the first of Mary's victims were ten clergyman, and their stories inspired an industry of martyrology, most famously *Actes and Monuments of These Latter Perillous Dayes, Touching Matters of the Church*, better known as Foxe's *Book of Martyrs*. The *Book of Martyrs* first appeared in English in 1563, although it had appeared in various forms from 1554, including a shorter Latin version in 1559. Such was its popularity that it underwent no fewer than six editions within 50 years. Foxe had a profound influence on English Protestantism, and Queen Elizabeth I (r. 1558–1603), rather unrealistically, ordered that a copy be placed in every parish church.

Mary's accession to the throne put the prominent Protestant Reformers on the back foot. After all, they had put much store on the right of the monarch to determine a country's religion, and it is possible that herein lay the root cause of the former Archbishop of Canterbury Thomas Cranmer's (1489–1556) frequent recantations. Even so, although the lead Reformers had been quickly arrested, their executions had to wait until the Church of England had reunited with Rome, and the heresy laws of the previous century re-enacted. It was this delay of more than a year that enabled the condemned men to craft a communal theology of their own deaths. Sending letters to one another and to friends they urged each other to die well and to see themselves as martyrs for the true Church.

The delay gave the martyrs time to build support, and their deaths became eagerly anticipated. Martyrdom, as it had been in the early Church, became a very public spectacle between the resolve of the Protestants and the authority of the queen, and her now Roman Catholic State. Mary and her advisors assumed that when faced with the flames, and the choice to 'turn or burn' in the words of Nicholas Ridley, the Protestant leaders would make very public recantation, sending a powerful message to the public that Roman Catholicism was the true religion. However, if Mary thought the stake would lead to the collapse of the Protestants' resolve and return the country to a united faith, those hopes would be dashed by the manner of the martyrs' deaths. If anything, English Protestantism was created in accounts of Mary's funeral pyres.

In February 1555 John Rogers became the first Protestant martyr created by Mary. The theatrical nature of his death was recorded by the French ambassador, who described Rogers being led out as if to a wedding rather than execution. He was met by his wife and eleven children. At the last minute, he was offered an opportunity to have his life spared if he would renounce his faith and accept the queen's pardon. He refused her offer and was burned. According to the Spanish ambassador, the crowds clamoured to gather up his bones and ash as relics.

Mary's advisors understood all too late that the Protestants, through martyrdom, were winning the propaganda war. Realizing the damaging effect of having the queen's offer of pardon so publicly renounced, the offer was eventually withdrawn, and an effort was made to ban the collecting of the remains of the martyrs. Edmund Bonner, the bishop of London, sought to abandon public executions altogether, suggesting they should be carried out quickly and privately, such was the negative effect of Protestant martyrdom on reclaiming England for Rome. Foxe's martyrology of Hugh Latimer and Nicholas Ridley (d. 1555) suggests as much, as Latimer is made to say to his fellow martyr, 'Be of good comfort, Master Ridley, and play the man. We shall this day light such a candle, by God's grace, in England, as I trust shall never be put out'.

Protestants were able to cast their deaths in the role of the early Christian martyrs, who had remained resolute in the faith against a hostile ruler. Reports of the resolve of martyrs gave the Protestant movement credibility. When Lawrence Saunders (d. 1555) came to be executed, he rushed forward to embrace and kiss the stake, a ritual that became standard for those who died after him.

The propaganda coup Mary longed for appeared to be within her grasp in the case of Thomas Cranmer. Cranmer was sent to the Tower in September 1553, and having been transferred to prison in Oxford, was tired for heresy exactly two years later under the jurisdiction of Rome. He was not sentenced immediately as he recanted some of his views, recognizing the pope as the head of the Church. Nonetheless, he was sentenced to death in February 1556, after which he issued a full recantation of all his Protestant views, asked to be received back into the Catholic Church, received absolution, and participated in Mass. Despite these and further recantations, Mary insisted that he still be burned, probably motivated by revenge for his support for Queen Jane, and his denunciation of both Mary and her sister Elizabeth as bastards, and in doing so, overplayed her hand, losing her advantage.

Cranmer was told three days before his death that his final recantation would be made in public immediately prior to his execution. However, when the time came, he dramatically departed from his approved script, and distanced himself from his previous recantations.

And now, forasmuch as I am come to the last end of my life, whereupon hangeth all my life past and all my life to come, either to live with my master Christ forever in joy, or else to be in pain for ever with wicked devils in hell, and I see before my eyes presently either heaven ready to receive me, or else hell ready to swallow me up; I shall therefore declare to you my very faith how I believe, without any colour of dissimulation, for now is no time to dissemble, whatsoever I have said or written in times past. First I believe in God the Father Almighty, maker of heaven and earth . . . and I believe every article of the catholic faith . . . and now I come to the great thing, that so much troubleth my conscience . . . I renounce and refuse, as things written with my hand, contrary to the truth which I thought in my heart, and written for fear of death, and to save my life . . . such bills and papers which I have written or signed with my hand since my degradation . . . and forasmuch as my hand offended, writing contrary to my heart, my hand shall first be punished . . . it shall be first burned.

He was dragged from the pulpit and taken to the stake. Foxe's account goes on:

And when the wood was kindled, and the fire began to burn near him, stretching out his arm, he put his right hand into the flame, which he held so steadfast and immovable that all men might see his hand burned before his body was touched. His body did so abide the burning of the flame . . . he seemed to move no more than the stake to which he was bound: his eyes were lifted up unto heaven, and often times he repented his unworthy right hand, so long as his voice would suffer him: and using often the words of Stephen, 'Lord Jesus receive my spirit'; in the greatness of the flame he gave up the ghost.

This was martyrdom as spectacle at its best. For the queen, the spectacle of the former archbishop of Canterbury, the architect of Henry's divorce from her mother, Katherine of Aragon, and author of the Protestant prayer book, publicly affirming the Roman Catholic faith before his death would have been a catastrophic blow to the English Protestants. Instead, she handed Cranmer, who in many ways had nothing to lose, a platform from which he could dramatically recant of his recantations. Despite publishing his recantations, Mary's attempt to claim Cranmer as a symbol of the perils of Protestantism failed; the story of Cranmer's dramatic death spread, and the former archbishop was proclaimed to be a true and faithful martyr. The prevarication, confessions, and retractions counted for nothing. All that was necessary was his death.

Cranmer's image of the cosmic theatre of angels above and devils below was precisely that in which early Christians set their own decisions to die. It was relatively easy for English Protestants to cast themselves plausibly as the heirs of the persecuted, and therefore true, Church, and Mary and her regime in the same role as the persecuting Roman Empire. For Protestants, martyrdom signified the rediscovery of the Gospel. As the first Christians were persecuted, so the same should be expected when the Church rediscovered its true mission. God's hand was seen at work when Mary died in 1558 to be replaced by Elizabeth I; the martyrs were vindicated. History repeated itself. As the persecuted Church became the religion of the Roman Empire, so with the dawning of a new age of security, Elizabeth was portrayed by Foxe as the new Constantine.

2.6 Roman Catholic Martyrs

Whereas Protestant martyrs were tried and executed for points of doctrine, very few English Catholics were executed for 'religious belief' and none were killed for heresy. Under Elizabeth, most Roman Catholic martyrs were tried for treason rather than any religious cause. Of course, the English government's case that Catholicism represented primarily a political threat was strengthened by the Northern Rebellion of 1569 and the papal bull, *Regnans in Excelsis* (1570), in which Pius V excommunicated Elizabeth and threatened the same for any Catholic who obeyed her. Pius, in doing so, effectively defined loyalty to the papacy as treason in England; one could not be a good Catholic and a good Englishman.

And moreover (we declare) her to be deprived of her pretended title to the aforesaid crown and of all lordship, dignity and privilege whatsoever. And also (declare) the nobles, subjects and people of the said realm and all others who have in any way sworn oaths to her, to be forever absolved from such an oath and from any duty arising from lordship, fealty, and obedience; and we do, by authority of these presents, so absolve them and so deprive the same Elizabeth of her pretended title to the crown and all other the abovesaid matters. We charge and command all and singular the nobles, subjects, peoples and others afore said that they do not dare obey her orders, mandates and laws. Those who shall act to the contrary we include in the like sentence of excommunication.

Elizabeth until then had demonstrated relative toleration of the significant pockets of Catholicism around the country. However, faced with new political threats, she acted, first by outlawing the importation of papal documents, and then eventually by equating loyalty to the pope as treason. In response to the execution of priests, Roman Catholic martyrologies began to emerge and circulate.

Even during Mary's reign, there had been an effort to 'make' Roman Catholic martyrs. Thomas More was rehabilitated in preparation for his nomination for beatification. More, who had been Henry's lord chancellor, refused to affirm the Act of Supremacy, although neither did he speak against it. However, silence was not enough to please the king and he was executed in 1535. Towards the end of Mary's reign, Nicholas Harpersfield wrote of More, whose head had been displayed on a pole after his execution:

> Sir Thomas More's head had not so high a place upon the pole as had his blessed soul among the celestial holy martyrs in heaven. By whose hearty and devout intercession and his foresaid co-martyrs, and of our proto-martyr St Alban, and other blessed martyrs and saints of the realm . . . [we are restored] to the unity of the Church that we had before abandoned.[13]

Ironically, although it was to be the cause for which he came to be recognized as a martyr, More had earlier advised the king against too great an enthusiasm for papal authority. In 1521, Henry had written a treatise, *Defence of the Seven Sacraments*, in which he enthusiastically supported the supremacy of the pope, and for which had been awarded the accolade, Defender of the Faith, by Leo X.

Also remembered were the Carthusian martyrs, the monks of the London charter house, who similarly refused to assent to the act. Some were hanged, while others were left to starve in prison. Roman Catholic martyrs' loyal to the pope paved the way for the reunification of England with Rome. Of course, despite Henry's break with Rome, he was no Protestant. Indeed, under Henry, Protestants were executed for heresy.

If the primary purpose of the Roman Catholic martyrs under Mary was to inspire devotion and loyalty to Rome, when Elizabeth came to the throne, the need for martyr models became more pressing. In 1559, Parliament repealed the heresy laws, which had been revived under Mary, passed the Act of Supremacy, restoring the independence of the English Church, and the Act of Uniformity, authorizing only the use of the 1552 *Book of Common Prayer.* Nonetheless, before the mobilization of Roman Catholic political forces to attempt to depose her from the throne, Elizabeth was tolerant of private observance of the Roman Mass. Following her famous words, 'I will not put windows on men's souls', Elizabeth chose not to follow her sister's example and build her reign on the blood of martyrs. None of the 14 bishops who refused to assent to the Act the Succession were executed.

However, after the uprisings led by the earls of Westmorland and Northumberland in Durham and York (1569), and in response to increasing political threats, many of them focussed on the now imprisoned Mary, Queen of Scots, Elizabeth began to pass laws increasingly targeted at Roman Catholic priests. Importation of papal correspondence had already been outlawed in retaliation for the 1570 bull. In 1581, it became an offence to reconcile a subject to the Roman Church, and after the assassination of William of Orange in 1584, simply being a Roman Catholic priest or aiding a priest became a treasonable offence. When Mary was implicated in the Babington Plot of 1586, Elizabeth eventually agreed to her execution, which was carried out the following year.

England was the only country in Europe where Roman Catholics were formally tried before being executed. Most premature Roman Catholic deaths on the continent occurred through military conflict in the Wars of Religion. However, English legislation against Catholics in England was cast in purely political terms. To express loyalty to the pope was regarded as treasonously offering fealty to any other foreign ruler. The political machinations of Catholic conspirators made protestations that Jesuit missions to England were not political but religious rather incredulous. The attempted invasion by Spain in 1588, repelled by the English fleet, put the matter beyond any doubt. Nonetheless, not only did Catholic martyr narratives begin to emerge, but a zeal for martyrdom was inculcated in the newly formed English seminaries of Douai-Rheims (1568) and the English College, Rome (1576).

These seminaries, established for the purpose of saving souls in England, instilled in those they trained the very real possibility that to venture to England would result in death. Martyrologies and other tracts promoting the benefits of martyrdom became popular, such as Robert Southwell's *Epistle of Comfort* (1587/8), which asked, 'What greater pre-eminence is there in God's Church than to be a martyr? What more renowned dignity than to die in this cause of the Catholic faith'[14]. One of the most famous of the Catholic martyrs of this period was Edmund Campion, a Jesuit priest, who having trained at Douai, returned to England in 1580. He wrote a widely circulated pamphlet, 'A Challenge to the Privy Council', more famously known as Campion's Bragg, in which he denied any political motivation for his mission. However, whatever Campion's private intentions, his and others' mission was interpreted in the light of wider political events, not least the French support of the rebellion in Ireland. In 1581, Campion was arrested, paraded through the streets with the charge, 'Campion, the seditious Jesuit', and was later hanged, drawn, and quartered.

A huge volume of Catholic literature celebrating the martyrs appeared. So between 1580 and 1640 more than 200 editions of accounts of Catholic martyrs in England and Holland appeared. The priests were incorporated into the panoply of saints in heaven, available for intercession for the faithful. Campion is eulogized as a martyr in the famous poem of Henry Walpole, who witnessed his death.

> Why do I use my paper, ink, and pen,
> And call my wits to counsel what to say?
> Such memories were made for mortal men.
> I speak of saints whose names shall not decay . . .
> England look up: thy soil is stained with blood.
> Thou hast made martyrs many of thine own.
> If thou have grace, their death will do thee good;
> The seed will take that in such blood is sown.[15]

Campion and other English Catholic martyrs were used as models for other seminarians to imitate. The martyrs were exemplary disciples of Jesus, and to go to England was to obey Christ's command to take up the cross. William Allen, the founder of the Douai-Rheims College spurred on his students with Campion's example:

His quarters hung on every gate do show,
his doctrine sound through countries far and near,
his head set up so high doth call for more
to fight the fight which he ensured here,
the faith thus planted thus restored must be
'Take up thy cross', sayeth Christ, 'and follow me'.

Similarly, woodcuts and graphics compared the death of Christ with the martyrdoms of priests and their helpers. However, some would-be martyrs found their efforts thwarted. When priest Roger Dicconson and layman Ralph Milner were arrested at Winchester in 1591, a group of women appeared demanding to be executed, since they had also aided the priest and partaken in Mass. However, they were never put to death. As ever, martyrdom depended on finding a willing executioner!

However, as well as making martyrs of those judicially tried and executed in England, priests who died in battle were also regarded as martyrs. Furthermore, the assassins of William of Orange and Henry IV of France were also described as Catholic martyrs. Baltasar Gerard was tortured and executed for murdering William in 1584; yet there soon emerged pamphlets published throughout Europe calling him a martyr. The Welsh priest Richard Gwyn, who was executed in Wrexham in 1584, wrote a poem welcoming the killing. Similarly Jacques Clément, the slayer of Henry, was made a martyr by pamphlets and engravings in Paris. Martyrs, as in the Crusading era, could kill as well as die for God.

2.7 Contesting Death at the Reformation

In Thomas More's *Utopia* (1516), a world is envisaged where a plurality of religious views is tolerated. Moreover, an adherent of religion would be permitted to proselytize, 'provided he did so quietly, modestly, rationally, and without bitterness toward others'. Overzealousness, even for right religion, would result in exile. There would be no compulsion in religion, and exile, slavery, and violence are explicitly ruled out against those who decide not to follow the commended religion. Unfortunately, More did not live up to these ideals in his role as lord chancellor, and was as violent and zealous in his prosecution of heresy as any could be, and certainly had no qualms regarding the merits of burning heretics alive. More was also aware that those he executed not only attracted some public sympathy, but also died well. In his *Dialogue Concerning Heresies* (1529), More acknowledged that some regard those he burned to be martyrs. However, he dismissed them as 'the Devil's stinking martyrs'. Luther also dismissed those killed, whom he thought held erroneous beliefs, as 'martyrs of the Devil', regardless of how well those executed died.

For Catholics, Protestants, and Anabaptists, the manner of the deaths of their own tribe was proof enough for the truth of their religion. Efforts to discredit the so-called martyrs of the other factions by promoting stories of dreadful and ignoble deaths failed because of the power of competing narratives. Like those in the early Church, sixteenth-century Christians had to contend with rival groups producing martyrs. The Anabaptist leader, Nicolas Meynderts van Blesdijk, writing around 1546, and therefore long before the creation of Elizabethan martyrs, neatly summed up the problem, by comparing the Henrician martyrs with European Protestants and Anabaptists.

Within the last ten years some of the most learned and noblest people of the country [England] have been killed for the sake of the papist faith, indeed preferred to let their heads be chopped off rather than confess and consent to the king that he had the power to change the popish ceremonies without the pope's order. The same thing has been done by others for the sake of the freedom of the Gospel and water baptism; in Italy, France, Spain, Upper and Lower Germany, innumerable followers of Luther and Zwingli have been killed and are still being killed because they believe that their cause is just . . . And all of them, I say, although they all call upon the scriptures . . . and however prepared they are to defend their cause with the scriptures, are nevertheless opposed to the others. It is not and cannot be that all of them have and follow a proper understanding of God.[16]

This would be a problem that would only get worse as the sixteenth and seventeenth centuries unfolded.

Anabaptists could claim that since Christians were always the persecuted and never the persecutors (aside from a short period in the kingdom of Münster), theirs was the true religion. Protestants could point to the obvious abuses of the Roman Church through the sale of indulgences, and with the printing of the Bible in the vernacular, expose unbiblical practices. Catholics could point to the diversity of opinions within Protestantism, as well as the miracles attributed to their own martyrs. All three traditions attached huge significance to the deaths of their faithful, interpreting every successful martyrdom as a vindication of their truth. For those sentenced to death, dying as a martyr was preferable to living as a traitor to Jesus. As the martyrs of one tradition filled up the pages of the ever-burgeoning genre of martyrology, the other faith groups denied the significance of their death. The difference between a heretic and a saint, a martyr and a traitor was simply one of perspective. Each faction in their own way returned to Augustine's apologetic dictum that it was the cause rather than the punishment that made a martyr. However, it should be clear by now, that this is not to say very much at all. Whose cause counts?

The fate of Thomas Becket neatly captures the problem. As a result of a dispute over the relative authority of the Church and king, Becket was murdered in Canterbury Cathedral in 1170. Whether he was more concerned about the rights of the Church or his own position within it, or even whether Henry II intended the archbishop to be assassinated matters little. Within three years, he was canonized by Pope Alexander III, and Henry, on the verge of military disaster, made a very public act of penance at Becket's tomb. The turn of fortune on the battlefield was attributed to the new saint's intervention. However, nearly 400 years later, Becket was ordered to appear before Henry VIII for crimes against the king. When he (naturally) failed to appear, Henry ordered his remains to be burned and all mention of his name was banned. He was reinstated under the Marian revival, and is one of *The Three Thomases* in John Stapleton's treatise of 1588, who died as Catholic martyrs, alongside Thomas More and the Apostle. Within a few hundred years, Becket had been a martyr and a traitor, twice!

The story of martyrdom in the Reformation period is a narrative about narratives and counter-narratives. Martyrs were made, unmade, and sometimes remade. Martyrdom has always been a contested concept, and one's claim to martyrdom would be only as strong as the martyr narrative it produced. For the 5,000 souls who lost their lives around the Reformation, the great martyrologies of Foxe told their dramatic stories of courage, faithfulness, and controversy.

3 KINGS AND MARTYRS

The contested nature of martyrdom during the Reformation period, particularly in England, revolved around the issue of the relative claims on the people by the Crown or State and the Church. Indeed, this conflict between Crown and Church goes as far back as the twelfth century with the iconic struggle between Henry II and Thomas Becket. So, for the most part, under Henry and Elizabeth 'martyrs' in England were not executed for any particular religious belief but for their lack of commitment to the Crown. Similarly, on the Continent, many Anabaptists who were killed were executed for revolutionary behaviour. To be sure, such behaviour, whether revolutionary or treasonous, was in the minds of the martyrs and their supporters, indistinguishable from religious commitment. As with the early Christian martyrs, both executor and executed interpreted the same event in two radically diverse ways, yet both saw their view of the world vindicated. Nonetheless, the manner of the martyrs' death in many cases, created some challenge to the executors' narratives.

3.1 King Charles 'the Martyr'

I have so far concentrated on England in this treatment of martyrdom during the Reformation. Before leaving the Reformation period, I wish briefly to turn my attention to Scotland, and mention two related martyrological events which led directly from the turmoil of Reformation Britain. The first radically altered the relationship between Crown and people: the execution of King Charles I. The second, the Scottish covenanter martyrs, helping to reinforce that change in that relationship, despite the restoration of the monarchy, and arguably helped define, or at least reinforce, the identity of the Scottish nation.

Charles I (1600–1649) was born in Dunfermline, Scotland, the second son of James VI (James I of England). When his older brother, Henry, died in 1612, he became heir to the throne, to which he acceded in 1625. Charles was an unpopular king, not least because of his marriage to the Catholic, Henrietta Maria of France, and his attraction to higher forms of Anglican worship, causing suspicion among his Protestant people. Moreover, he suspended Parliament on three occasions from 1625. Believing God had directly appointed him to the throne, Charles dissolved the 1629 Parliament altogether, and ruled alone for the next 11 years. In a move which made the king even more unpopular, he sought to raise taxes to fund wars abroad without the permission of Parliament.

In 1637, Charles and his archbishop, William Laud, attempted to force an Anglican-style prayer book on Scotland, leading to the famous riot beginning in St Giles Cathedral in 1637, where Jenny Geddes is alleged to have thrown a stool at the unfortunate minister, shouting, 'Daur ye say mass in ma lug?'[17] The resultant unrest, together with the decisions of the 1638 and 1639 General Assemblies of the Church of Scotland to ban the prayer book, depose all bishops, and assert independence from the monarch in ecclesial matters, led Charles to instigate the so-called Bishops' Wars (1639–1640). However, the result was a disaster for the king. By 1640, the Scots had occupied Northumbria and Durham. Charles had recalled Parliament in April 1640 to raise funds to support his endeavours, but dissolved it almost immediately when they demanded he cede some of his powers. However, when forced to pay the expenses of the invading Scots, he recalled it again in November 1640.

A weakened Charles had to accept some of the demands of the English Parliament. However, he became increasingly determined to use any means necessary to seek revenge for the lack of support he had received in the Bishops' Wars. When he unilaterally attempted to have five prominent Parliamentarians arrested, civil war looked inevitable. Charles himself signalled the opening of the war, when he raised his standard in Nottingham in August 1642. After four years of bloodshed, Charles was defeated, and in 1646 surrendered to the Scottish army, which eventually handed him over to the English Parliament, headed by Oliver Cromwell (1599–1658).

However, Charles engineered the events, which led to the second civil war in 1648, all but ensuring his death. Royalist forces combined with disaffected Scots attacked, but were defeated the following year. Cromwell concluded that Charles had to be tried for devising 'a wicked design to erect and uphold in himself an unlimited and tyrannical power to rule according to his Will, and to overthrow the rights and liberties of the People' and 'upholding of a personal interest of will and power and pretended prerogative to himself and his family against the public interest, common right, liberty, justice and peace of the people of this nation'. As such, he was a 'tyrant, traitor, murderer, and a public and implacable enemy to the commonwealth of England'. For the first time, a king was declared to be subject to a higher civic law, and treason was redefined as an offence against the people rather than the monarch. The people, rather than the king now represented the State.

However, even though he had been despotic, incompetent, and very unpopular, he was still the king. The Parliamentarians had to turn the king into a traitor and a common criminal. If the Reformation in England had anything to teach the Parliamentarians, it was surely that public trials and executions rarely succeed. They sought to make Charles I a traitor; instead, they made a martyr. The show trial at Westminster Hall was pure theatre, and the king played his part well. Although afflicted with a stammer (and a thick Scottish accent!), he refused to enter a plea, and denounced the Parliament as illegal without the abolished House of Lords. Instead, he asserted, 'I am your king, your lawful king'. Rather than assert the divine right of his kingship, which would have surely fallen on deaf ears, he cast himself in the role of the protector of the people's liberty: 'I stand more for the liberty of my people than any here that seateth to judge'. If this charade of a trial could happen to a king, then what protection could a commoner claim?

Parliament lost the propaganda war, and in the end, only 58 of the original 115 appointed to the trial signed the death warrant. Nonetheless, the king was found guilty of treason and executed on 30 January 1649. While France in the eighteenth century and Russia in the twentieth overthrew their monarchs more efficiently, in the more polite seventeenth-century England, the condemned king was permitted to utter final words before his execution and was even provided with two scribes skilled in shorthand to record them.

The people's liberty and freedom consist in having government, in having those laws by which their lives and their goods may be most their own. It is not their having a share in the government. If I would have given way to an arbitrary way, to have all laws changed by the power of the sword, I needed not to have come here; and therefore I tell you that I am the martyr of the people . . . I go from a corruptible to an incorruptible crown, where no disturbance can be.

After the king's death, Parliament passed an act preventing the succession of his son, Charles. Eventually Cromwell was appointed to the lord protectorate, but after his death in 1658, the restoration of the monarchy became inevitable, and two years later Charles II was proclaimed king.

Within six months of his death, a cult of Charles the Martyr emerged with claims that a handkerchief stained with the king's blood had cured a young girl of blindness. After the restoration in 1660, in an almost precise reversal of Henry's humiliation before the tomb of Thomas Becket, Parliament decreed that the anniversary of Charles' death should be a day of fasting and humiliation by the people of England. Charles was canonized by the Church of England, and a service for his commemoration day's observance was incorporated into the 1662 *Book of Common Prayer*. The day was removed from the calendar in 1858, in protest of which, the Society of Charles the Martyr was founded. The society remembers Charles as a martyr for the Church, claiming he was offered his life in return for abandoning the historic episcopacy. Effectively, Charles is claimed for the Anglo-Catholic wing of the Church of England. That historically this is actually untrue, and that Charles, in fact, agreed to impose Presbyterianism on the Church of England in return for the support of the Scots, hardly matters; what matters is the narrative that not only 'creates' the martyr, but determines the type of martyr, and the cause for which he died. Charles' own words demonstrate his anti-democratic belief against the people being involved in government. That is the issue for which he died. Charles I is a good example of my claim in Chapter 1 that martyrs do not require a good life, only a good death.

3.2 The Scottish Covenanters

When the 1640 General Assembly of the Church of Scotland dispensed with the need for the monarch in religious matters, they were asserting a peculiarly Scottish tradition, stretching back to at least the Declaration of Arbroath (1320). Indeed, whereas every other country or city state in Europe generally affirmed the principle that the ruler determined the religion of his subjects, Scotland had a Protestant parliament and a Catholic monarch, Mary, Queen of Scots. In 1560, under the leadership of John Knox (c. 1510–1572), the Church of Scotland abolished bishops, and adopted a proto-democratic model for electing ministers. This democratic principle together with the separation of Church and Crown meant the

Reformation in Scotland was relatively bloodless. The lynching of Cardinal Beaton (c. 1494–1546) in retaliation for the burning of the protestant George Wishart (1513–1546), an event Foxe puts down to God's vengeance, stands out in this regard.

Between 1560 and 1690, the Church of Scotland switched between a Presbyterian and Episcopal polity several times, but the bishops' actual powers were checked by its initial democratic principle. The 1637 revolt against the prayer book was an assertion of that principle, and led to the signing of the National Covenant at Greyfriars Kirk in 1638 by ministers, nobles, and thousands of ordinary Scots. The covenant was in effect a contract between the Scottish nation and God, over and against the claims of Charles I to be God's prince, and it was adopted by the Scottish Parliament of 1640. Nonetheless, while the covenant certainly curtailed the king's power over matters religious, it did make expressions of loyalty to the monarch. However, loyalty to the king was contingent on his undertaking to defend 'true religion':

That we shall in like manner, without respect of persons, endeavour the extirpation of Popery, prelacy (that is, Church government by Archbishops, Bishops, their Chancellors and Commissaries, Deans, Deans and Chapters, Archdeacons, and all other ecclesiastical officers depending on that hierarchy), superstition, heresy, schism, profaneness, and whatsoever shall be found to be contrary to sound doctrine and the power of godliness, lest we partake in other men's sins, and thereby be in danger to receive of their plagues; and that the Lord may be one, and His name one in the three kingdoms.

We shall with the same sincerity, reality and constancy, in our several vocations, endeavour with our estates and lives mutually to preserve the rights and privileges of the Parliaments, and the liberties of the kingdoms, and to preserve and defend the King's Majesty's person and authority, in the preservation and defence of the true religion and liberties of the kingdoms, that the world may bear witness with our consciences of our loyalty, and that we have no thoughts or intentions to diminish His Majesty's just power and greatness. (Articles II and III)

Although when in exile, Charles II signed the National Covenant, in 1662 he declared it to be unlawful and demanded that all his subjects denounce it. Those who would not were stripped of their livelihoods. Archibald Campbell, the Marquess of Argyll, and one of the architects of the covenant, was executed for treason. After the re-imposition of episcopacy, covenanters held open-air meetings, which had been declared to be illegal, and many were hunted down and executed. At the height of the covenanting uprisings, the king instituted a policy of extra-judicial killing. Once again, where a British monarch saw dangerous sedition, the covenanters saw martyrs. However, the covenanters were not only martyrs for God, the National Covenant made them martyrs for Scotland. So, a report of the last covenanter, James Renwick, to be killed includes among his final words, the prayer:

Lord, I die in the faith that thou wilt not leave Scotland, but that thou wilt make the blood of the witnesses the seed of thy church, and return again, and be glorious in our land. And now, Lord, I am ready – 'the bride, the Lamb's wife, hath made herself ready'.

Just as the martyr Jan Hus became an important marker of Czech nationalism, so the covenanting martyrs reinforced a distinctively Scottish sense of religious identity. In a move that would have pleased Renwick, Presbyterianism was restored to the Church of Scotland by an act of Parliament in 1690 after William and Mary deposed James VII (and II of England).

Although the covenanters were driven by a religious cause, they were part of a much more significant political shaping of the nation. When blood is spilled for a particular cause or tradition in times of conflict, the issues for which martyrs died becomes difficult to set aside in times of peace. Martyrdom has an undoubted political dimension. Mel Gibson's portrayal of William Wallace (c. 1272–1305) in the film *Braveheart* casts Wallace not only as a martyr for Scotland, but of the general principle of freedom, and by extension, democracy.

4   MODERN MARTYRS

It has been said that more Christians died for their faith in the twentieth century than the previous 19 taken together. Many martyr stories come from the mission fields, in a tradition begun by the Franciscans in the Middle Ages. Wherever Christianity has spread martyrs have been created. The bloodiest episode occurred in Japan, after a mission led by the Portuguese in the 1660s. From 1662 to 1666, some 20,000 Christians are reported to have been massacred for allegedly destabilizing the empire in a move which effectively wiped out a Christian presence in the country since Francis Xavier's missionary enterprise in 1549. Christianity had suffered at the hands of the state, and in 1597, many Christians were crucified, the so-called 26 martyrs of Nagasaki. When such large numbers are killed, the individual martyr narrative gives way to a collective narrative.

Many massacres since have been recounted as martyrdoms, such as Stalin's assault on the Orthodox churches in 1922, when more than 8,000 died. Even where the stories of individuals are highlighted, they tend to represent a much larger group. The accounts usually lack any supernatural intervention, and even the dimension of cosmic conflict is played down or entirely absent. Holy War has all but disappeared from the rhetoric of missionary martyrdom. Martyrs are models of extreme bravery, and almost always passive resistance.

Christian martyrdom over the last 200 years suffers from ambiguities of definition. Many commentators are concerned that their deaths were political rather than spiritual, that they could have avoided the situation they found themselves in, and even if their motivations were religious, their deaths did not mirror the demand to confess or deny Christ. One account from Madagascar stands out, but in doing so runs into inevitably questions of historicity. The London Missionary Society brought Christianity to Madagascar in 1818, and was initially successful. However, after a change of regime, missionaries were expelled in 1836, and the indigenous peoples who had converted faced massacre. A visitor to the region, William Ellis, recounts the trial of 18 Christians, which he not only self-consciously casts after the model of the Diocletian persecutions, but retells the trial in the style of the ancient martyr act:

On the 14th March 1849 the officer before whom the Christians were examined said, 'Do you pray to the sun, or the moon, or the earth?' [The Christian] answered, 'I do not pray to these, for the hand of God made them'

'Do you pray to the twelve mountains that are sacred?
'I do not pray to them for they are mountains' . . .

The trial continues in a similar vein. The Christians are condemned and sentenced to death, 14 to be thrown over a precipice, and four, to be burned alive. As the 14 are taken to the place of execution, the report notes 'their faces were like the faces of angels'. The four who were burned

> sang a hymn after they were in the fire. Then they prayed, saying, 'O Lord, receive our spirits, for thy love to us has caused this to come to us; and lay not this sin to their charge'. Thus they prayed as long as they had any life. Then they died; but softly, gently: indeed gently was the going forth of their life. And astonished were all the people around that beheld the burning of them there.

The story appears in W. Bramley-Moore's 1869 revision of Foxe's *Book of Martyrs*, and also in R. Backhouse's, *Christian Martyrs: A Handbook of Believers Who Have Dared to Die for God* (1996). In both its 1869 and 1996 manifestations it plays an apologetic and exhortative function. As these Christians demonstrated loyalty to Christ to the point of death, so contemporary readers, whether in the nineteenth or twentieth century, might compare their rather insipid religious lives and be inspired to deeper conviction against the unnamed foe of secularism.

Another contemporary edition of an ancient martyrology has the opposite intention. Father Antonio Gallonio's *Tortures and Torments of the Christian Martyrs* (1591) has been republished as recently as 2004 by Feral House, which plays up the pornographic elements of both the original writing and, in particular, woodcut illustrations. These two recent publications capture the controversial aspect of martyrdom to both inspire and attract, as well as repulse.

The category 'martyr' has continued to disintegrate, as political and religious causes become blurred. Even post-colonial martyrdom in Africa may be interpreted not so much as the results of the persecution of the Christian faith, but the intolerance of autocratic regimes of the alternative political power base the Church represents. But even Christian martyr narratives have blurred the distinction between religious and political causes. The abolitionist agitator John Brown's (1800–1859) ill-fated attempt to lead a slave uprising in the American South was inspired by a belief that God had called him to take direct action against an oppressive system. He was tried for treason against the state of Virginia, and for the murder of five slave owners. He was hanged in 1859. The extent to which his actions led to the American Civil War are disputed, but in the aftermath of his execution, some churches rang their bells, meetings praising Brown's actions were held, and Brown was acclaimed a martyr, not least in the famous song, the 'Battle Hymn of the Republic' (1861):

John Brown's body lies a-moulderin' in the grave . . .
His soul is marching on!
Glory, Allelluia . . . His soul is marching on.
He's gone to be a soldier in the army of the Lord . . .
His soul is marching on!

The second verse's imagery of fighting in God's army recalls the Holy War tradition of the Crusades, and a salutary reminder that both killing and dying for God has a long history in Christian martyrological tradition.

The First and Second World Wars resulted in the martyr cults of soldiers in both Britain and France, where all who resisted occupation had a claim to the martyrs' crown. Similarly, those who die in Iraq and Afghanistan are honoured by rudimentary elements of martyr devotion. Killing, even in secular causes, does not bar one from qualifying as a martyr. We have already noted the some of the ambiguity in Dietrich Bonhoeffer's claim to martyrdom, yet he is now uncritically accepted as such. Similarly the other nine martyrs in the Westminster memorial for twentieth-century martyrs all met deaths that have an unavoidable political element. Each, with the exception of the South African Manche Masemola (d. 1928), are examples of heroic individuals who stood up against oppressive regimes or systems. Even the way in which Manche's death is retold resonates with the much later injustices of apartheid South Africa. Martin Luther King, Janani Luwum, Oscar Romero, and all the others, although memorialized in a Christian context, are essentially modern secular martyrs. Yet, in their stories, unlike the passivity of missionary martyrs, they, like the early Christian martyrs, were each the protagonist in a wider struggle or conflict. In terms of the overall history of Christian martyrdom, it is more recent stories of missionary martyrs, which by their accounts of the martyrs' passivity, represent the exception to the presence of the Holy War motif in Christian martyrology.

CHAPTER 5

MARTYRDOM IN JUDAISM

1 EARLY JEWISH MARTYRDOM

Although Judaism was once described as 'eine Religion des Martyriums',[1] when taken as a whole, we find within the scope of Jewish history some ambivalence towards martyrdom. In Jewish thought there are many instances, in both antiquity and in more modern periods, where the value of martyrdom is downplayed. Indeed, there is no set Hebrew term for martyrdom: *Kiddush hashem* (sanctification for the name) comes closest. Nonetheless, martyrdom has cast a long shadow over the development of Judaism.

In common with Islam, the foundational formation of Judaism is set in the battle. Conquest and Holy War narratives dominate the books of the Deuteronomist. However, like Christians, Jews also experienced intense periods of severe persecution, the responses to which had a profound influence on the development of Jewish martyrology. What was perhaps unique to Judaism, mirrored only in the last 50 years or so in Islam, were experiences of persecution and military Holy War possibilities coexisting simultaneously. Both traditions, present in the martyrdom narrative of Samson discussed above, are found throughout the Hebrew Scriptures. This is because Jewish theology usually interpreted suffering as just desserts visited by God on his people in response to periods of national apostasy. Such suffering was deserved and principally corrective. National disobedience resulted in defeat on the battlefield, loss of land, and exile. However, there was always restoration as God returned his blessing on Israel after due punishment and repentance. Whilst the seeds of resistance to this theology are found in some psalms and the development of the theme of the righteous sufferer, it endured as the dominant explanation for suffering until the second century BCE.

1.1 Persecution under Antiochus

In 167 BCE, Antiochus IV (Epiphanes), king of the Seleucid Empire, entered Jerusalem to put down a revolt. After retaking the city, he issued a decree banning the observance of many distinctive Jewish identity markers:

Then the king wrote to his whole kingdom that all should be one people, and that all should give up their particular customs. All the Gentiles accepted the command of the king. Many even from Israel gladly adopted his religion; they sacrificed to idols and profaned the Sabbath. And the king sent letters by messengers to Jerusalem and the towns of Judah; he directed them to follow customs strange to the land, to forbid burnt offerings and sacrifices and drink offerings in the sanctuary, to profane Sabbaths and festivals, to defile the sanctuary and the priests, to build altars and sacred precincts and shrines for idols, to sacrifice swine and other unclean animals, and to leave their sons uncircumcised . . . He added, 'And whoever does not obey the command of the king shall die'. (1 Macc. 1.41–50)

The author of 1 Maccabees clearly disapproves of this action, but even through his negative assessment, we get a hint that the king's motivation was not primarily persecution, but cultural unity. Furthermore, the text reflects the many Jews who had already become Hellenized to the extent of abandoning such Jewish practices. Nonetheless, a great many Jews refused to obey the king's commands.

According to the decree, they put to death the women who had their children circumcised, and their families and those who circumcised them; and they hung the infants from their mothers' necks. But many in Israel stood firm and were resolved in their hearts not to eat unclean food. They chose to die rather than to be defiled by food or to profane the holy covenant; and they did die. Very great wrath came upon Israel. (1 Macc. 1.60–64)

The first and second books of the Maccabees chart the revolt against the Seleucids until independence was established in 142 BCE. They narrate not only successful military uprisings, but stories of individuals who would rather die than transgress the Laws of Moses. These conflict stories are reflected not only in the books of the Maccabees, but other apocryphal and pseudepigraphal writings. From this period onward, stories began to circulate about Jews who preferred death rather than transgress the Law. For example, the story of Taxo and his seven sons:

And there shall come upon them a second visitation and wrath, such as has not befallen them from the beginning until that time, in which He will stir up against them the king of the kings of the earth and one that rules with great power, who shall crucify those who confess to their circumcision: and those who conceal (it) he shall torture and deliver them up to be bound and led into prison . . . Then in that day there shall be a man of the tribe of Levi, whose name shall be Taxo, who having seven sons shall speak to them . . . 'My sons, hear me: for observe and know that neither did the fathers nor their forefathers tempt God, so as to transgress His commands. And you know that this is our strength . . . Let us fast for three days and on the fourth let us go into a cave which is in the field, and let us die rather than transgress the commands of the Lord of Lords, the God of our fathers. For if we do this and die, our blood shall be avenged before the Lord'. (*Testament of Moses* 8–9)

The *Testament*, narrated as prophecy, reports a time of persecution when those faithful to the Law will die. Taxo and his sons willingly die in the belief they will be avenged. The most famous of these conflict stories is found in the book of Daniel.

1.2 Daniel

Strictly speaking there are no martyrs in Daniel; it is a book concerned with faithfulness and miraculous deliverance. Daniel, Shadrach, Meshach, and Abednego face the same pressure to abandon their Jewish identity markers as the readers at the time of Antiochus. They stand firm in response to decrees from the king and, when they refuse to eat polluted food or abandon the worship of God, are sentenced to death. However, the heroes are miraculously delivered. For those reading the book of Daniel in the second century BCE there was no such spectacular deliverance. The lack of such deliverance is acknowledged in the narrative itself. As the three youths are threatened with the fiery furnace, they reply:

> If it be so, our God whom we serve is able to deliver us from the burning fiery furnace; and he will deliver us out of your hand, O king. *But even if he does not*, be it known to you, O king, that we will not serve your gods or worship your idols. (Dan. 3.17–18; emphasis added)

The fact that God does not always deliver his people from danger is accounted for, but even so, the three remain resolute. Nonetheless, in Daniel, the redemption of the righteous sufferer does occur, but it is postponed to a post-mortem eschatological time.

> At that time . . . there shall be a time of anguish . . . [but] your people shall be delivered, everyone who is found written in the book. Many of those who sleep in the dust of the earth shall awake, some to everlasting life, and some to shame and everlasting contempt. Those who are wise shall shine . . . like stars. (Dan. 12.1–3)

In the face of experiences of terrible suffering and martyrdom of the faithful, previous theological accounts of suffering collapsed. Faithfulness in the face of persecution, torture, and execution demanded vindication. This vindication came through a developing theology of resurrection. Daniel 12.1–3 are the only verses in the Hebrew Bible to speak of a general resurrection, but that theology was substantially developed in the aftermath of the Maccabean revolt.

1.3 The Maccabees

While both 1 and 2 Maccabees describe the military exploits of the family of Judas Maccabeus, it is in the second book where martyrdom plays a pivotal role.[2] First the historical background is rehearsed: King Antiochus, having taken the Jerusalem Temple after an unsuccessful Jewish uprising led by Jason (2 Macc. 5.5–16), decreed that the Jews were to abandon their ancestral traditions

(6.1), but many stand firm and are executed (6.9). Women who had their sons circumcised were thrown off the ramparts with their babies around their necks (6.10), while a group of secret Sabbath observers were betrayed and burned alive in caves, refusing to defend themselves because of the holy nature of the day (6.11). The heart of 2 Maccabees is the more detailed account of eight martyrs: Eleazar, a 90-year-old teacher of the Law, who chooses to die rather than eat pork (6. 18–31; also 4 *Macc.* 5–7); and the torture and execution of seven brothers (7.1–42; also 4 *Macc.* 8–18).

First, Eleazar was forced to eat pork, but spat it out 'preferring a glorious death to a life of defilement' (6.19). The author, approving of this course of action, cautions his readers that even the 'love of life' should not cause the faithful to transgress the Law (6.20). His persecutors offer a compromise. He need not eat the meat if he only pretends to do so. However, Eleazar refuses. To do so, he argues, would lead the young astray, and leave him liable to God's judgement:

> By bravely giving up my life now, I will show myself worthy of my old age and leave to the young a noble example of how to die a good death willingly and nobly for the revered and holy laws. (2 Macc. 6.27–28)

Enraged by Eleazar's stubbornness, his captors take him to the rack, beat him, and execute him. The author commends his action as an example how all the nation should act. 'This is how he died, leaving in his death a model of courage and an unforgettable example of virtue not only for the young but for the whole nation'. (2 Macc. 6.31)

The stories of Eleazar, Daniel, and the three friends are clearly similar. All five model resistance against a tyrant king's command to defile Jewish Laws. Unlike the characters in the Daniel narrative, there is no miraculous deliverance for Eleazar. The scribe's dying concern for the young is then dramatized as seven brothers become the next martyrs for the Law. Despite horrific tortures, each brother, encouraged by the others and their mother, resist all demands to transgress the Law. The brothers endure being roasted, scalped, having their hands and feet amputated, and their tongues cut out, yet welcome further torture and death.

The youngest brother said: 'What are you waiting for? I will not obey the king's command. I obey the command of the law given to our forefathers through Moses'. (2 Macc. 6.30)

Like Eleazar, the seven brothers left an example to all who heard their stories that even under the most extreme pressure, it was better to die for the sake of the Law.

The account of the seven brothers also leaves a more theological legacy in the development of the afterlife. Each brother is given a speech before his death providing insight into the developing doctrine. The first and second brothers affirm God will raise the righteous to everlasting life (2 Macc. 7.9), while the fourth claims there is no resurrection for the wicked (7.14). These themes are already found in Daniel. However, with the third brother there is a new development: bodies mutilated through torture will be restored:

When it was demanded, he quickly put out his tongue and courageously stretched forth his hands, and said nobly, 'I got these from Heaven, and because of his laws I disdain them, and from him I hope to get them back again'. (2 Macc. 7.10–11).

The experience of suffering and martyrdom necessitated a more robust doctrine of vindication than had previously existed within Jewish theological thought. That said, those who died for the Law do not simply leave a noble example to be followed and a theological legacy. In 2 Maccabees, the martyrs contribute to the winning of the temporal revolt.

At first, the battle does not go well for the Jews.

Raging like a wild animal, he [Antiochus] set out from Egypt and took Jerusalem by storm. He ordered his soldiers to cut down without mercy those whom they met and to slay those who took refuge in their houses. There was a massacre of young and old, a killing of women and children, a slaughter of virgins and infants. In the space of three days, eighty thousand were lost, forty thousand meeting a violent death, and the same number being sold into slavery.

Not satisfied with this, the king dared to enter the holiest temple in the world . . . He laid his impure hands on the sacred vessels and gathered up with profane hands the votive offerings made by other kings for the advancement, the glory, and the honor of the Place. Puffed up in spirit, Antiochus did not realise that it was because of the sins of the city's inhabitants that the Lord was angry for a little while and hence disregarded the holy Place . . . The Lord, however, had not chosen the people for the sake of the Place, but the Place for the sake of the people. Therefore, the Place itself, having shared in the people's misfortunes, afterward participated in their good fortune; and what the Almighty had forsaken in his anger was restored in all its glory, once the great Sovereign became reconciled. (2 Macc. 5.15–20)

For the writer, this military disaster, including the defiling of the Temple is caused by the unfaithfulness of the people. The blame is put on those who had sought Hellenization to the extent of abandoning outward signs of Judaism. Such disregard for the Law provoked God's wrath and caused him to withdraw his protection even from the sanctuary. Only when God is reconciled to his people, he argues, will the Temple be restored once again.

The people may have thought that as well as abandoning the Temple, God had also abandoned them. The calamitous experiences of invasion and military defeat mirrored the period of exile, the setting of the book of Daniel. However, the author of 2 Maccabees urges his readers not to interpret their experiences as God's abandonment of them.

Now I beg my readers not to be disheartened by those tragic events, but to reflect that such penalties were inflicted for the discipline, not the destruction of our race. It is a sign of great benevolence that the acts of impiety should not be overlooked for long but rather should meet their recompense at once. The Lord has not seen fit to deal with us as he does with other nations: with them he patiently holds his hand until they have reached the full extent of their sins, but on us he inflicts retribution before our sins reach their limit. So he never withdraws his mercy from us; although he may discipline his people by disaster, he does not desert them. (2 Macc. 6.12–16)

Suffering is not a sign of abandonment but of discipline. In intervening with punishment before their sins become too great, argues the author, God ensures the people will not be destroyed. Experiences of suffering now and throughout history, though severe, put off far worse punishment at the end of the ages.

The martyr narratives of Eleazar and the seven brothers are placed into this context. During their tortures, the brothers affirm the notion they suffer as part of God's disciplining of the people (7.18, 32). However, their suffering is not merely an expression of God's wrath, it is its fulfilment. The youngest brother answers the king:

> It is for our own sins that we are suffering, and, though to correct and discipline us our living Lord is angry for a brief time, yet he will be reconciled with his servants . . .
> I, like my brothers surrender my body and my life for our ancestral laws. I appeal to God to show favour speedily to his people and by whips and scourges to bring you to admit that he alone is God. May the Almighty's anger, which has justly fallen on our race, end with me and my brothers. (7.31–32; 37–38)

The sacrificial language of the youngest brother's intercession is striking. The martyrs are not only obedient to the Law, they take upon themselves the guilt of the people, and focus God's anger towards the nation onto themselves. The Temple, having been defiled, was no longer the place of restoration and atonement between the people and God. Instead, the martyrs' bodies become not only the sacrifice for sin, but the locus of that sacrifice; they take on the role of both the sin offering and the Temple. The martyrs' obedience and sacrifice replace the defiled Temple, enabling God to be reconciled with his people and prepare the way for the Temple to be restored and re-dedicated.

The youngest brother's prayer is answered. With his death, the anger of God is satisfied, and the time of wrath is ended. The martyrs' atonement triggers a change in fortune for the Jewish people in battle. Once the narrator has finished with the martyrs, he immediately moves on to the account of Judas Maccabaeus' successful campaign. He explicitly links the two events: 'the Gentiles found Maccabaeus invincible, *now that the Lord's anger had turned to mercy*' (2 Macc. 8.5). In dying for the Law, the martyrs died for the Jewish people and turned God's anger to mercy. Disobedience brought military disaster, and faithfulness resulted in victory; the martyrs' deaths were the ritual transaction marking the transition from one to the other.

Clearly, in dying for the fatherland, the sacrifice of the Maccabean martyrs fits the category of Noble Death. Taking place in the context of battle, their sacrifice closely resembles examples of *devotio*. A more clear-cut example of volitional death for others takes place on the battlefield, when the king's armies employ elephants in their advance against the Jews.

> Eleazar, called Avaran, saw one of the beasts bigger than any of the others and covered with royal armor, and he thought the king must be on it. So he gave up his life to save his people and win an everlasting name for himself. He dashed up to it in the middle of the phalanx, killing men right and left, so that they fell back from him on both sides. He ran right under the elephant and stabbed it in the belly, killing it. The beast fell to the ground on top of him, and he died there. (1 Macc. 6.43–46)

Eleazar's voluntary death is both heroic and, according to the author, for the benefit of his people. However, there is another lens through which the martyrs' deaths could be interpreted: Jewish Holy War.

1.4 Holy War and Ancient Israel

In Jewish tradition, God fought exclusively on behalf of Israel, and through battle, led his people into Canaan, the divinely appointed land. Their enemies, the occupants of the land, were defeated and cleared. However, nowadays, the Holy War tradition in the Old Testament is often treated with some understandable embarrassment; the bloody conquest of Canaan is at best the mythic exuberance of later scribes, at worst divinely sanctioned genocide. Clearly the principle aim of Holy War in the book of Deuteronomy was to take the land appointed by God to the Hebrews.[3] However, another major justification for Holy War was to keep the people free from idolatry.

> When the LORD your God shall bring you into the land where you are entering to possess it, and shall clear away many nations . . . greater and stronger than you, and when the LORD your God shall deliver them before you, and you shall defeat

them, then you shall utterly destroy them. You shall make no covenant with them and show no favour to them. Furthermore, you shall not intermarry with them . . . For they will turn your sons away from following me to serve other gods; then the anger of the LORD will be kindled against you, and He will quickly destroy you. But thus you shall do to them: you shall tear down their altars . . . and burn their graven images with fire. For you are a holy people to the LORD your God; the LORD your God has chosen you to be a people for His own possession out of all the peoples who are on the face of the earth. (Deut. 7.1–6)[4]

So long as the people remained faithful to God, they would enjoy military victory even against superior forces. However, the price of such victory was the annihilation of all temptations to idolatry. To do otherwise would threaten contamination and risk Yahweh's anger.

For if you are careful to keep all this commandment which I am commanding you, to do it, to love the LORD your God, to walk in all His ways and hold fast to Him; then the LORD will drive out all these nations from before you, and you will dispossess nations greater and mightier than you . . . See, I am setting before you today a blessing and a curse: the blessing, if you listen to the commandments of the LORD your God, which I am commanding you today; and the curse, if you do not listen to the commandments of the LORD your God, but turn aside from the way which I am commanding you today, by following other gods which you have not known. (Deut. 11.22–23, 25–28)[5]

War or violence was not only justified but demanded in order to keep the people free from contaminating influences.

Possessing and retaining the land was dependent on obeying God's will, and so, all traces of idolatry, including idolaters themselves, were to be completely destroyed. Crucially, the people of Israel were included in this threat. Anyone who threatened to lead the people astray was to be executed (13.6). Even family members were to be slain should they serve other gods:

If your own full brother, or your son or daughter, or your beloved wife, or your intimate friend, entices you secretly to serve other gods, whom you and your fathers have not known, gods of any other nations, near at hand or far away, from one end of the earth to the other: do not yield to him or listen to him, nor look with pity upon him, to spare or shield him, but kill him. Your hand shall be the first raised to slay him; the rest of the people shall join in with you. (13.7–10)

In the grand scheme of things, mass slaughter, including of one's own family, was preferred to idolatry.

The importance of the Hebrews keeping themselves free from idolatry is well illustrated by the story of Achan (Josh. 7). After the spectacular victory against Jericho (Josh. 6), God commanded the people not to take any of the spoils. However, Achan disobeyed this command. Despite the act being committed by an individual in secret, the sin is taken to be corporate: 'But the Israelites acted unfaithfully' (Josh. 7.1). Despite having superior military strength, the Israelites suffer defeat against Ai. It is only when Achan is discovered, stoned, and burned along with his sons, daughters, and livestock, that 'the LORD turned from the fierceness of his anger' (Josh. 7.26). Only the death of the transgressor, along with all traces of his crime, reconciles God to his people, and enables them to defeat the forces of Ai (Josh. 8). The martyrdoms of Eleazar and the seven brothers fulfil a similar function in 2 Maccabees. In order to prosper in Holy War, the people must be made holy through the spilling of blood.

1.5 Holy War in the Books of the Maccabees

Both 1 and 2 Maccabees portray the Maccabean revolt as Holy War, but in different ways. In the first book, Judas Maccabeus, his troops vastly outnumbered by the Syrians, confronts his men's fear with the conviction that God fights for them.

'How can we, few as we are, fight so great and so strong a multitude? And we are faint, for we have eaten nothing today'.

Judas replied, 'It is easy for many to be hemmed in by few, for in the sight of Heaven there is no difference between saving by many or by few. It is not the size of the army that victory in battle depends, but strength that comes from Heaven. They come against us in great insolence and lawlessness to destroy us and our wives and children, and to despoil us; but we fight for our lives and our laws. He himself will crush them before us; as for you, do not be afraid of them. (1 Macc. 3.17–22)

Judas' speech has obvious resonances with Jonathan's (1 Sam. 14.6) and Gideon's (Judg. 7.2) in similar circumstances. With God on their side, Judas' army wins the battle. [6] After his victory, 'Judas and his brothers began to be feared, and terror fell on the Gentiles all around them' (1 Macc. 3.25) in the same way the Israelites were feared after their Old Testament conquests.[7]

It was Judas's father, Mattathias, who sparked the revolt, tearing down false altars (2.44–45), and slaying renegade Jews who had abandoned the Law. Following the Deuteronomic imperative, Israel had to be purged of idolatry. Burning with zeal, he led the warriors of Israel – 'all who offered themselves willingly for the Law' – into battle (2.42–43). If in 1 Maccabees the heroes are those who fight for the Law, in 2 Maccabees, those who turn the fortunes of Israel are those who die for the Law.

Second Maccabees develops this concept of classical Deuteronomistic Holy War tradition. The pattern of sin and disaster is emphasized in a way in which it is not in the first book of Maccabees. Military disaster has befallen the Jews because of their sin of disobedience to God. The locus of the action is still battle, and as in 1 Maccabees, a battle which Judas will win. However, in contrast, holy warriors zealous for the Law do not achieve victory. In 2 Maccabees, God's favour is turned towards his people because of the faithfulness of a handful of individuals, whose shed blood causes God 'to hearken to the blood that cries out to him' (8.3). God then enables Judas to win the military conflict, for 'his wrath had turned to mercy' (8.5). Therefore, in 2 Maccabees, the context of the battle was still primarily conventional. Uprisings had failed while God's anger burned against his people because of idolatry, but the martyrs through the spilling of their blood, caused God to turn again to the people, leading to a successful military campaign. Just as the sin of individuals brought collective punishment, so the faithfulness of individuals led to salvation.

However, like the persecuted righteous of Daniel 12, there is also personal eschatological reward for the martyrs. The traditional

Holy War ideology has been combined in 2 Maccabees with developing eschatological promise, creating a potent apocalyptic matrix within which to interpret the deaths of the faithful. They affected the cosmos by turning God's anger away from the people, and in 2 Maccabees, for the first time, a military struggle is placed in an apocalyptic framework. In a startling departure from the tone of 1 Maccabees, the second book has heavenly armies appearing to fight for the Jews.

As soon as dawn broke, the armies joined battle, the one having as pledge of success and victory not only their valor but also their reliance on the Lord, and the other taking fury as their leader in the fight. In the midst of the fierce battle, there appeared to the enemy from the heavens five majestic men riding on golden-bridled horses, who led the Jews on. They surrounded Maccabeus, and shielding him with their own armour, kept him from being wounded. They shot arrows and hurled thunderbolts at the enemy, who were bewildered and blinded, thrown into confusion and routed. Twenty-five hundred of their foot soldiers and six hundred of their horsemen were slain. (2 Macc. 10.28–31; cf. 11.6–10 and 12.17–25)

Even so, idolatry remained a constant danger, and when some Jews fell in an otherwise successful battle at Idumea, they were found to be concealing idols under their tunics (2 Macc. 12.39). Fortunately on this occasion, the disobedience of a few did not have catastrophic consequences for the whole army.

There are obvious contrasts between the martyrs of the Maccabees and the heroes of Daniel. Daniel has miraculous deliverance stories, whereas in 2 Maccabees, the heroes die. Nonetheless, God's miraculous deliverance is still present in Maccabees in two ways. In the first instance, the martyrs are miraculously delivered through resurrection. Secondly, military victory is granted for the whole people, so that with God's help, the land is purged of the oppressive and idolatrous Gentiles. The author of 2 Maccabees explains the suffering of the Jewish people in terms of discipline and punishment; a temporary turning his face away from his people and the Temple. The individual suffering of the martyrs atone for the people's sin in the absence of the Temple; their deaths are apocalyptic; they make the cosmic transaction causing God once again to intervene on the side of the Israelites in the Deuteronomistic Holy War tradition.

The martyrs demonstrate unswerving loyalty to the Law. Indeed, the books of the Maccabees set the entire conflict as one in defence of God's Law. However, it is worth noting that the warriors had to compromise the Law for which they were fighting in order to win victory. After the initial rebellion, those zealous for the Law fled to the desert. The king's armies pursued them and attacked on the Sabbath. Rather than profane the Sabbath, the Jews resolved not to fight.

> Then the enemy attacked them at once; but they did not retaliate; they neither threw stones, nor blocked up their own hiding places. They said, 'Let us all die without reproach; heaven and earth are our witnesses that you destroy us unjustly'. So the officers and soldiers attacked them on the Sabbath, and they died with their wives, their children and their cattle, to the number of a thousand persons. When Mattathias and his friends heard of it, they mourned deeply for them. 'If we all do as our kinsmen have done', they said to one another, 'and do not fight against the Gentiles for our lives and our traditions, they will soon destroy us from the earth'. On that day they came to this decision: 'Let us fight against anyone who attacks us on the Sabbath, so that we may not all die as our kinsmen died in the hiding places'. (1 Macc. 2.35–41)

The reasoning of Mattathias, whose zealousness had sparked the revolt, that ultimately parts of the Law, which they were defending, had to be set aside in order for the people to survive and ultimately win becomes a critical piece of reasoning in later Jewish martyrological tradition. Dying for the Law was indeed noble, but in a critical departure from the example of Daniel and the three friends, and indeed, in distinction to Christian theologies of martyrdom, death was not always preferred to life.

2 ROMAN PERSECUTION

The Maccabean Revolt led to a period of Jewish independence. The Temple was 're-dedicated' in 164 BCE by Judas Maccabeus. After the death of Judas, his brother Jonathan wrested further control of

Israel from the Seleucids, before Simon, the last surviving son of Mattathias, won outright independence in 142 BCE, and took the titles of ethnarch and high priest. As Simon was not of the Zadokite line, his ability to become high priest was disputed, leading to tensions among the elite. His son, John Hyrcanus I (r. 134–104), became priest/king after an attack by the Seleucids was repelled, and advanced his kingdom into Samaria and Idumea. However, the Hasmonean dynasty lasted only a few generations. Troubled by family strife, John's grandsons, Hyrcanus II and Aristobulus II, vied for power, each appealing to the now powerful Romans to intervene on their behalf. So, in 63 BCE, General Pompey entered Jerusalem beginning the Roman occupation of Judea that would last seven centuries.

Herod the Great (r. 40–4 BCE), who had married Hyrcanus' granddaughter, was appointed king over Judea, Galilee, Idumea, Samaria, and Perea by the Roman Senate. In 37 BCE, he added Israel to his kingdom by having his wife's uncle, the High Priest Antigonus II, executed. Under Herod's reign, the kingdom enjoyed relative stability, and the Temple underwent extensive renovation as part of a prolific building programme. After Herod's death, his kingdom was divided between the sons he had not executed: Archelaus (r. 4 BCE–6 CE) became ethnarch of Judea, Idumea, and Samaria; Philip (r. 4 BCE–33 CE) was appointed tetrarch of the regions north of the Sea of Galilee; and Antipas (r. 4 BCE–39 CE) became tetrarch of Galilee and Perea. In 6 CE, Archelaus was deposed, and Judea, Idumea, and Samaria came under direct Roman rule.

2.1 The Jewish War

Memories of the Maccabean period, combined with the celebration of Passover, with its theme of liberation from foreign bondage, ensured tension flared up from time to time. This tension manifested itself most explosively when the Temple appeared to be threatened. Opportunities once more presented themselves to the Jews to die for the Law and the Temple. Initially, procurators appeared sensitive to Jewish sensibilities. This all changed when Pilate was appointed in 26 CE.

> Pilate . . . introduced Caesar's effigies, which were upon the ensigns, and brought them into the city; whereas our law forbids

us the very making of images; on which account the former procurators were wont to make their entry into the city with such ensigns as had not those ornaments. Pilate was the first who brought those images to Jerusalem, and set them up there; which was done without the knowledge of the people, because it was done in the night time; but as soon as they knew it, they came in multitudes to Caesarea, and interceded with Pilate many days that he would remove the images; and when he would not grant their requests, because it would tend to the injury of Caesar, while yet they persevered in their request, on the sixth day he ordered his soldiers to have their weapons privately, while he came and sat upon his judgment-seat, which seat was so prepared in the open place of the city, that it concealed the army that lay ready to oppress them; and when the Jews petitioned him again, he gave a signal to the soldiers to encompass them, and threatened that their punishment should be no less than immediate death, unless they would leave off disturbing him, and go their ways home. But they threw themselves upon the ground, and laid their necks bare, and said they would take their death very willingly, rather than the wisdom of their laws should be transgressed; upon which Pilate was deeply affected with their firm resolution to keep their laws inviolable, and presently commanded the images to be carried back from Jerusalem to Caesarea. (Josephus, *Antiquities* 18.3.1)

Pilate's induction into Judean politics was not a happy one. Whether exaggerated or not, Josephus records an incident not only of mass civil disobedience, but preparedness to die on a mass scale. Pilate's intended action mirrored that of Antiochus IV, the incident which sparked the Maccabean revolt. Pilate had been poorly briefed. Presented with the opportunity to slaughter so many Jews, Pilate backed down, and the Temple remained unmolested for the time being.

However, soon after, Pilate took money from the Temple to build the aqueduct, and this time when a riot broke out, many thousands were killed (*War* 2.9.2-4–177; cf. Lk. 13), one of a number of massacres that took place under Pilate. After Pilate had slaughtered a group of Samaritans who intended to assemble at Mt Gerazim, the Emperor Tiberius recalled Pilate in 36 CE. By the time Pilate returned to Rome the following year, Tiberius, rather fortunately for Pilate, had died.

Jewish resolve to die for the Temple was tested once again when Caligula, Tiberius' successor, ordered a statue of himself to be set up in the Temple in 41 CE. This may have been in response to some Jews tearing down an imperial ensign in Jamnia. However, the intervention of Herod Agrippa and the successful procrastination of the Governor Petronius until the death of the emperor, probably delayed the Jewish War.

In the 50s and 60s, sections of the Jewish community became further radicalized. Prominent among the radicals were the *sicarii* (the dagger men), assassins who targeted those they regarded as collaborators in Roman rule. Tension continued to grow until it eventually boiled over. The garrison at Masada was overrun by sicarii and the Roman soldiers massacred. In 66 CE, the Temple captain, Eleazar ben Ananias, ordered the cessation of all Temple sacrifices for foreigners, including the emperor. This was a declaration of independence. The small number of Roman troops fled to the palace and surrendered in return for safe passage out of Jerusalem. However, as they lay down their weapons, they were slaughtered. The region was in turmoil and Rome intervened. The Syrian legate Cestius assembled an army and marched on Jerusalem to lay siege against the city. But the siege was abandoned. While the soldiers retreated, an outnumbered army from Jerusalem came against them, and killed around 5,000 Roman soldiers. Euphoric with victory, the radicals set up a revolutionary government, and pronounced Simon Ben Giora to be the messianic king. For the first time since Pompey entered Jerusalem, Judea was independent.

In response, Nero sent his general Vespasian to the region. Vespasian recaptured much of the lost territory, but turmoil in Rome following the assassination of Nero halted his progress as he waited for news of how to proceed. The succession of short-lived emperors brought no resolution from Rome, so in June 69, Vespasian resumed his attack, only to be proclaimed emperor by the army the following month. His appointment was confirmed by the senate later that year. Vespasian's son, Titus, laid siege to Jerusalem. Inside the city, rival factions competed for power as the population were ravaged by famine that killed half a million. In 70 CE, the walls of the city were breached, and Jewish deserters were crucified in many positions along the city walls to deter the resistance. When the Romans reached the Temple, it was set alight, and as Josephus testifies, even then some Jews were prepared to defend the Temple with their lives:

As for the priests, some of them plucked up from the holy house the spikes that were upon it, with their bases, which were made of lead, and shot them at the Romans instead of darts. But then as they gained nothing by so doing, and as the fire burst out upon them, they retired to the wall that was eight cubits broad, and there they tarried; yet did two of these of eminence among them, who might have saved themselves by going over to the Romans, or have borne up with courage, and taken their fortune with the others, throw themselves into the fire, and were burnt together with the holy house. (*War* 6.5.1)

2.2 Masada

Aside from the destruction of the Temple, the most famous event of the Jewish War was the taking of Masada. Rebel forces had captured the fortress in 66 CE, from where they launched a series of raids on the Romans. After the fall of Jerusalem, the Romans surrounded the fortress and constructed a ramp by which to enter the settlement. When they succeeded, they found 960 inhabitants dead. There were only seven survivors of what had been a mass suicide. The only account of the incident is by Josephus, and care must be taken in assessing his testimony. His main aim was to demonstrate to his Roman audience that Judaism was a noble religion. Masada is put forward as an example of peculiar bravery in the face of defeat. In order to defend the inhabitants' actions, he put a speech into the mouth of the zealot leader, Eleazar:

Since we, long ago, my generous friends, resolved never to be servants to the Romans, nor to any other than to God himself, who alone is the true and just Lord of mankind, the time is now come that obliges us to make that resolution true in practice . . . Let our wives die before they are abused, and our children before they have tasted of slavery; and after we have slain them, let us bestow that glorious benefit upon one another mutually, and preserve ourselves in freedom, as an excellent funeral monument for us. But first let us destroy our money and the fortress by fire; for I am well assured that this will be a great grief to the Romans, that they shall not be able to seize upon our bodies, and shall fall of our wealth also; and let us spare nothing but our provisions; for they will be a testimonial when we are dead that we were not subdued for want of necessaries, but that, according to our original resolution, we have preferred death before slavery. (*War* 7.8.6)

For Josephus, death was better than slavery to the Romans. He is concerned to stress this is a noble choice not borne out of desperation, so includes the detail about not destroying the food. Josephus expects his readers to interpret the events in the light of Noble Death, and provides a prompt for how he expects his readers to react by noting the attitude of those who found the corpses:

Nor could they do other than wonder at the courage of their resolution, and the immovable contempt of death which so great a number of them had shown, when they went through with such an action as that was. (*War* 7.9.2)

Notably, Josephus did not take this course of action when he found himself in similar circumstances. When the Romans took Jotapata, Josephus, who was the commander of the Jewish troops, found himself trapped with forty others in a cave. They agreed to draw lots and kill each other until the last survivor killed himself rather than hand themselves over to the Romans. However, when only Josephus and another soldier were left, they handed themselves over to Vespasian rather than kill themselves.

After the fall of Masada, many sicarii fled to Alexandria and continued their campaign against the Romans. When they were captured, some handed over by other Jews, the Romans sought to force them to confess Caesar as lord. They were tortured, but resisted.

Their courage, or whether we ought to call it madness, or hardiness in their opinions, everybody was amazed at. For when all sorts of torments and vexations of their bodies that could be devised were made use of to them, they could not get any one of them to comply so far as to confess, or seem to confess, that Caesar was their lord; but they preserved their own opinion, in spite of all the distress they were brought to, as if they received these torments and the fire itself with bodies insensible of pain, and with a soul that in a manner rejoiced under them. But what was most of all astonishing to the beholders was the courage of the children; for not one of these children was so far overcome by these torments, as to name Caesar for their lord. So far does the strength of the courage [of the soul] prevail over the weakness of the body. (*War* 7.10.1)

Although Josephus is highly critical of these dagger men, he commends their courage under torture to resist.

2.3 Rabbinic Martyrdom

The destruction of the Jerusalem Temple left an indelible scar on the Jewish psyche. With the 'hardware' of the cult no longer available, Judaism had to 'reinvent' itself. Factions made rival claims to power and authority. Although it was the rabbis who won out, the priestly class were influential in the early years after the Jewish War, especially in supporting further revolts, notably that led by Bar Kochba in 132 CE. Martyrdom played a role in the creation of Jewish rabbinic identity, although as we shall see, it is not as enthusiastically embraced by Jews as it was by their Christian cousins. The accounts are from the Talmud and are therefore far later than the stories they narrate. Tales of rabbinic martyrdom from the earlier centuries advance the claims of the place of the rabbis over the priests in fifth- and sixth-century Judaism. Listed among the faithful of each generation, including the friends in the fiery furnace, are 'Rabbi Akiba and his companions who gave themselves up to immolation for the sake of the Torah' (*b. Sanhedrin* 100b).

The martyrdom of the seven sons resurfaces as a template for Jewish martyrdom. However, the mother, who is largely peripheral in 2 Maccabees becomes more prominent in the story's retelling. Furthermore, the story is taken out of its Hasmonean context so that the sons are ordered to transgress the Law by Caesar.

For you we are being killed all day long. We are taken as a flock for slaughter. And R. Yehudah said: This means the woman and her seven sons. They brought the first before the Emperor and said to him, Serve the idol. He said to them: It is written in the

Law, I am the Lord your God. So they led him away and killed him. They then brought the second before the Emperor and said to him, Serve the idol. He replied: It is written in the Torah, You shall have no other gods before me. So they led him away and killed him . . .

The tortures and elaborate eschatological pronouncements have been removed from the template. All the brothers simply refuse to commit idolatry and are executed. The emphasis turns from the sons to the mother after sentence is pronounced on the final son.

> . . . They were leading him away to kill him when his mother said: Give him to me that I may kiss him a little. She said to him: My son, go and say to your father Abraham, You bound one [son] to the altar, but I have bound seven altars. Then she also went up on to a roof and threw herself down and was killed. Then a voice came out of heaven saying, 'A joyful mother of children'. (*b. Gittin* 57b)

The story of Abraham's near sacrifice of Isaac (*aqeda*) is invoked as a model (Gen. 22). The mother is favourably compared to Abraham, who was called to sacrifice only one son. She notes that her sacrifice is seven times that of Abraham. Moreover, she also kills herself, an act which appears to win divine approval. This unnamed mother is eventually given the name Miriam, and she appears to stand for all mothers who lose children in times of calamity.

Immediately prior to this story in the Talmud is an account of 400 boys and girls being shipped off to Rome to the brothels. When they realized where they were going, they contemplated jumping overboard and drowning themselves.

> They said to themselves, 'If we drown in the sea we shall attain the life of the future world'. The eldest among them expounded the verse, The Lord said, I will bring again from Bashan, I will bring again from the depths of the sea . . . When the girls heard this they all leaped into the sea. The boys then drew the moral for themselves, saying, 'If these for whom this is natural [i.e. being the passive partner in sexual encounter] act so, shall not we, for whom it is unnatural?' They also leapt into the sea. (*b. Gittin* 57b)

As with the Masada incident, and the mother of the seven sons, the normal Jewish injunction against suicide is overridden in order to avoid a worse fate, in this case being used as prostitutes. There is a further interesting case of suicide reported approvingly, this time of a Roman executioner. In the time of Hadrian, Rabbi Hanina was arrested for teaching the Law in public. He was sentenced to be burned at the stake, wrapped in a Torah scroll. Sadistically, woollen sponges soaked in water were to be placed over his heart so he would die more slowly. When the fire was lit, his disciples urged him to breathe in the smoke in order that he may die more quickly, but R. Hanina refused on the grounds that only the one who gave him life should end it. However, the executioner then asks him:

'Rabbi, if I raise the flame and take away the tufts of wool from over your heart, will you cause me to enter the life to come?' 'Yes,' he replied . . . He thereupon raised the flame . . . and his soul departed speedily. The executioner then jumped and threw himself into the fire. And a voice from heaven exclaimed, 'R. Hanina b. Teradion and the executioner have been assigned to the world to come'. (*b. Abodah Zarah* 18ab)

For his act of kindness to the rabbi, even a Roman executioner is granted a place in the life to come. Also noteworthy is that it is rabbis who stand in the tradition of the Maccabees in protecting and dying for the Law. In another version of Hanina's death, his daughter screamed when she saw her father burning. However, his concern was for the Law scroll:

My daughter, if it is for me that you are weeping and for me that you throw yourself on the ground, it is better that a fire made by man should consume me, rather than a fire not made by man . . . But if it is for the Torah scroll that you are weeping, lo, the Torah is fire, and fire cannot consume fire. Behold, the letters are flying into the air, and only the parchment itself is burning. (*Semahot* 8.12)

In this version, the Law is untouched by the flames, flying back to heaven, leaving only the parchment and the rabbi to burn.

Rabbi Hanina is listed in the story of 'The Ten Martyrs', rabbis who were said to have been executed under Hadrian. However, in the tradition there are various lists of the ten, and some lived at a different time. Nonetheless, their story is paradigmatic of rabbinic martyrdom. One of the ten, Rabbi Akiba, becomes the most celebrated martyr of Judaism in this period.[8] Akiba was executed after Hadrian's suppression of the Bar Kochba revolt, a revolt supported by Akiba. It is unclear precisely why Akiba was arrested and charged. However, the tract *Berakhot* suggests the government had outlawed all teaching of the Law. When Pappos b. Yehudah encountered Akiba with a group of students teaching the Law, he questioned whether he ought not to be afraid of the empire. Akiba told a parable:

A fox was once walking alongside of a river, and he saw fishes going in swarms from one place to another. He said to them: From what are you fleeing? They replied: From the nets cast for us by men. He said to them: Would you like to come up on to the dry land so that you and I can live together in the way that my ancestors lived with your ancestors? They replied: Are you the one that they call the cleverest of animals? You are not clever but foolish. If we are afraid in the element in which we live, how much more in the element in which we would die! So it is with us. If such is our condition when we sit and study the Torah, of which it is written, For that is thy life and the length of thy days, if we go and neglect it how much worse off we shall be! (*b. Berakhot* 61b)

For Akiba, not to study Torah was to be already dead. Akiba was arrested and when he was led out to be killed, it was the time to recite the *Shema*:

While they combed his flesh with iron combs, he was [reciting the *Shema*] . . . His disciples said to him: Our teacher, even to this point? He said to them: All my days I have been troubled by this verse, 'with all thy soul', [which I interpret] 'even if He takes thy soul'. I said: When shall I have the opportunity of fulfilling this? Now that I have the opportunity shall I not fulfil it? He prolonged the word *ehad* (one) until he expired while saying it. A voice from heaven went forth and proclaimed: Happy are you, Akiba . . . you are destined for the life of the world to come'. (*b. Berakhot* 61b)

There is an element of melodrama in this account, and similarly in the other, where the rabbi appropriately dies on the word *nepesh*, emphasizing that he has just served God with all his *soul/life*. However, although there are many other stories of rabbinic martyrdom as well as the execution of Jewish rebels, the appeal of martyrdom lessened after the Bar Kochba revolt.

The Romans had no desire to prevent Jews from being Jews. At no time was Judaism outlawed. Roman attitudes towards Jews probably owed more to the aftermath of revolt rather than any concerted effort to destroy the religion. Perhaps in reaction to the growing prominence of Christian martyrdom, Jews, as they had in order to win the Maccabean War, struck a balance between dying and living for the Law. Unlike the Christians, Jews were not to surrender themselves to arrest even on account of the Law: 'no halachic matter may be quoted in the name of one who surrenders himself to meet death for words of the Torah' (*b. Baba Kamma* 61a). In fact, transgression was encouraged in certain circumstances rather than martyrdom.

> By a majority vote, it was resolved in the upper chambers of the house of Nithza in Lydda that in every law of the Torah, if a man is commanded: 'Transgress and suffer not death' he may transgress and not suffer death, excepting idolatry, incest, and murder. (*b. Sanhedrin* 74a)

The rabbis go on to discuss whether even these proscribed Laws may be violated to save one's life, and whether only private or public transgression was permitted.

This decision decisively separated Jewish and Christian reflection on martyrdom. With dire threats of eschatological punishment for deniers, and the saying of Jesus that there was nothing one could do to save one's own life (Mk 8.35–38), Christians could not easily judge choosing life through denial over death to be the better choice. The Jewish ruling that in some cases transgressing the Law in order to live was permissible would come to be crucial in the history of Jewish martyrdom. Limited transgression when faced with Roman persecution was one thing; Romans never expected Jews to stop being Jews. However, when the Roman Empire became Christianized, and the first age of Christian martyrdom ceased, Jews had to contend with persecution coming not from pagan quarters, which had never desired the end of Judaism, but from Christians, who ideally wished the conversion of all Jews.

3 CHRISTIAN PERSECUTION OF JEWS

In 388, the Jewish synagogue in Callinicum was burned down by a mob, including monks, at the instigation of the local bishop. The Emperor Theodosius I demanded the synagogue be rebuilt at the bishop's expense. However, Ambrose of Milan intervened and argued that the order should be rescinded. In his letter to the emperor, Ambrose reasons that should the bishop acquiesce with the emperor's command, he would be an apostate; should he stand firm, he would become a martyr. Neither outcome would be in the emperor's best interests. Ambrose questions whether the destruction of a synagogue 'a place of unbelief, a house of impiety, a receptacle of madness, which God Himself has condemned' should be rebuilt at Christian expense. (*Letter* 40.14)

> Will your Majesty give this triumph to the Jews over the Church of God; this victory over the people of Christ, this joy to the unbelievers, this felicity to the Synagogue, this grief to the Church? They will place this solemnity among their feast-days; numbering it among those where they triumphed over the Ammonites, or Canaanites, or over Pharaoh king of Egypt, or which delivered them from the hands of Nebuchadnezzar king of Babylon. This festival they will add in memory of the triumph they have gained over Christ's people. (*Letter* 40.20)

If the emperor allows the Jews to triumph over the Church in this way, Ambrose wonders what Christ might say to Theodosius come Judgement Day. The order to rebuild the synagogue was never enforced.

The lack of reprisals for the burning of the synagogue effectively sanctioned violence against Jews. Following Nicaea, legislation had increasingly restricted rights of Jews especially in terms of legal representation and property ownership. Jews had suffered sporadic violence, but Ambrose's defence of the bishop of Callinicum's actions was the first time such violence had official Church sanction. Until then, conflict between Christian and Jew had largely been with words, but now Jews would suffer well over a millennia and a half of violence predominantly, though not exclusively, at the hands of Christians.

In 415, Bishop Cyril expelled all Jews from Alexandria. For centuries there had been a large Jewish centre in that city, but this incident brought the increasing anti-Jewish sentiment that had been developing in the new Christianized empire to a new stage. Only three years later, the Jewish communities in Minorca faced forced conversion. After the relics of Stephen were brought to the island, the bishop led a campaign to convert the Jews. After attacking, looting, and burning the synagogue, according to a Christian source (*Letter of Severus of Minorca*), 540 Jews were miraculously converted. Christians elsewhere were urged to follow this example.

Persecution continued in the empire: The Code of Theodosius (439) codified anti-Jewish legislation, including a ban on building new synagogues, while Justinian's *Corpis Juris Civilis* (529–534) declared Jews, indeed all non-Christians, to be non-citizens, and banned recitation of the *Shema*. Jews were given the choice of conversion or expulsion in Clermont (576) and Spain (613). However, in the seventh century, under the Emperor Heraclius (r. 610–641) Judaism, was for the first time banned, and all Jews ordered to undergo baptism. This policy was restated by Leo III (r. 717–741), Basil I (r. 867–886), and Romanos (r. 932–944). Although some died rather than accept baptism, and others fled, most Jews simply went through the motions of conversion. The chronicler, Theophanes, reports,

In this year [721–722] the Emperor forced the Hebrews and the Montanists to be baptized. The Hebrews ate and partook of the holy gift but, as they had not been baptized of their own free will, washed off their baptism and defiled the faith. (*Annus Mundi* 6241)

After Basil's death, most Jews simply returned openly to Judaism. For the most part, during these periods of persecution, mock observance of Christian rituals or exile to Islamic Spain rather than death appears to have been the preferred option taken by Jews. But when Pope Urban II inaugurated the period of the Crusades in 1095, Jews once again embraced martyrdom as a means of resistance to the oppressor.

3.1 The Crusades

As crusader armies marched to the Holy Land in response to Urban's rallying call to liberate Jerusalem from the enemies of the cross, some pointed out that other 'enemies of the cross' were right on their doorstep. Guibert of Nogent describes the slaughter of the Jews of Rouen.

On a certain day when the people of Rouen who had joined in that expedition under the badge of the cross, began to complain to one another, 'We, after travelling great distances towards the East, desire to attack the enemies of God there. But this is wasted labour, since before our eyes there are Jews, of all races the worst foes of God.' Saying this and seizing their weapons, they herded them into a certain church, driving them in either by force or guile, and without discrimination of sex or age put them to the sword, but allowed those who accepted Christianity to escape slaughter. (Memoirs 2.5)

Massacres like this appear to have taken place all over France. The Crusaders reasoned that there was no need to wait until encountering Muslims, when those responsible for killing Christ could be encountered and converted or slain on the way. No doubt many Jews did go through the rituals of conversion. However, many accounts describe resistance, resulting in martyrdom. So, for example, a Jewish account describes the plight of Rhenish women, who faced forced baptism.

The saintly ones were brought before the courtyard of the church and they implored them to immerse themselves in their sullied water. When they arrived at the church, they did not wish to enter the shrine of idolatry and they stuck their feet . . . at the threshold . . . when the Crusaders saw that they did not wish to be baptised and that they increasingly trusted with all their heart in the living God, then the enemy jumped on them and struck them with axes and blows. There the pure ones were killed for the sanctification of the Name. (*Sefer Gezerot*, 38)

As armies journeyed down the Rhine Valley, they attacked and slaughtered thousands of Jews until they reached Mainz, the site of one of the most notorious incidents of the First Crusade.

Breaking the bolts and doors, they killed the Jews, about 700 in number, who in vain resisted the force and attack of so many thousands. They killed the women, also, and with their swords pierced tender children of whatever age and sex. The Jews, seeing that their Christian enemies were attacking them and their children, and that they were sparing no age, likewise fell upon one another, brother, children, wives, and sisters, and thus they perished at each other's hands. Horrible to say, mothers cut the throats of nursing children with knives and stabbed others, preferring them to perish thus by their own hands rather than to be killed by the weapons of the uncircumcised. (Albert of Aix)[9]

This Christian account of the incident suggests that in the face of the slaughter, the Jews of Mainz killed themselves rather than wait to be killed by the Christian Crusaders. Conversion may also have spared some of their lives, but that does not appear to have been contemplated in the retellings of the massacre.

Self-killing as an alternative to being slain by the enemy naturally recalls the tradition of Masada, and the events of the Jewish War were present in the Jewish popular imagination. The *Sefer Yosippon*, an account of Judaism from Adam to the war, written in the ninth century, was widely read by Jews in the Middle Ages, and promoted martyrdom in the face of outsider threats. Accounts of the Jews under Roman rule offered models for medieval Jews. In a scene reminiscent of the first rebellion under Pilate, the Jews in Orléans faced the choice between conversion or death under King Robert in 1009. Representatives of the Jews gave an uncompromising response:

Our Lord, we will not heed you in this regard. We shall not deny it [the Torah]. Treat us as you wish. Then they stretched out their throats for the sword for the sanctification of his name and His great Unity. (*Sefer Gezerot* 19)[10]

Whereas Pilate's forces had drawn back when presented with the multitude of Jews who bore their necks for the sword, the Jews of Orléans were not so fortunate. Robert killed them immediately. In response to the massacres, a group of women resolve to die for the Law by drowning in the river in an echo of the 400 who drowned by leaping from the ship on the way to the brothels of Rome.

The account of persecution advanced in the *Sefer Yosippon*, just as in Old Testament theology, was that it was in some way caused by the sins of the people. In Crusader literature, the slaughter of Jews is justified by attributing the atrocities to righteous vengeance for their ancestors killing Christ. In Jewish thought, their experiences related more to the 'Jewish original sin' of selling Joseph into slavery. Nonetheless, martyrs, as we find in 2 Maccabees, somehow atone for the sins of the people. In an account of the slaughter of priests in the Temple by the Romans, while they continued to offer the Temple sacrifice, the sacrificers became the sacrificed. Similarly, those who took their own lives at Masada are regarded as fitting sacrifices before God.

They gathered their wives, sons, and daughters to slay them on the ground. They will be considered a burnt offering before God, because for His Name they went, not to be killed before the Romans. (*Sefer Yosippon* 1.430.[11])

It was, therefore, relatively easy to cast those who suffered martyrdom, even at their own hand as offerings to God.

As well as the example of Masada, the *Aqeda* is also a valuable interpretative resource. In a Jewish account of the slaughter of Mainz, those who killed their children, rather than allow them to fall into the hands of Christians are cast in the role of Abraham, and by extension the holy mother of the Maccabees who similarly had urged her children on to death.

Behold and see our Lord, what we do for the sanctification of Your holy Name without exchanging You with the crucified one . . . The precious children of Zion, the children of Mainz, were tested ten times, like our ancestor Abraham . . . They sacrificed their children as Abraham had sacrificed his son Isaac. (*Sefer Gezerot* 31–32.[12])

Abraham was prepared to sacrifice his son in faithfulness to God, so rather than exchange their faith in God for the false one presented by the Christians, they sacrificed their children and themselves. In rabbinic sources, the Maccabean mother pointed out that her sacrifice bettered Abraham's sevenfold. The Mainz account claims for the people a tenfold repetition of Abraham's example, probably recalling the tradition of the ten martyrs under Hadrian. A litany of persecution provided Jews with a rich matrix within which they could interpret their experiences of suffering. The Maccabean mother, Masada, and the *Aqeda* proved to be the favoured models for those who chose death, with some form of sacrificial atonement for the people's (generally unspecified) sins often found to be the theological interpretative framework for their deaths. Death at the hands of the Crusaders, and even self-killing was designated *kiddush ha-Shem*.

For the best part of the 1,000 years since Robert's slaughter of the Jews of Orléans, Jews faced opportunities for martyrdom as one atrocity followed another. In every part of Europe at one time or another, Jews faced expulsion, forced conversion, and massacre. In Flanders (1121), York (1190), Naples (1288), England (1290), France (1306), Hungary (1360), and Austria (1421) Jews faced expulsion or death. Jews were blamed for the plague in the mid fourteenth century, and from 1391, Jews in Spain faced forced conversion, leading eventually to brutal treatment under the Spanish Inquisition, until they were expelled in 1492. Models of martyrdom were re-enacted, but equally important was the rabbinic idea that it was permissible to save one's life and commit idolatry. In the thirteenth century, Judaism had its own 'lapsed' crisis, when it was determined that the martyrs covered the sins of the lapsed, and in Spain, many converted to Catholicism while still openly practising Judaism.

For 500 years after the Reformation, European Jews faced bouts of persecution and expulsion interspersed with periods of protection. In the twentieth century, there were pogroms in Eastern Europe, and further expulsions from Moscow, Kiev, Lithuania, and Poland. By the middle of the twentieth century, European anti-Semitism reached its awful climax in the death camps and the slaughter of six million Jews in the Nazi Holocaust, the event which, for Emile Fackenheim, 'murdered Jewish martyrdom itself'.[13]

4   THE HOLOCAUST

In an address delivered in 1990, the *Lubavitcher Rebbe*, Menachem Mendel Schneerson, declared that all who had lost their lives in the Holocaust were martyrs.

Looking at all our fellow Jews with a favourable eye is in place especially now, for our generation is 'a firebrand saved from the blaze', the smouldering remnant preserved from the horrors of the Holocaust. After so many of our people have perished, we must try to appreciate – and in this manner, help reveal – the positive potential that every Jew possesses. This potential is enhanced by the luminous legacy bequeathed to us by the martyrs of the previous generation. Our Sages teach that the very fact that a person dies *al Kiddush ha-Shem*, in sanctification of G-d's Name, elevates him to such a level that 'no creature can stand in his presence'. Thus, every man and woman who died in the Holocaust is a holy martyr.[14]

Of course, some may see sentiments such as this as an oversimplification. Many died not knowing they were going to their deaths, and very few died voluntarily. Many of the characteristic elements of a martyr act are absent: there is no confrontation with an evil tyrant, no declaration of faith, and crucially, no choice. However, to declare all Jews who died martyrs is not without precedent. Maimonides in the twelfth century had ruled that all Jews killed for being Jews were to be regarded as martyrs. Even if a body of a Jew was found by the road, Maimonides argued, he should be regarded as a martyr since it should be assumed that he died for his Jewishness.

For most people, regarding the six million Jews who lost their lives in the death camps as martyrs is uncontroversial. As I argued in the first chapter, to create martyrs one needs a martyr narrative. The official English title of the *Yad Vashem, The Holocaust Martyrs' and Heroes' Remembrance Authority*, helps create this martyrology by retelling individuals' stories, and crucially, in naming as many victims as possible. The authority also creates a collective martyr narrative for the Six Million. In some ways, this collective martyrology lifts the Holocaust out of history, for as Jonathan Weber notes, Six Million is a shorthand attempt to understand something completely incomprehensible.[15] Martyrology, as we have already observed, is not so much to do with reporting historical facts, but offering an interpretation of conflict or death. The testimony of Holocaust survivors contributes to what one writer has called a 'sacred myth'[16]. Holocaust martyrology does not so much answer the question, 'What happened?' The stories of the martyrs demand that lessons be learned. Martyr accounts, as we shall see, are told in different ways depending on what the narrator wishes to commend as the ultimate meaning of the atrocity.

The question has been raised whether the two titles, martyr and hero, of *Yad Vashem* are intended to represent the same or different groups. Is a distinction to be drawn between different kinds of martyrs: those who offered resistance against those who displayed particular religious devotion, for example? Stories are told of both devotion and resistance, but what makes these martyrs different from other Jewish martyrology is the fact that the Nazis were not principally attempting to convert Jews to Christianity, but to destroy them. Reflection on martyrdom had to take account of this significant factor. What could *Kiddush ha-Shem* mean when faced with mass slaughter? There are a variety of responses to this question, all found within martyr narratives of the Holocaust.

For some, it meant faithfulness to the Law, even if it resulted in death. Rabbi Ephraim Oshry recommended the continuation of praying and studying the Talmud when these were outlawed in the Kaunas ghetto in modern Lithuania in 1942. He reasoned that since the Germans were attempting to destroy an element of the faith, it was appropriate to continue with religious devotion despite the consequences. Clearly Rabbi Oshry's recommendation stands within a long-established tradition of Jewish martyrdom from Daniel and the three friends, in disobeying an edict to abandon Judaism even if it meant death.

Many stories have emerged from the ghettos and camps telling of unswerving devotion to the faith. Some Hasidim went to extraordinary lengths to avoid eating the non-kosher food from the communal pot, selling their soup for bread and raw potatoes, from which they made their own meals. Prayers were kept despite prohibitions banning religious rituals. Other accounts tell of those on the way to the 'showers' being urged to sing songs of faith to assert not only their Jewishness, but their humanity, the very thing the Nazis sought to strip from them.

Stories of faithfulness in the depths of suffering inevitably read like hagiography; martyr narratives become part of the quest for meaning, and in doing so adopt many familiar elements of Jewish martyrology. A small number of Jewish commentators place the suffering in the classical context of *Mippenei Hata'einu* (because of our sins). Although this view has been criticized, many martyrologies employ the related Maccabean concept of the martyrdom and atonement. An example of this is Rabbi Oshri's account of the martyrdom of Rabbi Elhanan and his pupils.

Rabbi Elhanan spoke quietly, with his customary spiritual tranquillity . . . 'In Heaven they apparently regard us as righteous ones, since we have been chosen to atone with our bodies for all Israel. Accordingly, we must return to the Lord in complete repentance, immediately, here. The time is short . . . We must know that our sacrifices will be made more acceptable by repentance . . . We shall not, God forbid, have any improper thought that would . . . invalidate the sacrifice. We are now fulfilling the greatest commandment . . . The fire that will burn in our bones is the fire that shall re-establish the house of Israel'.[17]

Rabbi Oshri was an eyewitness to the event and there are doubtless strong historical roots in his retelling. That said, what we have here is a martyrology that seeks to make sense not only of the rabbi and his pupils, but the deaths of many other millions. The narrative of Rabbi Elhanan's death is explained in terms of atonement for the Jewish people, and the re-establishment of the house of Israel, probably a reference to the formation of the Israeli State. The interpretation of the death of the faithful is put in the mouth of the rabbi himself, lending the interpretation greater theological weight. Of course, it is entirely possible Rabbi Elhanan said something along these lines. Whether he did, or whether the speech is like that which Josephus put in the mouth of Eleazar at Masada, it is Rabbi Oshri's account and its subsequent retelling in the form of martyrology that offers possible meaning for the millions of lives lost.

Like those in the fort of Masada, other Jews employed suicide as an act of resistance. In the face of mechanized slaughter where choice was removed from millions, there are many stories of suicide, where martyrs chose the means and time of their death. Ninety-three women, who had been detained in Beit Yaakov in Cracow, made and drank poison rather than endure the fate of being sexually exploited by German soldiers. In this act, they stand in the tradition of Jewish women who had done likewise, beginning with the 400 bound for the brothels of Rome.

However, for many rabbis such suicide had its appropriate place in the past. In the Middle Ages when Christians attempted to convert Jews, martyrdom and even suicide was an appropriate way to thwart this goal. In the face of the systematic slaughter at the hands of the Nazis, rabbis debated whether Jews should use bribery, or obtain certificates of baptism in order to survive. Early rabbinic discussions on when it was permissible to transgress the Law to survive became an important source of theological reflection. As one author puts it, 'what need was there for voluntary death if life itself was a capital crime?'[18] Many came to the view that the goal of being a Jew in the midst of death was not to attempt to die as a martyr, but to survive. This instinct was encapsulated in the term coined by Rabbi Yizhak Nissenbaum: *Kiddush ha-Hayyim*:

This is the time for *Kiddush ha-Hayyim*, the sanctification of life, and not for *Kiddush ha-Shem*, the holiness of martyrdom. Previously, the Jew's enemy sought his soul and the Jew sacrificed his body in martyrdom; now the oppressor demands the Jew's body and the Jew is obliged to defend it, to preserve his life.

Even R. Oshry ruled that contraception and abortion, both normally forbidden, could be permitted, when in Kaunus it was decreed that any woman who was pregnant would be killed. It is probably also the case that most Orthodox Jewish men did cut off their beards and sidelocks when ordered to do so by the Germans rather than preserve them as acts of defiance. The stories of the Hasidim going to extraordinary lengths to avoid eating non-Kosher food are likely to be exceptional.[19] These exceptional stories of fidelity to the faith, for those who narrate them, demonstrate the importance of that faith in the face of an attempt to exterminate it. The purpose of such martyrology is not to shame those who did not make the same choice, but to exhort contemporary Jews to greater devotion. Many heroes died for the faith; that is all the more reason for Jews today to live faithfully.

The *Aqeda* is yet another ancient tradition invoked to interpret the Holocaust. The binding of Isaac has proved to be an enduring interpretative lens for Jewish suffering from the earliest times, from Josephus, through the rabbinic sources, to the medieval crusading period. We have already seen how the Maccabean mother in rabbinic tradition compares herself favourably with the sacrifice Abraham was called to make. The purity of the sacrifice, the blamelessness of the people in this interpretation stands in sharp relief against the view that somehow the Jews suffer because of their sins. Bernard Maza writes, 'The history of the *Shoah* is the history of the Binding of Isaac repeated six million times. Six million martyrs died, not with complaints, not with questions, but with love and faith'.[20] Clearly, Maza's characterization is problematic in both historical and theological terms, and may be balanced by the traditions of protest and complaint found in the Psalms, and in particular, Job. Maza's martyrology gives choice back to those who in actuality had none by setting them in the role of Isaac, who according to Josephus' account of the *Aqeda*, was

of such a generous disposition as became the son of such a father, and was pleased with this discourse; and said, 'That he was not worthy to be born at first, if he should reject the determination of God and of his father, and should not resign himself up readily to both their pleasures; since it would have been unjust if he had not obeyed, even if his father alone had so resolved'. So he went immediately to the altar to be sacrificed. (*Antiquities* 1.13.4)

Although historically implausible, in Maza's retelling of the horrors, those who died become less passive by being placed in the tradition of the willing self-sacrifice of Isaac.

Ancient theological accounts of Jewish suffering have proved remarkably enduring. Maccabean martyr theology, the Masada suicide tradition, and rabbinic reflection of transgression of the Law to survive provided the theological tools for both martyrdom, where the victims made a choice to die, but also in the face of the massacres of the Crusades and the Holocaust. The one tradition which has not proved so enduring is that of the Holy War. It is not difficult to see why. Yet voices during the war did to some extent recapture the Jewish warrior instinct, dissenting against the predominant passive acceptance of martyrdom in the *Aqeda* and suffering servant traditions. Some contemporary Jewish voices have questioned the passivity of the Holocaust victims – the sheep to the slaughter – even suggesting that in not taking up armed resistance those who died bore some responsibility for their own deaths.[21] Indeed, there were armed uprisings in the ghettos of Warsaw, Bialystock, and Vilna in 1943, as well as Treblinka, Sobibor (both 1943), and Auschwitz (1944). As early as 1941, the poet Abba Kovner wrote a proclamation, which was read out to a youth movement gathered in a Dominican convent in Vilna:

Jewish youth, do not believe those that are trying to deceive you . . . Before our eyes they took away our parents, our brothers and sisters [to Ponar]. Of those taken through the gates of the ghetto not a single one has returned. All the Gestapo roads lead to Ponar, and Ponar means death. Ponar is not a concentration camp. They have all been shot there. Hitler plans to destroy all the Jews of Europe, and the Jews of Lithuania have been chosen as the first in line. We will not be led like sheep to the slaughter. True, we are weak and helpless, but the only response to the murder is revolt! Brothers! It is better to die fighting like free men than to live at the mercy of the murderers. Arise! Arise with your last breath![22]

The call to armed struggle led to the formation of the *Fareynikte Partizaner Organizatsye* (United Partisan Organization) led mainly by Zionists and Communists. However, even where uprisings took place, the loss of Jewish lives was high. Nonetheless, even the Maccabean revolt tradition could be found in the ghettos of occupied Europe. Missing from that Holy War paradigm was the notion that God fights for the people. Indeed, in the face of the evil of the Holocaust, some have simply given up on God.[23]

5. CONCLUSION

Jews responded in many different ways to the threat of extermination under the Nazis. With courage and dignity, many demonstrated what it meant to live and die like a Jew, through devotion and ritual. Others did what they could in order to survive, while radicals took up arms against their oppressors. The vast majority probably responded with bewilderment and confusion. All who died, however they approached death, are remembered as both martyrs and heroes. The way in which others reflect on the manner of their death, retelling their stories, says much about what the narrators value. Martyr stories, whether of the Holocaust, the Crusades, the rabbis, or the Maccabees, are used to interpret not only events of the past, but point to both present and future.

Judaism has for most of its history experienced persecution. The stories of suffering and martyrdom have to some extent shaped Jewish identity, through the use of consistent martyrological paradigms. However, the late Jewish historian Salo Wittmayer Baron recently rejected 'the lachrymose conception of Jewish history'. Even this view is to explicitly engage in the stories of the martyrs by rejecting models of patient suffering in favour of a more active confidence. Similar is the way in which the Masada martyrs are incorporated into the initiation ritual of the Israeli Defence Force. New recruits spend the night at the fortress and swear that Masada will not fall again. The soldiers stand in the Holy War tradition while at the same time rejecting what was ultimately a defeat. Both accounts of Jewish suffering for others, and the rejection of them can reinforce the need for a secure and militarily powerful Jewish State.[24] Martyrology recounts the past, but also undeniably shapes the future.

CHAPTER 6

MARTYRDOM IN ISLAM

1 INTRODUCTION

1.1 Religion in a Secular Age

If martyrdom is dying for one's religion, then for most people in the modern world, the Islamicist suicide bomber is today's image of the martyr. In many ways, the modern phenomenon of killing as well as dying for God through employing these 'sacred explosions', as their supporters call them, has rendered all martyrdom suspect. Increasingly, secularist adherents, when they are not calling (however fancifully) for the complete abandonment of religion, fasten the blame for all conflict in the world on religious belief.[1] More moderate thinkers emphasize the role religion can play in contributing to social capital. The secular contract with religious believers, it would appear, is that in return for suppressing any 'underbelly' hostility to 'secular' progressive norms, such as tolerance and plurality, including any missionary impulse, religious groups may contribute to the public intellectual arena with a distinctive if not always honoured voice.

In countries where there are majority national Christian churches, to which the populous nominally belong without having to demonstrate high, or even *any* level of commitment, such as in England, Scotland, and Scandinavia, this contract has worked well. National churches provide civic religion for the State at times of national celebration, concern, and mourning. However, these 'contracts' are under pressure, not only from committed secularists, but from within religious communities.

Where a broad national Church, whose values have largely contributed to the general ethos of a society, occupies a relatively significant structural position within a nation, the sense of 'otherness' adherents (however committed) feel in relation to that society are low; there are few causes for conflict with the State. However, in other faith communities, particularly those whose presence is largely due to immigration, the sense of 'otherness' from 'mainstream' values may be enhanced, particularly where there are or have been intra-community conflicts over questions of acculturation and assimilation. Attitudes to such questions are themselves prone to be influenced by the general attitude of the majority population to that group. Hostility can, paradoxically, lead to both an anxiety to assimilate in some, while provoking an entrenchment in traditions and practices that make that community distinctive in others. For example, although over the past few generations Muslims in Europe have tended to become progressively acculturated, general Western hostility to Islam, together with specific attacks on the wearing of the *hijab,* appear to have caused *hijab* wearing to increase among young British Muslim women, which comprises a challenge to acculturation.[2]

Feelings of 'otherness' are by no means restricted to 'immigrant' faith communities. In the United Kingdom, conflict has arisen over the refusal of a British Airways employee to wear a cross, and the refusal of the State to allow Roman Catholic adoption agencies to debar potential adopters on the grounds of sexual orientation. As Christianity is increasingly marginalized as a resource for political decision making, some Christian traditions stress areas of distinctiveness which emphasize their own difference from secular society, and so, positively 'other' themselves. Where the Christian community enjoys some level of political dominance, as in the United States, the resulting clash of religious and secular ideology can lead to all out 'culture wars'.

This was the dynamic at work within Judaism prior to the Maccabean revolt. Where some Jews, particularly the aristocracy and leadership, attempted to assimilate to a greater or lesser degree, from the perspective of the books of the Maccabees, they were traitors for abandoning distinctive religious indicators. Similarly, in Western Muslim communities there are found varying degrees of commitment to 'otherness' in the construction of Muslim identity. Many competing factors are at work, including geopolitical issues in relation to the Occupied Territories, as well as the concern for influence.

Western governments have tended to take no account of Islamic religious polity, where no appointed individual can speak on behalf of all or a significant group of Muslims, with the result that those who are generally chosen to speak *as if* they represented the views of their communities, are those who are most fully acculturated. As we saw in the first chapter, one response to 'Islamic terrorism' has been to deny the actions of a suicide bomber have any claim to Islamic tradition. It is usually a condition of entry to the table that Muslim 'representatives' adhere to this view. In the War on Terror ideology, a Palestinian attack on an Israeli military installation, which may enjoy widespread Muslim support, or an Indonesian targeting a crowded night club, less likely to find general Muslim approval, essentially belong to the same category. This lack of nuance risks alienating the 'leader' who agrees to this ideology from his community.

1.2   Talking about Islamic Martyrdom

It should now be clear to readers who have ventured this far that the common distinction made between 'violent Islamic martyrdom' and passive non-violent Christian martyrdom cannot be maintained. I hope I have demonstrated that even aside from the active and divinely sanctified killing fields of the Crusades, Christian martyrdom, even in its so-called passive form, was originally set firmly within a Jewish Holy War tradition. This is not to say the legacy of the martyrs has not been controversial. Some martyr narratives have been confronted with anti-martyr narrative. Where Christians welcomed martyrs, Romans saw criminals, and Gnostics, fools. Even competing groups of early Christians sought to control who should and who should not be called a martyr. Martyrs are at the mercy of competing narratives that seek to 'make' or 'unmake' them. Often, there is no justice in who is remembered and who is forgotten.

Islamic martyrdom is a sensitive topic, and as I begin my historical examination of martyrdom and Holy War in the Islamic tradition, I am anxious not to be misunderstood. I have already rejected as inadequate any attempts to define martyrdom. Therefore, I will make no distinction between what the West might consider acts of terrorism from acts of martyrdom. The anti-martyr narrative of War on Terror ideology is a competing narrative with those Islamic stories that seek to create martyrs.

To anticipate some of my conclusions, it will be found that although there are good political reasons for doing so, there is little intellectual justification for divorcing Islamic tradition from contemporary martyrological activity which claims Islam as a resource. On the contrary, we will see, as we have with both Judaism and Christianity, that both killing and dying for God enjoys a clear religious trajectory within Islam. It seems to me that attempts to do so, while politically understandable, are ultimately unhelpful. This is not to say that Islam is inherently violent, or that all Muslims support or are sympathetic to acts of 'terror', any more than Christians are bound to support the actions of abortionist killer Paul Hill. Hill's act of murder, while repugnant to most Christians, is still rooted within Christian reasoning. If there is a political solution to religiously inspired violence in all its forms, it seems to me there is little value in pretending it does not exist.

2 MARTYRDOM IN EARLY ISLAM

2.1 Early History and the Life of Mohammad

According to Islamic historiography, Mohammad received the first of his revelations from the angel Gabriel in 610 CE.[3] He began to preach a strict form of monotheism, although his mission was initially restricted to his immediate family. He later expanded his mission to tribal elders, but his message against Meccan polytheism was met with hostility. Mecca around the time of the first revelations was marked by a tribal and clan system, with warfare between tribes common. Hostility towards Mohammad's movement was so intense that he had to send some of his followers to Abyssinia to seek refuge under the protection of the Christian king there. Mohammad, though subjected to ridicule, remained physically free from violence because of the protection of the powerful Banu Hashim clan. As his followers became more numerous, Mohammad's opponents attempted bribery, offering him wealth and position, but when that failed, they attempted to pressurise his clan to withdraw their protection through an economic boycott. Finally, a failed attempt was made on Mohammad's life.

Eventually, in 622, Mohammad and the faithful emigrated (*hijra*) to Medina, some 150 miles north of Mecca. This was an event of such importance that it marks the beginning of the Islamic calendar.

The tribesmen of Medina are reported to have invited Mohammad to make peace between warring tribes and the Jewish community. Eventually, an Islamic polity was established in Medina, so that within five years the bulk of the population of Medina were Muslim. Now established, Mohammad turned his attention back to Mecca. The trade routes on which Mecca depended could be barricaded from the strategic oasis of Medina, and Mohammad's attack on Meccan caravans led to the now iconic Battle of Badr in 624. Mohammad led an army of around 300 men against a much larger Meccan army that included a cavalry of camels and horses. Despite being outnumbered, Mohammad and his army routed the Meccans. This victory reinforced the belief that God was with Mohammad.

> There has already been for you a Sign in the two armies that met (in combat): one was fighting in the cause of Allah the other resisting Allah; these saw with their own eyes twice their number. But Allah doth support with his aid whom He pleaseth. In this is a warning for such as have eyes to see. (Qu'ran 3.13)

However, Mohammad was unable to press home his advantage as he lacked the resources to mount a full-scale invasion. Just two years later, he suffered his first major loss at the battle of Uhud. The Meccans, following their defeat at Badr, mustered an army of more than 3,000 warriors and 400 horses and camels. Mohammad faced them with just 700 men. Despite being outnumbered, for a spell, the Muslim forces held their own before retreating. For Mohammad, who believed his campaign to be blessed by God, this defeat created a theological problem. As the Hebrews had done centuries before, Mohammad interpreted defeat in battle as a sign God was punishing a lack of faith. As we will see, this reverse also in some way contributed to a developing theology of martyrdom.

The Meccans inexplicably, rather than complete their victory, returned home. There were two further skirmishes between the Muslims and the Meccans which proved indecisive: a poorly planned Meccan siege of Medina, and an attempted pilgrimage led by Mohammad to Mecca in 629. However, by incorporating the surrounding Bedouin tribes and Jewish settlements, Mohammad at last gained sufficient military superiority to enter Mecca, and in 630, the pagan tribes of Mecca converted to Islam. By the time of Mohammad's death in 632, virtually the whole of the Arabian Peninsula was Islamic.

Mohammad's death created a crisis of succession. The power vacuum opened fissures between tribes whose loyalty appeared to belong to Mohammad rather than to any notion of a state or a religion. Mohammad's close friend and father of his wife Aisha, Abu Bakr, was eventually elected the first caliph at a controversial meeting which took place during Mohammad's funeral. Abu faced tribal revolts in what became known as the War of Apostasy, although clearly the cause of revolt was political rather than religious. Further resentment against Abu's leadership was fostered by those who believed not only had Mohammad already appointed his son-in-law Ali to be his successor, but that in any case, the leadership of the community should be restricted to the prophet's immediate family. This tension would become critical for Islamic martyrology. Nonetheless, Abu successfully faced down tribal and personal revolts and consolidated Arabia as a single political entity.

Abu died two years later, and his own appointed successor, Umar ibn al-Khattub, became the second caliph. Under Umar's leadership, Islamic forces invaded both the Byzantine and Sassanid Empires, so that by 637, Syria, Palestine, and Lebanon had been conquered, and Umar gained an important foothold in Iraq.

Civil unrest marked the period of the third caliph, Uthman (r. 644–656), who was murdered at prayer after a violent uprising. In order to bring peace, Ali was finally appointed leader of the community. However, Ali faced opposition from those who thought his investigations of the murder of Uthman were somewhat half-hearted, including from Mohammad's wife, Aisha. However, he repelled her supporters at the Battle of Camel in 656, after which she retreated to her home town. Ali faced more substantial opposition from Uthman's cousin, Mu'awiya Ummayad, and when he was unable to subdue the rebellion, he sought a peace treaty. However, Ali's more ardent supporters saw this compromise as a betrayal and Ali was later killed in 661, like Uthman before him, at prayer. Mu'awiya assumed the caliphate until his death in 680.

Ali's eldest son, Hassan, had agreed not to press his own claims to leadership in return for an agreement that he would succeed Mu'awiya. However, within a year of that agreement, Hassan was dead, probably through poisoning. When Mu'awiya died, there were two claimants to the caliphate: his own son Yazid, and Ali's younger son, Hussein, the grandson of Mohammad. The decisive battle between the two took place on the plains of Karbala in 680. Despite being vastly outnumbered, Hussein and his band of 72 held out for six days, engaging in one-on-one combat, before Hussein was himself killed.

This episode marks the main fault line between Sunni and Shi'a Islam. Politically, the Shi'at Ali (Party of Ali) was decisively defeated, and their experience of oppression helped created a Shi'a identity as a suffering and persecuted grouping. Hussein's martyrdom is remembered in the Shi'a tradition on the Day of Ashura. However, the events also fostered a narrative of grievance, which would prove an important contributor to modern Islamic reflections on martyrdom. After Hussein's death, Yazid established the Ummayad Dynasty which lasted only until 750, when the entire family were massacred. It was replaced by the Abbassid dynasty, which endured until the mid thirteenth century until the attack of the Mongols.

We will return to the Battle of Karbala shortly. For the time being we note that warfare was an important element in the formation and expansion of early Islam. It is not true to say that early followers of Mohammad faced no persecution;[4] for the first ten years after Mohammad's revelation, Muslims, particularly the poor and slaves, faced hostility and persecution in order to dissuade them from their faith, and 'passive' martyrs were made in that period. Nonetheless, it is the case that after the move to Medina, both offensive and defensive warfare was a constituent element in the theological formation of Islam. Indeed, after the *hajj*, Islamic martyrdom was likely to occur *only* in the context of battle.

2.2 Jihad

Although the term *jihad* is often associated in the modern mind with violent Holy War, in fact, it essentially means 'striving'.[5] In the Qu'ran, it is usually found in the sense of striving for the sake of Islam, often having in mind an internalized struggle against evil; jihad by the heart (*bil qalb* or *nafs*). Religiously motivated war – jihad by the sword (*bis saif*) – is, of course, one way in which one might strive on behalf of religion, but it by no means exhausts the range of meaning. As well as jihad by the heart and sword, there is also found jihad of the mouth (*bil lisan*) and the hand (*bil yad*).

The former relates to speaking out against injustice and peacefully spreading the message of Islam, while the latter refers to nonviolent struggle to right a wrong or overturn injustice. The primary purpose of jihad is to create a world of justice and peace, where all submit to the will of Allah, by transforming the non-Muslim world (*dar al-harb*) into a Muslim world (*dar al-Islam*). In order to achieve this aim, one Hadith claims that 'jihad is the peak of religion'. Importantly, the peaceful internal struggle is regarded as the greater jihad (*al-jihad al-akbar*), while military adventures constitute the lesser struggle (*al-jihad al-asghar*). Nonetheless, given that it was in the lesser jihad that most Muslim martyrs were created, this will be the focus of our study.

In the Qu'ran, there are several commands concerning jihad in the sense of warfare. However, they are not at all consistent. At this point it is worth noting that the method of compilation of the Qu'ran is not thematic or chronological. Therefore, the order in which the material was composed is not immediately obvious. Some verses advocate all-out aggression against enemies of the faith, while others counsel the endurance of suffering and persecution. These different attitudes to war probably reflect different periods in the prophet's life and Islam's development.

It is generally accepted, though not without challenge, that there were four main stages of development. These stages reflect the relative military strength of or perceived threat to the early Muslim communities. The first cluster of texts is not enthusiastic about engaging enemies in battle. This strata probably dates from the earliest stage of Islamic history when Mohammad's preaching was enjoying only limited success, and the early adherents of Islam faced significant hostility and persecution from the Meccans. Although Muslims were to profess their faith, conflict was to be avoided.

Profess openly what you have been commanded, and turn away from the Polytheists. For we are sufficient for you against the scoffers. (Qu'ran 15.94–95)

Summon to the way of your Lord with wisdom and good admonition and argue against them with what is better, for your Lord knows best who has strayed from his path and who has been guided. (Qu'ran 16.125)

The second strand advocates conflict, but only in self-defence.

Permission is given to those who have been fought against in that they have been wronged; those who have been wrongly expelled from their homes only because they say, 'Our Lord is Allah'. For God is most powerful for their aid. (Qu'ran 22.39–40)

Fight in the way of God those who fight you, but do not transgress limits, for God does not love transgressors. (Qu'ran 2.190)

These verses, as well as legitimating warfare, probably also reflect the experiences of violence perpetrated against Muslims by Meccan raids. Nonetheless, in neither of the first two stages is idolatry mentioned as something which needs to be actively attacked other than with speech. Again, it is probably the case that the Muslim community was simply too small to confront the idolatrous Meccans head on. In the final two stages of the development of jihad, this changes.

Within the third stage, strictly limited offensive conflict was permitted. Idolatry is now a prominent motive for attack.

Slay them wherever you catch them, and turn them out from where they have turned you out, for idolatry is worse than killing. But do not fight them at the Sacred Mosque unless they fight you there. But if they fight you, then kill them. Such is the recompense for the unbelievers. (Qu'ran 2.191)

Violence is cast as retaliation. The Muslim community had gained sufficient numbers that it could now launch assaults in return for violence perpetrated against them. Nonetheless, fighting at the mosque is prohibited unless they are first attacked. Even the prohibition during the sacred months is provisional:

They ask you concerning fighting in the prohibited months. Say, 'Fighting during it is a grave (offence); but preventing access to the path of God, disbelief in God, and expelling his people from the Sacred Mosque is worse in the sight of God. (Qu'ran 2.217)

There is an order of offence to God. Killing is a sin, but allowing idolatry to flourish is worse. Fighting during the prohibited months is forbidden. However, if believers are being prevented from worshipping, violence even at this time is justified.

Finally, in what have become known as 'the sword verses', war against believers is not only tolerated, but commanded.

Fighting is prescribed upon you, (although) you dislike it. But it is possible that you dislike a thing which is good for you, and that you love a thing which is bad for you. God knows, and you know not. (Qu'ran 2.216)

The verse indicates some resistance to the command to war, which is overcome by appealing to the superior wisdom of God. In the most far reaching of the sword verses, hunting down and slaying idolaters becomes a routine activity outside the sacred months.

When the forbidden months are past, fight and slay the idolaters wherever you find them, and seize then, beleaguer them, and lie in wait for them in every stratagem (of war) . . .

However, the Qur'an even here does not advocate indiscriminate slaughter. If idolaters abandon idolatry, then this is to be welcomed.

. . . but if they repent and establish regular prayers and pay the alms tax, then open the way for them, for God is oft-forgiving, most merciful. (Qu'ran 9.5)

Admittedly, what we find here looks suspiciously like 'conversion by the sword'. Although offensive to modern sensibilities, it may be observed that the opportunity of conversion was not open to those whom the Hebrews encountered and massacred in the conquest narratives of Deuteronomy and Joshua![6] Even so, later in *sura* 9, it becomes clear that survival does not depend on conversion.

Fight those who do not believe in God or the last day, nor hold what has been forbidden by God and his messenger to be forbidden, nor acknowledge the religion of truth from among the people of the book, *until they pay the jizya* (poll tax) with willing submission, and feel themselves subdued. (9.29)

Clearly, these verses potentially universalize the Islamic struggle. In the initial stages of the development of jihad the concern was to defend a small, peculiarly monotheistic sect within a more powerful and hostile polytheistic setting by either endurance or carefully targeted retaliation. As Islam spread throughout the Arabian Peninsula, what required defending was not a small community, but a potentially universal faith. This defence necessitated the active elimination of idolatry through conquest and conversion. The historical political ascendency of Islam at the close of the revelation obviously leaves Qur'anic notions of Holy War untempered in the way those of the Hebrew Bible were by experiences of decline and exile, or indeed the total lack of political power in the period the Christian scriptures were composed. This historical contingency would have a profound effect on Islamic theology of martyrdom.

2.3 Martyrdom in the Early Islamic Period

Martyrdom in Islam, as in Christianity, is related to the concept of 'witness'. The Greek word *martus*, which originally had the import of witnessing in court, eventually became a technical term for 'martyr' in Christianity. Although some scholars believe the first technical use of the term is found in the mid-second-century text, *The Martyrdom of Polycarp*, I have demonstrated that there is already a strong connection between witnessing and death in the book of Revelation. Furthermore, the use of *martus* in relation to Antipas (Rev. 2.13) appears quite close to a technical usage.

Similarly, there is no single term for martyrdom in the earliest Islamic period. There is recognition that Muslims may be killed while struggling in the path of God, but the closest technical term is also the Arabic term for a legal witness, *shahid* (pl. *shahdua*). It is possible, but by no means certain there was some Christian influence in connecting the concepts of witness and death. Mirroring the scarcity of the term being employed in a technical sense in the New Testament, the Qur'an similarly has only one clear occurrence of *shahid* where it most likely has the technical sense of martyr.

Do not be faint-hearted and do not grieve; you will have the upper hand, if you are true believers. If you have been afflicted by a wound, a similar wound has afflicted the others. Such are the times; we alternate them among the people, so that Allah may know who are the believers and choose martyrs (*shuhada'*) from among you. (Qu'ran 3.140)

This saying probably dates to the period after the Battle of Uhud in 625, the only significant military defeat endured by Mohammad. The victory at Badr the previous year had raised expectations, and reinforced in the Muslims the conviction that God was on their side. The unexpected defeat at Uhud caused a theological crisis, which, in the main, *sura* 3 addresses.

First, some of the fighters disobeyed Mohammad's and Allah's orders, and became more concerned with raiding the Meccan camp for treasure:

And Allah had surely made good to you His promise when you were slaying and destroying them by his leave, until, when you became lax and disagreed among yourselves concerning the order and you disobeyed after He had shown you that which you loved, *he withdrew his help.* Among you were those who desired the present world, and among you were those who desired the next. Then He turned you away from them, that he might try you – and he has surely pardoned you, and Allah is Gracious to the believers. (Qu'ran 3.153)

The cause of the defeat, therefore, is here and elsewhere explained by God's protection being withdrawn because of disobedience. Next, those who doubted God still favoured the Muslims are chastised.

What! When a single disaster befalls you, although you defeated (your enemies) it was twice as great, what do you say? 'It is from yourselves: For God has power over all things. What you suffered on the day the two armies met was God's will, in order that he might test the believers. (Qu'ran 3.165–166)

Finally, the place of the dead are assured; God has chosen them to be martyrs (3.140). Even in the face of defeat, those who die fighting for God are martyrs and will be rewarded.

Do not think those who have been killed in the way of Allah are dead; they are rather living with their Lord, well-provided for. Rejoicing in what their Lord has given them of His bounty, and they rejoice for those who stayed behind and did not join them, knowing that they have nothing to fear and that they shall not grieve'. (Qu'ran 3.169–170)

Developing a martyrology in the face of defeat was particularly important after Uhud. Not only were the numerical losses great, but a number of prominent figures were killed, not least, Mohammad's uncle Hamza. Hamza had killed a number of Meccan leaders at the Battle of Badr, and his death at Uhud was a particular blow. During the battle, he had been killed by a spear thrown by the slave Wahshi and had died in some agony. Furthermore, Hamza's body was mutilated; his liver being removed from his body and eaten by Hinda, the wife of a former Meccan leader whom Hamza had killed. Despite his ignominious end, Hamza demonstrated the qualities of a warrior-martyr, by far the most common type of martyr in early Islam. Even in battles where the Muslims were victorious, there would always be casualties. However, those who fell in war would be remembered as victorious martyrs.

Allah has bought from the believers their lives and their wealth in return for paradise; they fight in the way of Allah, kill and get killed. This is a true promise from Him . . . Rejoice then at the bargain you have made with him; for that is the great triumph. (Qu'ran 9.111)

This is not to say that there are no examples of 'passive' martyrs in Islam. In revenge for the loss at the Battle of Badr, Khubayb ibn Ali, along with some other men, was captured by men from the Lihyab clan. Despite being promised they would not be harmed if they surrendered, Khubayb was sold to the sons of a man he had killed at the battle. There are several versions of his death in the Hadith literature, but each recounts his resolve under torture and death.

When they took him out . . . to kill him . . . Khubayb said to them, 'Allow me to pray two *raka'as*' and they left him, so he prayed two *raka'as*, and said, 'By Allah, if it were not for the fact that they would think that I am apprehensive, I would have prayed more'. He said, 'O Allah, Count them each one, kill them separately and do not leave one of them'. Then he said, 'I do not care what part of my struggle for Allah was, since I am being killed as a Muslim, since this is part of the essence of godhood; if he wills, he can bless the severed members of (my) body'.

Other versions recount a conversation between Khubayb and his torturers about whether he would prefer Mohammad to be in his place and for him to go free, to which he replied, 'By Allah, I would not like to be among my relatives and sons enjoying all the world's health and well-being while even a tiny thorn hurts the Prophet'. Khubayb's self-identification as a Muslim is critical. Although Khubayb is not asked to renounce his faith, it is as a Muslim that he dies, and this makes him a martyr.

There are other cases of early passive martyrdom from the initial period of Islam. Followers of Mohammad, particularly slaves, experienced a high degree of hostility and torture. One of the earliest paradigmatic stories of one of the faithful suffering for Islam is that of the Ethiopian slave Bilal. Also remembered as the first *muezzin*, Bilal was tortured by his master, Ummayah. He was made to lie unprotected in the sun with a large rock on his chest in order to make him renounce Islam. However, he remained faithful, and was bought and emancipated by Abu Bakr (the successor to Mohammad). He is later said to have killed his former master in the Battle of Badr. Similarly, another slave, Ammar ibn Yasir, in Shi'a tradition, one of the four companions, was one of the few survivors of the brutal persecutions of Abu Jahl, a leading member of the Quraysh. Despite the fact that neither of the two slaves died, their struggle and faithfulness are paradigmatic of martyrological suffering.

However, martyrs *were* created during this period of persecution, including Mohammad's wife and father-in-law. One of the first martyrs, Ammar's mother, Sumayya bint Khayyat, was tortured and fatally stabbed by Abu. It was in response to these persecutions that Mohammad sent some of his followers to Abyssinia. It is likely these experiences of persecution, as well as the attempt on Mohammad's life, provided some of the motivation to conquer Mecca when the Muslim armies became large enough to do so.

2.4 Shi'a Martyrdom

Active and passive forms of martyrdom come together in the Shi'a narrative of the Battle of Karbala, and the death of Hussein. The confrontation between Hussein and Yazid was a struggle for political control between two contenders for the caliphate. However, for the Shi'a, the struggle was between true and more lax expressions of Islam. In Shi'a tradition, Yazid was leading the people back into the habits of polytheism, and so Hussein and a band of 72 fighters confronted his forces. Travelling across the desert with his family and so few men, it is historically, unlikely that Hussein intended to engage in military conflict. Nonetheless, although vastly outnumbered, and under siege with no access to water, Hussein's army fought bravely.

In accounts of the martyrdoms, each of Hussein's party dies well, often accompanied by dreams assuring the fallen of paradise. Hussein withstands many blows, before finally being killed after 33 wounds were inflicted upon him. His body was then mutilated, before his head was cut off and sent to Yazid. Interpretations of the Battle of Karbala are essentially concerned with legitimacy. For Shi'a, that the contemporaries of Hussein did not support him leaves a sorrowful stain on Islam that manifests itself on the Day of Ashura. The remembrance of Hussein's martyrdom was institutionalized in the ninth century, and involves ritualized mourning, and the shedding of blood through flagellation.

For Shi'a Muslims, the defeat of the virtuous Hussein, representing the blood line of the prophet, stands as an example of the fate of a minority faithful sect against a more powerful, illegitimate, and persecuting majority. Hussein's martyrdom was paradigmatic of a whole line of imams, persecuted and martyred by their Sunni rivals. The history of Shi'a Islam is a history of martyrdom. The revered 12 imams all died unnatural deaths. The tenth-century martyrology, *Slaughter of the Talibites* (*Maqatil al-Talibiyyin*), lists almost 200 of the Prophet's descendants who were martyred, reinforcing the Shi'a idea that persecution, or indeed martyrdom, is the fate of the descendants and true followers of Mohammad, mostly at the hands of other Muslims.

2.5 Rewards of the Martyrs

We have already noted that in the Qur'an, those who die as martyrs are not to be mourned, for they live in paradise, and receive of God's bounty. Further verses hint at these rewards:

And those who believe in Allah and His messengers – they are the loyal, and the martyrs (*shuhada'*) are with their Lord; they have their reward and their light; while as for those who disbelieve and deny Our revelations, they are owners of hell-fire. (57.19)

To be sure, *shuhada'* need not have the specific meaning of martyr here, and Yusuf Ali renders it as the more generic 'witnesses'. Nonetheless, many Islamic exegetes take it in its martyrological sense here. A more fulsome picture of paradise is given elsewhere:

And those Foremost (in Faith) will be Foremost (in the Hereafter). These will be those nearest to Allah in the Garden of Bliss . . . (They will be) on thrones encrusted (with gold and precious stones), reclining on them facing each other. Round about them will (serve) youths of perpetual (freshness) with goblets, (shining) beakers, and cups (filled) out of clear flowing fountains. No after-ache will they receive therefrom, nor will they suffer intoxication . . . And there will be Companions (*houris*) with beautiful, big, and lustrous eyes like unto pearls well-guarded; a reward for the deeds of their past (life). No frivolity will they hear therein, nor any taint of ill – only the saying 'Peace, Peace'. (56.10–26)

Once again, in the Qur'an, it is not clear that this description of paradise is a specific reward for martyrs rather than all faithful Muslims. However, in the Hadith and later exegetical tradition, martyrs are singled out for special reward.

The martyr receives six good things from Allah: he is forgiven at the first shedding of his blood; he is shown his abode in Paradise;

he is preserved from the punishment in the grave; he is kept safe from the greatest terror; he has placed on his head the crown of honour, a ruby of which is better than the world and what it contains; he is married to seventy-two wives of the maidens (*houris*) with large dark eyes; and is made intercessor for seventy of his relatives. (*Al-Tirmidhi Hadith* 1067)

Of all the rewards of the martyrs, the *houris*, that is, the virgins attained in paradise, have proved controversial. Many contemporary Western enemies of Islam have seized upon the vision of the reward of virgins, dubbing Islam a sensuous religion, recruiting immature, sexually starved young men to sacrifice themselves for posthumous sex. It is difficult to ascertain what is precisely on the minds of suicide bombers as they reach their final moments. Although many martyr posters call the act of martyrdom the 'wedding' of the protagonist, many videos and notes focus instead on themes of injustice and oppression. Furthermore, this explanation fails to offer a persuasive account of women and secularists who have engaged in suicide attacks.

The Hadith exalt the position of martyrs in heaven, and accord them a special spiritual status. Like the early Christian martyrs, their own blood plays a role in the forgiveness of their sins; they possess a special place in heaven, and because of this purity, have an intercessory role. So, in present-day Afghanistan, people bring prayers to the graves of Taliban martyrs. The martyrs' special status in heaven has a knock-on effect for the treatment of their remains.

The body of a martyr, that is, a Muslim killed in battle at the hands of disbelievers, may not be washed even though it is in a state of major ritual impurity. His body should be enshrouded in the clothes he wore when he died if they are good enough for the purpose. Otherwise some additional cloth may be used to enshroud his body according to the *sunnah*. The body of such a person should be buried in its blood-stained state. None of his blood should be washed off. (*Fiqu-us-Sunnah Hadith* 4.27)

The Hadith goes on to explain that this was the course of action ordered by Mohammad for the dead at the Battle of Uhud: 'Do not wash those who die as martyrs, for every wound or drop of blood will exude a fragrance like musk on the Day of Judgement'.

Before moving onto the development of martyrdom in the modern age, there is one important point of clarification that must be made. So far, I have focussed on one particular type of martyr in Islam; the one who loses his life in battle. However, martyrdom in classical Islam encompasses a far greater diversity of circumstances of death. Indeed, according to the Hadith, when this definition of martyrdom was put to the prophet, he replied, 'Then the martyrs of my Ummah will be small in number' (*Sahih Muslim Hadith* 891). A martyr can be made in all kinds of situations so long as one is faithful to Allah. In a well-attested Hadith, the definition of a martyr is expanded.

The Messenger of Allah . . . said, 'Allah has made his reward fall according to his intention. What do you consider dying a martyr to be?' They said, 'Death in the Way of Allah.' The Messenger of Allah, may Allah bless him and grant him peace, said, 'There are seven kinds of martyr other than those killed in the way of Allah. Someone who is killed by the plague is a martyr; someone who drowns is a martyr; someone who dies of pleurisy is a martyr; someone who dies of a disease of the belly is a martyr; someone who dies by fire is a martyr; someone who dies under a falling building is a martyr; and a women who dies in childbirth is a martyr'. (*Al-Muwatta Hadith* 16.36)

It would seem, then, that virtually anyone could be considered to be a martyr by this definition. However, as I have contended throughout, martyrs are not defined, martyrs are made. Martyrs require a martyr narrative, and the categories mentioned above rarely, if ever, receive such narratives. To be sure, it is noteworthy that women can be specifically incorporated into the category of martyr. Nonetheless, our focus will remain those who are killed in a situation of conflict, where the death is subsequently interpreted as a martyrdom.

3 TOWARDS THE MODERN AGE

3.1 Assassins

Although the capture of Jerusalem by Christian Crusaders in 1099 was met by a lack of interest in the Islamic world, Saladin's

(c. 1138–1193) eventual proclamation of a jihad in the mid twelfth century enabled Muslims once again to fight and die for God on the battlefield.[7] However, between the eleventh and thirteenth centuries, a variant form of battlefield martyrdom emerged in Islam which bears some resemblance to the Graeco-Roman Noble Death tradition, and the Jewish sicarii movement. The Order of Assassins of the Ismaili tradition, a branch of Shi'a Islam which revered only seven of the 12 imams, was founded by Hassan Sabbah in Iran, which was at the time ruled by the Seljuk Empire.[8] From his base in the Elburz Mountains, Hassan conquered the fortress at Alamut in 1090. Hassan reportedly never left the castle, but spent his days in prayer, while recruiting and training his followers with a strict regime of discipline and physical training.

Hassan challenged the sole authority of religious authorities to interpret matters of religion, especially as, from his perspective, they tended to ignore issues of injustice. In response, those rulers sent troops to quash the rebellion. However, they found the fortress impenetrable. Hassan knew that he could never succeed by confronting these troops in open warfare, so he set about devising a mode of attack designed to cause maximum anxiety and destabilization – the targeted assassination. And so, this tiny group created terror for nearly 200 years, killing princes, generals, caliphs, and any other persons of influence. Crucially, the assassins did not expect to survive their missions. They always used a dagger, never an arrow, and always allowed themselves to be killed at the hands of bodyguards, or face execution. To survive a mission was considered to be a disgrace.

The assassins were also marked by a particularly intense loyalty to their founder. The order appears to have adopted a strong eschatological belief that their actions somehow hastened the return of the hidden imam, who would establish a new order of pure Islam. Their ability to go about unnoticed before unleashing a very public attack on a prominent dignitary before either taking their own life or submitting to execution caused them to be particularly feared. Since the assassin did not fear death, it rendered any sanction ineffective. Although the assassins rarely failed in their task, they were unsuccessful in killing Saladin, against whom they made two attempts. The unswerving devotion to their task led to suggestions by, among others, Marco Polo, they may have been drugged (they were dubbed the *hashishin*). The order faced twin threats from Sunni Muslims and the Christian Crusaders, but remained a potent force until they were destroyed by the Mongols in the thirteenth century.

The assassins form an important link between early expressions of jihad and the contemporary manifestation of suicide bombing. Those who engaged in jihad by the sword did not wish to die. Although they knew they would win a martyr's reward should they die in battle, the primary object was to win the war. Significantly, losses on both sides of the wars with the Meccans were very low, so the odds of surviving battle were comparatively high. The assassins, on the other hand, would only survive if their mission was a failure. Indeed one story tells of a mother whose rejoicing at news of her son's death as an assassin turned to mourning when he returned home very much alive! The certainty that each successful mission would lead to the assassin's death, together with the recruitment methods of Hasan, bear some similarities with the modern phenomenon of suicide attacks, although by contrast, assassins never took their own lives.

3.2 Demise of the Islamic Empire

Aside from the first dozen years from its founding, Islam rarely had to deal with military misadventure. Once Mohammad had achieved a foothold in Medina, Islamic forces were able to expand their influence across much of the East. Such expansion demonstrated God's favour on Islam. This increased the Islamic belief that it represented the final revelation of God intended to supersede both Judaism and Christianity. Comparatively few Muslims faced a situation of being forced through torture to abandon their faith. Most who died in an active sense did so through battles which expanded Muslim territory.

However, this expansion was no more 'aggressive' than any other imperial expansion. Although the Qur'an advocated little tolerance for idolatry, it also forbade 'compulsion in religion' (2.256). On the payment of a poll tax, Jews and Christians could and did remain Jews and Christians. The Islamic Empire was also happy to make peace and trade accords with 'enemies', even the Crusaders. In the aftermath of the Crusades, and the establishment of the Ottoman Empire, Muslims remained politically and militarily superior, claiming Constantinople/Istanbul in 1453.

However, from the sixteenth century, Christian Europe began to push back. Tartars and Moors were expelled from Russia and Spain, and when in 1683, the Ottomans were forced to retreat from their siege of Vienna, more than a millennium of dominance was broken. The Ottoman Empire endured a string of defeats as the Europeans colonized Africa, India, and Asia. At the turn of the eighteenth century, European military superiority was demonstrated when first Napoleon conquered Egypt in 1798, and it took another European power, the British under Nelson, to evict them. Throughout the nineteenth and early twentieth century, the British and French invaded Algeria, Aden, Tunisia, Morocco, and the Persian Gulf, while Indonesia, another centre of Islam, came under Dutch colonial rule. After the First World War, the Ottoman Empire, which had sided with the Germans, was divided between the two European powers by the League of Nations, and when Turkey became an independent state in 1922, the empire was over.[9]

Although the European empires brought the benefits of infrastructure, public education, and health, that most Islamic population centres were dominated by foreign rule dented national and religious pride, and resentment against Western imperialism grew. However, although the language of jihad was employed in protest against foreign imperial power, in practice, secular nationalism was the vehicle with which the Muslim elite were most comfortable. However, secular nationalism gave way to a more radicalized form of Islam over the establishment of the state of Israel, especially after the Six Day War of 1967, where Arab nations, which had been granted independence from European colonial powers, now found sections of their countries, including Jerusalem, occupied by another foreign non-Islamic power, backed by Western imperialism. The humiliating defeat of the pan-Arab forces, taken together with all other twentieth-century military misadventures carried out in Arab nations, effectively ruled out national military action as a means of advancing either political or religious aims against foreign oppression, occupation, and injustice. A new mode of operation was therefore required. The Iran–Iraq War (1980–1988) highlighted the ineffectiveness of military conflict. However, it was also to contribute to the development of a new form of Islamic martyrdom in the region: the suicide attack.

4 CONTEMPORARY ISLAMIC MARTYRDOM

The discourse of martyrdom in the twenty-first century is almost completely dominated by Islamicist suicide attackers, whether it be in the form of the lone bomber setting off his explosives on a bus or café, the attacker who drives a car, van, or truck full of explosives into a strategic base, or most iconic, the hijacking and crashing of the aircraft into the Twin Towers and Pentagon on 11 September 2001. Such attacks have dampened public sympathy for all 'martyrs'; their unswerving loyalty to their faith to the point of losing their lives can appear extremist and inhuman. Martyrs display devotion and commitment to religion which is out of step, and even suspicious to modern Western minds. Furthermore, as I have shown, *all* martyrs encourage the interpretation of everyday life not only as a struggle, but a war, often with a cosmic apocalyptic spin. As such, suicide bombing represents a series of clashes between civilizations; between secular and sacred ideologies, and also of language. Can suicide bombers be martyrs? Any reader who has come with me this far will know the answer is affirmative. All martyrs require are martyr narratives, and in the case of modern Islamicist suicide attackers, these narratives exist.

A more difficult and sensitive question concerns the relationship between suicide bombers and Islam. Whatever mainstream Muslim opinion on such attacks may be, it is clear that martyr narratives claim an Islamic context, and in terms of historical Islamic martyrology, such claims are not impossible. Nonetheless, two elements of the phenomenon in particular require attention: the killing of others, especially the innocent; and the self-killing of the protagonist, which is specifically forbidden in Islam.

4.1 Martyrdom and Protest

The aims of most conflicts in which Arab nations took part in were essentially political. Nonetheless, the narratives created to both justify the attack and the attacker appeal to the traditional rhetoric of Islamic jihad. But as with both Christianity and Judaism, it is not always clear where the religious realm ends and the secular sphere begins. All three religions of the book have at some point in their history operated with a religio-political polity. Protest movements and revolts against the governing authorities in Islamic states have often taken religious inspiration for their actions, often in order to correct the ruling authorities' deviaton from 'true' Islam. This prophetic protest impulse is built into Shi'aism, but is also found throughout Islamic history. This is perhaps why essentially political causes can adopt a religious narrative, both in relation to the political goal, such as the attempts to expel foreign powers from Islamic lands, and to all who die in that struggle. There are sufficient resources in Islamic martyr theology to subsume political fighters who die in the most contemporary manifestations of struggling for Islam into the category of martyr (*shahid*); all that is necessary is that the martyr died struggling for Islam.

Because it lost out in the succession crises of early Islam, Shi'a Islam developed a potent tradition of resisting the political rule of those they regarded as deviant Muslims. The most significant recent example of religious rebellion to overthrow a lax Muslim government occurred in Iran.[10] In the Revolution of 1979, the Iranian people overthrew the shah, while the leaders of the revolution criticized both those who compromised with imperial powers, represented by America, but also the revolutionary left-wing People's Mujahedeen. The people had defeated the shah despite his possessing modern military equipment supplied by America. Iran's Shi'a Islam interpreted revolution as the time before the return of the hidden imam, and in order for the revolution to fully take effect, men had to become warriors again, and that included a readiness for martyrdom.

Ayatollah Khomeini developed the concept of 'red Shi'ism', in recognition of the blood-stained sacrifice of Karbala martyrs. Khomeini's mass martyrdom movement made possible the new wave of suicide bombing in Sunni Islam. Only Shi'ite Islam, with its devotion to Hussein, and recreation of his life as a quasi-saint cum revolutionary, could provide the impetous to propel the mass human waves of young men and even children to volunteer to face certain death on the front line and mine fields of the Iran–Iraq War.

After Saddam Hussein's invasion of Iran in 1980, Khomenei invoked the memory of Karbala in order to recruit 'volunteers' for the war. Saddam and his Western backers represented the pretender Yazid, while the Iranian people became the loyal 72 who stood with the Prince of Martyrs, Hussein, and who had refused to save their own lives and instead chose to die with him. Each of the suicide operations was named after that battle. Each wave was a re-enactment of the deaths of the prophet's true family and heirs against the infidel aggressor. Banners bore the words, 'Every land is Karbala; every month is Muharram; every day is Ashura'.[11] Parents were paid for their children's service in the war. If they died, they received a certificate of martyrdom. 'The tree of Islam', Khomenei claimed, 'can only grow if it's constantly fed with the blood of martyrs'.

Hundreds of thousands of young men volunteered to serve on the front line. They simply charged at the Iraqi machine-gunners until they had overrun them, or they were all dead. The soldiers all had keys around their necks; keys which they had been told would open the gates of paradise should they die a martyr's death. In Shi'a tradition, the veneration of Hussein had made him a model beyond human reproduction. Before the Iranian revolution, the dominant interpretation of Hussein was as someone who accepted death rather than face humiliation at the hands of the enemy. Martyrdom was therefore the preference to being humiliated at the hands of the enemy. After the revolution, Hussein's example became a model all Muslims could follow. Martyrdom is an act which is profoundly inclusive. All Muslims can be martyrs, rich or poor, educated or illiterate, men and women.

Despite having little in the way of military success to show for the thousands of lives sacrificed in the war against Iraq, the mode of suicide attack spread to the other place where there was a concentration of Shi'ite Muslims: Lebanon. In the early 1980s, around one thousand Iranian Revolutionary Guards entered Lebanon and brought suicide bombing as a new military tactic. It was in Lebanon that the phenomenon, carried out by Hezbollah, was first dubbed 'martyr operations'. Whereas in the Iran–Iraq conflict nearly one million people lost their lives with very little to show for their sacrifice, in the Lebanon just four martyrs caused the withdrawal of American, French, and Israeli troops by 1985. Importantly, Hezbollah only resorted to suicide attacks from a position of weakness. When they gained some political influence, the tactic was dropped. Nonetheless, the success of these martyrdom operations caused the phenomenon to spread to the Sunni Muslims of Palestine. Prior to the attacks on 9/11, suicide attacks were most commonly associated with the Palestinian cause.

4.2 Palestine and Israel

In 1988, the Palestinian organization Hamas was founded in direct competition to Yasser Arafat's Palestinian Liberation Organization

(PLO). The founding covenant casts the problem facing Palestine as a religious problem and calls for Muslims to rediscover the faith of their ancestors.

> The Islamic Resistance Movement . . . strives to raise the banner of Allah over every inch of Palestine, for under the wins of Islam followers of every religion can coexist in security and safety where their lives, possessions and rights are concerned. In the absence of Islam, strife will be rife, oppression spreads, evil prevails, and schism and wars will break out. (Article 6)

The document goes on to claim that the current Palestinian leadership had abandoned Islam, which was the cause of the Palestinians losing their land to the 'Zionist invaders' (Article 9). Furthermore, the peaceful solution was rejected, since the infidel Jews could not be expected to treat Muslims with any justice (Article 13). The only solution, according to the manifesto, is jihad.

> The day that enemies usurp part of Muslim land, Jihad becomes the individual duty of every Muslim. In the face of Jews' usurpation of Palestine, it is compulsory that the banner of *Jihad* be raised . . . It is necessary to instil the spirit of *Jihad* in the heart of the nation so that they would confront the enemies and join the ranks of the fighters. (Article 15)

Hamas, therefore, cast all Palestinians as fighters on the path of jihad. The PLO, it claimed, were erring brothers who had abandoned Islam.

Despite receiving early backing from Israel, the movement was soon banned, and in 1992, four hundred radicals were deported to South Lebanon, where they mixed with the Shi'a Muslims of Hezbollah. Although Hamas leaders had mooted the idea of suicide attacks, it was only after this encounter that the first suicide mission struck in Israel. Even so, the PLO leadership were able to contain and punish the ringleaders. However, strategic errors, such as supporting Saddam Hussein in the run-up to the First Gulf War, combined with the stalling peace talks, weakened Arafat's leadership. The Hebron Massacre in 1994 when an Israeli doctor, Baruch Goldstein, opened fire on worshippers at the Ibrahim Mosque, killing 29 before being overpowered and killed, fuelled Palestinian anger. That a shrine was erected for the martyr Goldstein, which became a place of pilgrimage for radical Israeli settlers, only compounded the humiliation of an occupied people, whose freedom of movement was restricted by check points.

At first, Hamas struggled to find legitimacy in Palestine. However, as suicide bombing became more frequent, Hamas's popularity and credibility grew, especially in Gaza. Israeli assassinations of prominent Hamas leaders, such as the quadriplegic Ahmed Yassin in 2004, only gave the movement more credibility. Hamas set in place a system of social security that rewarded families of martyrs. It is arguably the case that years of displacement, occupation, and humiliation has created in the Palestinian people a 'culture of death'. Martyrdom is a means by which the powerless can win back power, as it had been for some Jews against Christian Crusaders and Nazis. When one is prepared to sacrifice one's life, there is no sanction. 'To put it simply' stated a father of a Palestinian martyr, 'we love martyrdom; they [the Israelis] love life.'[12] When martyrdom transforms an oppressed person into a hero, it becomes a potent means of providing meaning for one's life. What Hamas achieved was to create a narrative that combined the Shi'a concept of martyrdom as a response to oppression together with Sunni notions of jihad in response to injustice.

As with South Lebanon, a cult of martyrdom developed in Palestine. Martyrs were both heroes and provided noble examples to be followed. Posters and graffiti recounted the brave deeds of the martyrs, effectively creating martyr narratives. One poster, 'announcing' the death of a martyr, reads:

One soldier killed and three wounded in a suicide operation carried out by a son of Fatah. O masses of our great people, this morning, 9/3/92, the Brother, the Son of Fatah 'Ala al-Mughrabi carried out a suicide operation against a group of soldiers and policemen . . . where he killed one of them on the spot and gravely wounded three others. With the utmost insistence and challenge in continuing on the road of struggle, Fatah announces the death of its martyr, the Martyr of Palestine, the Brother 'Ala al-Mughrabi. We first promise Allah and then the masses to continue on the road of giving until victory. [13]

The poster claims, perhaps even creates, a sense of solidarity among all Palestinians, whether they approve of the action or not. Similarly, 'martyr cards' complete with Qur'anic verses and photographs are distributed by the families of martyrs as commemorative tokens. The other principal way of creating a martyr narrative is the note or video left by the martyr. While these may be an unreliable source of an individual's actual motivations, they contribute to the community's conflict narrative. One example in the Palestinian struggle is Ismail Masawabi, who killed himself and murdered two Israeli soldiers in June 2001. Masawabi, like many Palestinian martyrs, was well educated and came from a relatively wealthy family. His last testament sets his death in the context of jihad against the unjust oppression of the Israelis, and contrasts the humiliation and disgrace of life compared to the glory and victory of death. Moreover, he offers himself as a model to be emulated by other Muslim youth.

Thanks be to God who brings about the mujahideens' victory and the dictators' defeat, and praise be to Muhammad, the faithful, honourable Prophet Muhammad, and all his friends, and all who have followed his footsteps.

Dear Muslim youth the world over: I greet you with the blessed greetings of Islam; greetings that I send to all of you who fight in the name of religion and the nation; greetings to all those who are convinced fighters and martyrs . . .

Dear brothers: there is no doubt about the situation prevailing in the . . . Muslim nation . . . It's a situation that makes us weep and makes our hearts ache because of what has happened to the Muslims. We are truly grieved about it.

Before we had power, then we became weak. We live in humiliation, where we once lived in dignity . . .

The wish to become a martyr dominates my life, my heart, my soul and my feelings . . . We are a nation living in disgrace and under Jewish occupation. This happened to us because we didn't fight them; we didn't fight for God.

I reject this terrible and dark situation . . . and I have decided to become a shining light, illuminating the way for all Muslims – and a blazing fire to burn to death the enemy of God. Just standing there and watching our Muslim people being slaughtered and not taking any action to change the situation is a dirty game that I will not tolerate . . . Therefore . . . I prefer to meet God and leave humankind behind . . . I have told myself that I will be with the Prophet Muhammad and his followers tomorrow . . .

God will not forgive you if you accept such a life. The alternative is the true life. God will not forgive you if you accept humiliation and don't fight to put an end to the situation and to strengthen Islam. [14]

The testimony goes on to assure those who may grieve for him that he is in paradise and they should not grieve, before outlining his wish that he will make the 'Jews feel some of the devastation they subject my people to every day'.

Ismail's eloquence is disarming, yet what we have in this note is a narrative of conflict that sustains a belief that for even educated men and women the most appropriate course of action is to kill Israelis and die in the process. The narrative is plausible enough that many Palestinians have followed Ismail's example. Moreover, it represents the real experiences of enough people to sustain a powerful cult of the martyrs in Palestine.

4.3 Martyrdom and Suicide

Western politicians and commentators are understandably horrified that the language of martyrdom is employed for what they regard as cold-blooded killers. The suicidal element also confronts the fundamental secular liberal principle of the impulse to protect (one's own) life. As I hope I demonstrated in the opening chapter, much of the objections to the principle of suicide bombing are rather superficial. Leaving aside Jewish and Christian conceptions of Holy War, those who hold to liberal Western (secular) ideologies have little problem killing those regarded as enemies in the context of war. Targeted assassinations have also been employed by Western powers. The articulation of the war aims for the ongoing conflicts in Iraq and Afghanistan include the rhetoric of nation building through the spread of democracy, and with it 'freedom' for the individual; in other words, the spread of Western liberal polity through military force. The Allied Forces have discovered that winning an armed conflict is far easier than 'winning hearts and minds' to the Western agenda. In this respect, the War on Terror may be categorized, with some legitimacy, as a Western liberal jihad.

Therefore, on secular Western liberal principles alone, it is not difficult to justify an ideologically driven conflict in which many people will be killed. The fact that a suicide bomber kills is not problematic per se. Neither is the fact that bystanders are killed. We in the West have developed a rhetoric of 'collateral damage', by which many thousands of civilian deaths can be accounted for within a moral framework. I have already suggested that even suicide killing, canonized by Samon's actions, can be incorporated into a Western ideology of 'Just War', so long as it is carried out against an agreed enemy. Talal Asad also points to the fact that some powerful nations hold the right to defend themselves with nuclear weapons effectively affirming that 'suicidal war can be legitimate'.[15] However, as in Christianity and Judaism, Islam offers a strong injunction against suicide. How then can suicide missions be justified within an Islamic narrative?

Opinion is divided among Islamic scholars whether or not suicide missions are a priori ruled out for a Muslim. Suicide is *haram* (forbidden) in Islam (4.29), but those Muslim voices which accept (at least some) suicide bombers into the ranks of the martyrs do not regard them as committing suicide. Rather, they sacrifice themselves in jihad by spilling their blood for the sake of the Muslim community. So while the respected Egyptian scholar Yusaf al-Qaradawi had no difficulty condemning the 9/11 attacks as a 'heinous crime in Islam', he leaves open the possibility that killing in the right circumstances, even by suicide attack, may be a legitimate operation for a Muslim. In respect of the Palestinian struggle, he is explicit. In 2004, on the BBC's *Newsnight* programme, he supported Palestinian suicide attacks as a

> type of martyrdom operation [which gives] an indication of the justice of Allah Almighty. Allah is just. Through his infinite wisdom he has given the weak what the strong do not possess, and that is the ability to turn their bodies into bombs like the Palestinians do.

Yusaf was not unaware this view is controversial. He explained:

> It is not suicide, it is martyrdom in the name of God. Islamic theologians and jurisprudents have debated the issue, referring to it as a form of *jihad* under the title of 'jeopardising the life of

the *mujaheed'* [holy warrior]. It is allowed to jeopardise your soul and cross the path of the enemy, even if it only generates fear in their hearts, shaking their morale, making them fear Muslims. If it does not affect the enemy then it's not allowed. [16]

Even though the martyr will only survive if he (or she) fails in the set mission, a distinction is made between this form of martyrdom operation and suicide. Similarly, an influential though anonymous *fatwa*, 'Islamic Ruling on the Permissibility of Martyrdom Operations', warns

> Not every martyrdom operation is legitimate, nor is every martyrdom operation prohibited. Rather, the verdict differs based on factors such as the enemy's condition, the situation of the war, the potential martyr's circumstances, and the elements of the operation itself. Thus, one may not give a verdict on such operations without having an understanding of the actual situation and this is obtained from the Mujahideen, and not the unbelievers.[17]

The fatwa also rejects the term 'suicide bomber' as an invention of unbelievers. Similarly, many Palestinian groups prefer terms such as holy or sacred explosions. The fatwa lists a few Qu'ranic verses, 40 Hadith, and other scholarly views to demonstrate the martyrdom operations are not suicide.

> It has transpired that scholars gave, to the issue of plunging single-handed into the enemy with reasonable certainty of being killed, the same verdict as in cases of death being certain, such that whoever permits the latter permits the former.

The crucial conditions for permission being: intention; inflicting losses on the enemy; creating fear; and strengthening the hearts of Muslims. Importantly, intention also separates a suicide from martyrdom.

> [T]exts prohibiting suicide related to killing oneself for worldly motives such as pain or anguish or lack of patience, and not for raising aloft the Word of Allah . . . Can one then say that one who kills himself in order to lift the Word of Allah . . . and with

a sincere intention – can we describe him as one committing suicide? That is a grave slander. We say that the prohibition of suicide is on account of its resulting from weakness or lack of faith, whereas the Mujahid in a martyrdom operation is killing himself on account of the strength of his faith.

Al-Qaradawi made a similar point in an Al-Jazeera broadcast in 1995.

A person who commits suicide kills himself for his own benefit. But a person who becomes a martyr sacrifices himself for the faith and the nation. Whereas a person who kills himself has given up all hope in himself and in God, the mujahid, the warrior, has total faith in God's mercy.[18]

Overall, the fatwa makes several important points. It is not for outsiders to judge the 'morality' of martyrdom operations. Indeed, since in many cases the actual motive will not be known, even Muslims should take care before 'slandering' a potential martyr. An act, even if it will certainly lead to death, if committed not out of fear and pain, but through faith and a desire to honour Allah, is not to be counted as suicide. Finally, in terms of historical precedent, the action of the assassins, or brave single warrior is most appropriate.

Unsurprisingly, this view has been challenged within Islamic scholarship. The website Fatwa-Online has compiled the views of several scholars who oppose in all cases the use of suicide bombing. Two arguments against the practice are particularly prominent. First, such actions cannot be separated from suicide, and are therefore forbidden. The argument here hinges on whether the killing of the self is primary or secondary. Does the martyr first kill himself and happen to kill the enemy, or is he principally attacking the enemy, with his own death simply the *result* of the attack. Often the lack of historical precedent in Islam is cited as a reason for forbidding this type of mission; even the assassins did not kill themselves.[19] However, it seems to me that this point is overplayed. No mechanism existed prior to the invention of explosives to simultaneously kill oneself and the enemy. Contemporary martyr operations are in their result precisely like the operations of the assassins, who could after all have used arrows to kill their targets at a far lower risk to their own lives.

Secondly, some scholars have pointed to the lack of success of the missions. They point to the weakening of support for the Palestinian cause as a result of the attacks, and also the failure of any such operation to fulfil its objectives. There is far more substance to this point. The dominant Western narrative after the 9/11 attacks regards the mode of suicide bombing as de facto terrorism, even though the death toll from such attacks is far less than either the conventional 'retaliatory' strikes by Israel, or Allied actions in Iraq or Afghanistan.

While fatwas for and against suicide missions/sacred explosions will no doubt continue to be made, the lack of a single Islamic polity whereby one voice or school can issue an authoritative ruling means this discussion is unlikely to be resolved. What is important is that in many places, particularly in Palestine, such attackers are recognized enthusiastically as martyrs.

As suicide missions spread throughout the world, led in the main by Al-Qaeda, the narratives of justification have become more diffuse. Indeed, the religious basis of the narrative has almost disappeared. This, combined with the more indiscriminate killing resulting from these attacks probably accounts for their lack of support among Islamic scholars. It is worth stressing again that suicide missions did not spring from Islam, and indeed the majority of such attacks in the twentieth century were secular rather than of religious motivation. In asymmetric warfare, where one's enemy possesses tanks, jets, and missiles, leaving aside all religious notions of martyrdom, it is not difficult to see the tactical appeal of human bombs. One person can inflict much damage at the cost of only one life, but can also spread fear and anxiety in the enemy.

Since the attack on the Twin Towers, suicide missions have increased. Wars in Iraq and Afghanistan have caused the radicalization of some Western Muslims, while the principal narrative of Islamicist grievance, the Palestinian cause, has been superseded by a much more ambitious narrative: the clash of civilizations, which radical Muslims have cast as a war for the survival of Islam. The West has responded with its own narrative: the War on Terror, itself redolent with quasi-religious Crusader vocabulary. Both wars require soldiers/mujahedeen, and neither shows any sign of ending. Seeking to understand martyrdom has never been more crucial.

POSTSCRIPT: NARRATING MARTYRDOM

'Martyrdom', writes New Testament scholar John Dominic Crossan,

> is an unfortunate necessity, an unwanted inevitability of conscious resistance to systematic evil. Otherwise, resistance itself colludes with the violence it opposes. Such collusion may entail, minimally, desiring or provoking martyrdom (but every martyr needs a murderer). It may entail, maximally, the hunger-striker or the suicide attacker . . . Such collusive actions are not . . . ethical.[1]

For Crossan, therefore, only death where it is not desired and in no way provoked is to be counted as an ethical act. Any provocation, however minimal, is collusion with violence that causes the martyrdom. Martyrdom is also cast as resistance to systematic evil. Here, Crossan finds an ally in Church historian Everett Ferguson, who regards early Christian martryology as the starting point of the non-violent tradition of civil disobedience.[2]

Most modern people will readily contrast the non-violent passive acts of endurance and bravery of the early Christians who endured martyrdom with contemporary manifestations of Islamic terror, on the grounds that the Islamic 'martyr' destroys not only himself, but aims to murder others. A radical distinction is often drawn between Islam and the martyrdom traditions of Judaism and Christianity. The latter are thought to be passive and peaceful, while in Islam, killing and dying for God have often gone together in the jihad tradition.

I began this book with the claim that martyrdom was one of the most important, yet neglected, contemporary issues in the study of religion. I hope I have demonstrated that a careless distinction between the three monotheistic religions should be abandoned. The martyrological traditions of Judaism, Christianity, and Islam have far more in common than separates them. Even those Christian passive martyrs, who endured horrific brutality at the hands of the Romans, believed they were engaged in a cosmic war, which they were ultimately winning by their deaths. Each death brought nearer a violent and cataclysmic overthrow of 'evil'. The early Christians certainly had their 'explosions', but theirs was on a longer eschatological fuse.

Early Christian reflection on martyrdom sprang from Jewish Holy War tradition, in which God fought on behalf of the Hebrews as they conquered lands and peoples, often with instructions not to spare any of the inhabitants of the land. Although the battles of Deuteronomy and Joshua almost certainly do not reflect actual historical events, the radical command to eliminate idolatry, with the belief God fought for them, was potent enough to fuel at least four full-scale revolts from the time of the Maccabees to Bar Kochba. Even the passive martyrdoms of the seven brothers in 2 *Maccabees* are theologically incorporated into the Holy War tradition, and in 2 *Maccabees* turn the direction of the battle.

That said, Islam never 'benefitted' from a period of sustained persecution or decline during the formation of its scriptures, in the same way as Judaism or Christianity. However, despite the New Testament being written exclusively in a time of weakness, and notwithstanding the beatitude on peacemakers, it was not long before the eschatological violence of Christian theology was actualized in the persecutions of Jews, Crusades against Muslims, and the fires and scaffolds of the Reformation era. Killing as well as dying for God has been part of the theological grammar of Judaism and Christianity as well as Islam.

However, it has not been my purpose to denigrate those held to be martyrs. Quite the opposite; this book represents an attempt to understand martyrdom as narrative. Too much time and ink has been spilled attempting to define martyrdom in order to find ways to include some and exclude others from the canon of martyrology. As I have demonstrated, this is an activity that goes back at least to Clement in the mid third century. There are laudable political reasons for attempting to exclude contemporary suicide bombers from the category of martyr, and to crowbar the movement away from any association with Islam. However, I do not believe either of these aims, however well intentioned, contributes to a better understanding of the phenomenon of martyrdom. Martyrdom can never be reduced simply to a death of which we approve. The category of martyr is controversial; it is a contested term. Joan of Arc and Dietrich Bonhoeffer were not immediately accepted as martyrs by all. Granted, the claim to martyrdom is often a claim for legitimacy, as with the ferocious attempts to 'make' and 'unmake' martyrs during the Reformation period. It mattered to Roman Catholics whether those who were executed were killed as martyrs or traitors, just as it was important to Protestants to claim those burned at the stake were martyrs rather than heretics. There is simply no satisfactory way to determine whether or not Thomas Cranmer, Charles I, Bobby Sands, Paul Hill, Matthew Shepherd, or Neda Solton are martyrs. So long as people recognize them as such, the only way to decisively settle the argument is for universal recognition, or to eliminate all voices of support. Only the almost unimaginable horror of the Holocaust threatened to bring about the 'end of martyrdom'.

The same is true of at least some contemporary suicide bombers. Although many Islamic scholars reject the idea that those who die in this way are martyrs, other scholars do allow the tactic in limited circumstances. There is little prospect that Western anti-martyr narratives will ever persuade those who celebrate Palestinians who kill both themselves and others as heroes and martyrs that they are misguided; the cult of the martyr is too deeply embedded. Similarly, it would be very difficult to persuade relatives of those killed in suicide bomb attacks that their loved one died in an act of 'resistance' rather than 'terrorism'.

The trouble with martyr narratives is that they turn defeat into victory, and weakness into strength. Furthermore, they encourage repetition. The early Christians saw their executed brothers and sisters winning a martyr's reward and contributing to a cosmic victory. However, the Romans were oblivious to this narrative. They saw the triumph of the Roman machine, executing criminals in public displays of humiliation. Both narratives, though one person could not hold both simultaneously, reinforced the other. Today, the War on Terror narrative and Islamicist martyrologies are similarly mutually incompatible ways of viewing the world, yet each contributes to the other. If the Palestinian martryology centres on themes of humiliation and oppression, Israel's attempts to protect itself from those attacks depend on adding to that humiliation and oppression. Anti-martyr narratives are very weak weapons against martyrology, but so are bombs, missiles, and the destruction of social and economic infrastructure. Christian martyrdom first ended when the early Christians gained positions of political influence. It may be that the level of political influence of power required to put an end to Islamic martyrology is simply too high for the West to grant. However, when action is taken that contributes to a backdrop where martyr narratives continue to be plausible, there can be no foreseeable end to the phenomenon of martyrdom.

NOTES

CHAPTER 1

1 For a collection of essays on the history of suicide attacks, see D. Gambetta (ed.), *Making Sense of Suicide Missions* (Oxford: Oxford University Press, 2005).

2 http://news.bbc.co.uk/1/hi/uk_politics/2051372.stm (all websites listed were accessed in January 2011).

3 J. W. van Henten and F. Avemarie, *Martyrdom and Noble Death: Selected Texts from Graeco-Roman, Jewish and Christian Antiquity* (London: Routledge, 2002): 3.

4 On noble death, see D. Seely, *The Noble Death: Graeco-Roman Martyrology and Paul's Concept of Salvation* (Sheffield: JSOT, 1990); A. Yarbro Collins, 'From noble death to crucified Messiah', *NTS* 40 (1994): 581–503; A. J. Droge and J. D. Tabor, *A Noble Death: Suicide and Martyrdom among Christians and Jews in Antiquity* (San Francisco: Harper, 1992).

5 A. J. L. van Hooff, *From Authothanasia to Suicide: Self-Killing in Classical Antiquity* (London: Routledge, 1990).

6 Diogenes Laertius, 6.76–77; Lucian, *Demonax*, 65.

7 L. W. Hurtado, 'Jesus' death as paradigmatic in the New Testament', *SJT* 57 (2004): 413–433.

8 B. Wicker (ed.), *Witnesses to Faith? Martyrdom in Christianity and Islam* (London: Ashgate, 2006).

9 Wicker, *Witnesses*, xi.

10 See S. Evans, *Mothers of Heroes, Mothers of Martyrs: World War I and the Politics of Grief* (Montreal: McGill-Queens University Press, 2007) and J. Davies, *The Christian Warrior in the Twentieth Century* (New York: Edwin Mellen Press, 1995).

11 Osama bin Laden, reported in *The Scotsman* (Friday, 2 November 2001).

12 George. W. Bush, Speech to the Joint Session of Congress, 20 September 2001.

13 http://news.bbc.co.uk/1/hi/world/americas/1547561.stm

14 Quoted in F. Schlingensiepen, *Dietrich Bonhoeffer 1906–1945: Martyr, Thinker, Man of Resistance*, trans. I. Best (London: T & T Clark, 2010): 380.

15 The other nine are: The Grand Duchess Elizabeth of Russia; Manche Masemola; Maximilian Kolbe; Lucian Tapiede; Esther John; Martin Luther King; Wang Zhiming; Janani Luwum; and Oscar Romero.

16 http://news.bbc.co.uk/1/hi/world/americas/3077040.stm.
17 www.mttu.com/Articles/Men%20of%20Courage%20%20Paul%20 Hill%20and%20 Dietrich%20Bonhoeffer.htm.
18 D. Cullen, 'Who said yes?' *Salon Magazine* (30 September 1999). http:// www.lhup.edu/~dsimanek/salon.htm, reproduced by the publisher of *Skeptic Magazine*.
19 M. Thernstrom, 'The Crucifixion of Matthew Shepard', *Vanity Fair* (March, 1999): 100–106, 145–153.
20 J. Joseph, 'Like the student in Tiananmen Square, Neda is image that becomes an icon' *The Times* (Wednesday, 23 June 2009): 4
21 Martin Fletcher, 'Video clip of student's last breath makes her martyr of Tehran', *The Times* (Tuesday, 29 June 2009): 4.

CHAPTER 2

1 The classic text on persecution is W. H. C. Frend, *Martyrdom and Persecution in the Early Church* (Oxford: Blackwell, 1965).
2 Paul lists his sufferings in Rom. 8.35–36; 1 Cor. 4.9–13; 2 Cor. 4.8–9, 6.4–5, 11.23–29 and 12.10. See J. S. Pobee, *Persecution and Martyrdom in the Theology of Paul* (Sheffield: JSOT Press, 1985); K. Y. Lim, *The Sufferings of Christ are Abundant in Us: A Narrative Dynamics Investigation of Paul's Suffering in Corinthians* (London: Continuum, 2009); P. Middleton, '"Dying We Live": Paul and Martyrdom' in P. Middleton, A. Paddison, and K. Wenell (eds), *Paul, Grace, and Freedom: Essays in Honour of John Riches* (London: T & T Clark, 2009): 82–93.
3 See, for example, Mk 3.31–35; Mt. 8.21–22; Lk. 12.51–53; Mt. 19.29–30; Lk. 14.26.
4 The literature on the early Christian's relationship with the synagogue is voluminous. See, for example, E. P. Sanders (ed.), *Jewish and Christian Self Definition*, 3 vols. (Philadelphia: Fortress Press, from 1980); S. G. Wilson, *Related Strangers: Jews and Christians 70 CE–170 CE* (Minneapolis: Fortress Press, 1995).
5 See, for example, S. Benko, *Pagan Rome and the Early Christians* (Bloomington: Indiana University Press, 1986); G. W. Bowersock, *Martyrdom and Rome* (Cambridge: Cambridge University Press, 1995).
6 Quoted by R. L. Wilken, *The Christians as the Romans Saw Them* (New Haven: Yale University Press, 2003): 18.
7 E. Pagels, *The Gnostic Gospels* (New York: Random House, 1979).
8 M. Reasoner, 'Persecution', in R. P Martin and P. H. Davids (eds), *Dictionary of Later New Testament* (907–914): 913.

CHAPTER 3

1 See also *M. Lyons* 1.36, 1.38; *M. Polycarp* 17.1, 19.2; *M. Potamiaena* 6; *M. Fructuosus* 1.4, 4.1; *M. Ignatius* 5; Tertullian, *Valentinians* 56;

On *Patience* 15; Pontus, *Life of Cyprian* 19. Martyr texts are from H. A. Musurillo, *Acts of the Christian Martyrs* (Oxford: Oxford University Press, 1972).

2 On the Roman games, see, for example, C. Edwards, *Death in Ancient Rome* (New Haven: Yale University Press, 2007); K. Welch, *The Roman Amphitheatre from Its Origins to the Coliseum* (Cambridge: Cambridge University Press, 2007); P. Plass, *The Game of Death in Ancient Rome: Arena, Sport, and Political Suicide* (Madison: University of Wisconsin Press, 1995); T. Wiedemann, *Emperors and Gladiators* (London: Routledge, 1992).

3 For example, Tertullian, *Scorpiace* 6; Origen, *Exhortation* 17–20; *M. Lyons* 42, 2: 6–8; *M. Fructus* 6:1.

4 For example, *M. Carpus* 35; *M. Lyons* 1, 17; *M. Perpetua* 10; Origen, *Exhortation* 1, 17–20, 34, 42, 49; *M. Ignatius* 5.

5 Ignatius, *Ephesians* 3.1; see also *M. Polycarp* 2; *M. Lyons* 1. 6, 7; *M. Potamioena* 4–5.

6 So especially J. C. Scott, *Domination and the Arts of Resistance* (New Haven: Yale University Press, 1990): 203–206; L. L. Thomson, 'Martyrdom of Polycarp', 38–41; K. Hopkins, *Death and Renewal*, 11.

7 For example, *M. Polycarp* 12.2; *M. Lyons* 1.3, 1.15, 1.17, 1.30, 1.39, 1.50, 1.53, 1.57; *M. Potamiaena* 3.

8 See *M. Polycarp* 3.2; *M. Lyons* 1.43.

9 *M. Polycarp* 12.2, 3; *M. Perpetua* 18.9.

10 *M. Polycarp* 8.3, 31.1; *M. Lyons* 1.7, 1.31, 1.44.

11 *M. Lyons* 1.57, 1.60.

12 See *M. Polycarp* 2.2, 13.3; *M. Carpus* 35; *M. Lyons* 19, 51, 56.

13 *M. Lyons* 1.11; *M. Apollonius* 47.

14 G. W. Bowersock, *Martyrdom and Rome* (Cambridge: Cambridge University Press, 2005): 66.

15 See also, Tertullian, *Scorpiace* 4; *On Modesty* 22; Clement, *Miscellanies* 4.7; Origen, *Exhortation* 34, 51.

16 See also 4.6–7, 10.11, 14, 20.1, 21.10; *M. Polycarp* 3.1, 17.1; *M. Carpus* 5, 6–7, 17; *M. Lyons* 1.3–6, 14, 16, 23, 25, 27, 35; *M. Apollonius* 47; *M. Fructus* 1.4, 7.2; *M. St Justin* (recension C) 1.2.

17 See also *M. Lyons* 1.27 where the devil devises his strategy.

18 See *M. Polycarp* 9–12; *M. Carpus*, passim; *M. Perpetua* 6; *M. Pionius* 4–5, 12, 20; *M. Conon* 3–4; *M. Agape* 5.2.

19 *M. Polycarp* 12.2.

20 *M. Carpus* (Latin) 4.2.

21 The contrast is clearly demonstrated in *M. Lyons* 1.27, where the jailers are filled with the devil, while the Christians are filled with the Holy Spirit.

22 Ignatius, *Ephesians* 3.1; see also 1.2; *Trallians* 5.2; *Romans* 4.2, 5.1; *Polycarp* 7.1. The same idea is found in *M. Polycarp* 17.3.

23 *M. Lyons* 30.

24 The following is from R. I. Pervo, *Acts: A Commentary*, Hermeneia series (Minneapolis: Fortress Press, 2009): 168.

25 Similarly, there are literary parallels between what Jesus predicts what will happen to believers (Mk 13) and his own Passion (Mk 14–15). For a tabulated comparison, see Middleton, *Radical Martyrdom*, 152–153.
26 Some of the following are also listed by L. L. Thomson, 'The martyrdom of Polycarp: death in the Roman games', *Journal of Religion* 82 [2002] , 48.
27 See also *M. Polycarp* 2.2–3 where the martyrs are not present in the flesh during torture.
28 *M. Justin* 3.4, 4.1, 4.3, 4.4, 4.6, 4.9.
29 See also the *Acts of the Scillitan Martyrs*, a trial narrative where the confession *Christianus/a sum* is prominent (9, 10, 13) and *M. Perpetua* 3.2, 6.4.
30 *M. Polycarp* 14, 15; *M. Lyons* 1.40, 51–52; *M. Conon*, 6–7; *M. Justin* 2.2; Origen, *Exhortation* 3; Ignatius, *Romans* 5, Ireneaus, *Against Heresies* 4.33.9; Tertullian, *Scorpiace* 6, 7; *De Fuga* 9.
31 On Martyrdom and questions of identity see M. P. Jensen, *Martyrdom and Identity: The Self on Trial* (London: Continuum, 2010); C. R. Moss, *The Other Christs: Imitating Jesus in Ancient Christian Ideologies of Martyrdom* (New York: Oxford University Press, 2010); J. Perkins, *The Suffering Self: Pain and Narrative Representation in the Early Christian Era* (London: Routledge, 1995).
32 *M. Polycarp* 1; *M. Carpus* (Latin) 6.1; *M. Apollonius* 47.
33 Origen, *Exhortation* 42; Tertullian, *Scorpiace* 6, 11; *M. Polycarp* 19; *M. Lyons* 1.36, 1.42, 2: 6–8; *M. Apollinus* 47.
34 *M. Lyons* 1.36; *M. Polycarp* 17.1, 19.2; *M. Pionius* 22.2; *M. Fructus* 4.1.
35 See Clement *Misc.* 4.7; Tertullian, *On Modesty* 22.
36 Origen, *Exhortation* 28; Tertullian, *On Prayer* 4; Irenaeus *A.H.* 3.18.5 where an inquisition is made of their blood.
37 Irenaeus, *Against Heresies* 3.18.5.
38 *M. Polycarp* 3; M. Carpus (A) 39; *M. Justin* (C) 4.6; *M. Perpetua* 11.4; *M. Ignatius* 4; Justin, *Trypho* 46; *Apology* 1.57; Origen, *Exhortation* 22.
39 *M. Lyons* 1.9; Tertullian, *Scorpiace* 8; *M. Ignatius* 1, 7; Origen, *Exhortation* 11.
40 *M. Pionius* 20.5, 21.4.
41 *Acts of Scillitian Martyrs* 15, 17; *M. Ptolemaeus* 17–18; *M. Ignatius* 2.
42 See P. Brown, *The Cult of the Saints: Its Rise and Function in Latin Christianity* (Chicago: The University of Chicago Press, 1981).
43 M. A. Tilley, *Donatist Martyr Stories: The Church in Conflict in Roman North Africa* (Liverpool: Liverpool University Press, 1996): 26.

CHAPTER 4

1 Quoted in C. Morris, 'Martyrs on the Field of Battle Before and During the First Crusade', in D. Wood (ed.), *Martyrs and Martyrologies*, Studies in Church History, 30 (Oxford: Oxford University Press, 1993) , 97.
2 In Morris, 'Martyrs', 101.

3 Quoted in J. Riley-Smith, *The Crusades: A History*, 2nd ed. (London: Continuum, 2005): 80.
4 *The Craft to Lyve and Dye Well* (1505), quoted in Gregory, *Salvation at Stake: Christian Martyrdom in Early Modern Europe* (Cambridge: Harvard University Press, 1999): 37.
5 On the Hussites, see Howard Kaminsky, *A History of the Hussite Revolution* (Berkeley: University of California Press, 1967).
6 *Letter* 6.
7 WA 23:474.16–19.
8 Gregory, *Salvation*, 17–18.
9 Johannes Fabri, 1550 trans. Gregory, 16.
10 Richard Tracy, *Of the Preparation to the Cross and to Death* (1540).
11 George Joye, *Present Consolation* (quoted in Gregory, *Salvation*, 162–163).
12 Heinrich Bullinger, 'A Sermon of the Confessing of Christe' (quoted in Gregory, *Salvation*, 130).
13 Quoted in Gregory, *Salvation*, 270–271.
14 Gregory, *Salvation*, 280.
15 Quoted in A. Shell, *Catholicism, Controversy, and the English Literary Imagination 1558–1660* (Cambridge: Cambridge University Press, 1999): 184.
16 Quoted in Gregory, *Salvation*, 322.
17 How dare you say mass within my earshot!

CHAPTER 5

1 W. Bousset and H. Gressman, *Die Religion des Judentums im späthellenistischen Zeitalter* (Tübingen: Mohr Siebeck, 1926): 374.
2 See especially J. W. Van Henten, *The Maccabean Martyrs as the Saviours of the Jewish People: A Study of 2 and 4 Maccabees* (Leiden: Brill, 1997).
3 Deut. 1.6–8, 2.25–37, 3.1–22, 6.10–12, 7.1, 9.1–3, 11.23–25, 20.1–18, 29.6–8, 31.3–6.
4 Deut. 7.1–5, 7.16–26, 12.1–3, 12.29–13:1, 13.2–19, 16.21–22, 17.2–7, 18. 9–14.
5 See also Deut. 7.1–4, 9–11, 8.19–20, 11.16–17, 28.1–68, 29.15–27, 30.17–18.
6 See also 1 *Macc.* 3.50–53, 3.60, 4.8–11, 4.24–25, 4.30–33, etc., where God is called to fight on behalf of Israel.
7 For the theme of terror falling on Israel's enemies, see Exod. 15.15–16 (cf. 1 Macc. 4.30–33), 23.27–28; Deut. 2.25, 11.25; Josh. 2.9.
8 See L. Finklestein, *Akiva: Scholar, Saint and Martyr* (New Jersey: Jason Aronson, 1990); D. Boyarin, *Dying For God: Martyrdom and the Making of Christianity and Judaism* (California: Stanford University Press, 1999).
9 In A. C. Krey, *The First Crusade: The Accounts of Eyewitnesses and Participants* (Princeton: Princeton University Press, 1921).

10 S. Shepkaru, *Jewish Martyrs in the Pagan and Christian Worlds* (Cambridge: Cambridge University Press, 2006): 147.
11 In Shepkaru, *Jewish Martyrs*, 120
12 In Shepkaru, *Jewish Martyrs*, 175
13 E. Fackenheim, *Jewish Return into History: Reflections in the Age of Auschwitz and a New Jerusalem* (New York: Schocken Books, 1978): 247.
14 Various versions of the address exist. See, for example, http://www. sichosinenglish.org/essays/35.htm
15 Jonathan Webber, 'Jewish Identities in the Holocaust: Martyrdom as a Representative Category', in A. Polonsky (ed.), *Polin: Studies in Polish Jewry*, vol. 13, *The Holocaust and its Aftermath* (London/Portland: The Littman Library of Jewish Civilization, 2000): 128–46, 129.
16 See especially P. Novick, *The Holocaust and Collective Memory* (London: Bloomberg, 2000); J. Neusner, *Stranger at Home: 'The Holocuast', Zionism and American Judaism* (Chicago: University of Chicago Press, 1997).
17 Quoted in N. Nadav, 'Lights of Faith and Heroism in the Darkness of the Holocaust', in Y. Fogel (ed.), *I will be sanctified. Religious Responses to the Holocaust*, trans. E. Levin (New Jersey: Jason Aronson, 1996): 25–36, 31.
18 Shepkaru, *Jewish Martyrs*, 276.
19 See also I. Trunk, *Jewish responses to Nazi Persecution* (New York: Stein & Day, 1979): 10–38.
20 B. Maza, 'Why?', in S. L. Jacobs (ed.), *Contemporary Jewish Religious Responses to the Shoah*, Studies in the Shoah 5 (Lanham: University Press of America, 1993): 136–156, 155.
21 See, for example, R. Hilberg, *The Destruction of the European Jews* (New York, Holmes & Meier, 1985). This is also a popular view among some Zionist movements. For a response, see D. H. Jones, *Moral Responsibility in the Holocaust: A Study in the Ethics of Character* (Lanham: Rowman & Littlefield Publishers, 1999).
22 Quoted in I. Gutman, *Resistance: The Warsaw Ghetto Uprising* (New York: Miles Lerman Center, 1994): 103.
23 See especially the classic by R. L. Rubenstein, *After Auschwitz: History, Theology, and Contemporary Judaism*, 2nd ed. (Baltimore: John Hopkins University Press, 1992; 1st ed., 1966).
24 See especially N. G. Finklestein, *The Holocaust Industry: Reflections on the Exploitation of Jewish Suffering* (London: Verso, 2000).

CHAPTER 6

1 See especially R. Dawkins, *The God Delusion* (London: Bantam Press, 2006) and C. Hitchens, *God Is Not Great: How Religion Poisons Everything* (London: Atlantic Books, 2007). For an excellent response, see D. Fergusson, *Faith and Its Critics: A Conversation* (Oxford: Oxford University Press, 2009).
2 Important on this question are S. P. Huntingdon, *The Clash of Civilizations and the Remaking of World Order* (New York: Simon & Schuster, 1996); A. Sen, *Identity and Violence: The Illusion of Destiny* (New York: W. W. Norton, 2006); and B. Tibi, *Islam between Culture and Politics* (Basingstoke: Palgrave, 2001).

3 See, among others, K. Armstrong, *Islam: A Short History* (New York: Modern Library, 2002); *Muhammad: A Biography of the Prophet* (London: Phoenix, 2001); H. Motzki (ed.), *The Biography of Mohammad: The Issue of Sources* (Leiden: Brill, 2000); D. Waines, *An Introduction to Islam* (Cambridge: Cambridge University Press, 2003).
4 So D. Cook, *Martyrdom in Islam* (Cambridge: Cambridge University Press, 2007).
5 See especially R. Firestone, *Jihad: The Origin of Holy War in Islam* (Oxford: Oxford University Press, 1999).
6 See the important comparative article by R. Firestone, 'Conceptions of holy war in biblical and Qur'anic tradition', *Journal of Religious Ethics* 24 (1996): 99–123.
7 See C. Hillenbrand, *The Crusades: Islamic Perspectives* (London: Routledge, 2000).
8 On the assassins, see B. Lewis, *The Assassins: A Radical Sect* (London: Phoenix, 1967).
9 On the Ottoman Empire see P. M. Holt (ed.), *The Cambridge History of Islam*, 2 vols. (Cambridge: Cambridge University Press, 1970); C. M. Philliou, *Governing Ottomans in an Age of Revolution* (Berkely: University of California Press, 2011).
10 See, for example, S. A. Arjomand, *Turban for the Crown: The Islamic Revolution in Iran* (Oxford: Oxford University Press, 1988); N. Keddie, *Modern Iran: Roots and Results of Revolution* (New Haven: Yale University Press, 2003).
11 Quoted in C. Reuter, *My Life as a Weapon: A Modern History of Suicide Bombing*, trans. H. Ragg-Kirkby (Princeton: Princeton University Press, 1994): 42.
12 Reported by Suzzane Goldenberg, 'The men behind the suicide bombers', *The Guardian* (Wednesday, 12 June 2002): 12–13.
13 A. M. Oliver and P. Stenberg, *The Road to Martyrs' Square: The Journey into the World of the Suicide Bomber* (Oxford: Oxford University Press, 2005), plate 5.
14 Quoted in Reuter, *Weapon*, 90–91.
15 T. Asad, *On Suicide Bombing* (New York: Columbia University Press, 2007).
16 Quoted by H. Haleem, 'What Is Martyrdom' in Wicker, 59.
17 An abbreviated translation is found at www.religioscope.com/pdf/martyrdom.pdf.
18 Quoted in Reuter, *Weapon*, 122.
19 Cook makes this point in *Martyrdom*.

POSTSCRIPT

1 J. D. Crossan, *The Birth of Christianity: Discovering What Happened in the Early Years Immediately after the Crucifixion of Jesus* (San Francisco: HarperSanFrancisco, 1998), 285
2 E. Ferguson, 'Early Christian martyrdom and Civil Disobedience.' *Journal of Early Christian Studies*, 1 (1993), 73–83

SUGGESTED FURTHER READING

Martyrdom in Christianity

Bergman, S. (ed.), *Martyrs: Contemporary Writers on Modern Lives of Faith* (New York: Harper Collins, 1996).

Castelli, E. A., *Martyrdom and Memory: Early Christian Culture Making* (New York: Columbia University Press, 2004).

Chenu, B. et al., *The Book of Christian Martyrs*, trans. J. Bowden. (London: SCM, 1990).

Crossan, J. D., *The Birth of Christianity: Discovering What Happened in the Years Immediately after the Crucifixion of Jesus* (Edinburgh: T & T Clark, 1999): 285.

Ferguson, E., 'Early Christian martyrdom and civil disobedience', *Journal of Early Christian Studies* 1 (1993): 73–83.

Freeman, T. S. and Mayer, T. F. (eds), *Martyrs and Martyrdom in England, c. 1400–1700* (Woodbridge: The Boydell Press, 2007).

Frend, W. H. C., *Martyrdom and Persecution: A Study of a Conflict from the Maccabees to Donatus* (Oxford: Blackwell, 1965).

Gregory, B. S., *Salvation at Stake: Christian Martyrdom in Early Modern Europe* (Cambridge: Harvard University Press, 1999).

Middleton, P., *Radical Martyrdom and Cosmic Conflict in Early Christianity* (London: Continuum, 2006).

Moss, C., *The Other Christs: Imitating Jesus in Ancient Christian Ideologies of Martyrdom* (Oxford: Oxford University Press, 2010).

Musurillo, H., *The Acts of the Christian Martyrs* (Oxford: Clarendon Press, 1972).

Salisbury, J. E., *The Blood of the Martyrs: Unintended Consequences of Ancient Violence* (New York: Routledge, 2004).

Smith, L. B., *Fools, Martyrs, Traitors: The Story of Martyrdom in the Western World* (New York: Knopf, 1997).

Martyrdom in Judaism

Abulafia, A. S. (ed.), *Religious Violence between Christians and Jews: Medieval Roots, Modern Perspectives* (New York: Palgrave, 2002).

Boyarin, D. *Dying For God: Martyrdom and the Making of Christianity and Judaism* (California: Stanford University Press, 1999).

Chazan, R., *European Jewry and the First Crusade* (Berkely: University of California Press, 1987).

Droge, A. J. and Tabor, J. D., *A Noble Death: Suicide and Martyrdom among Christians and Jews in Antiquity* (San Francisco: Harper Collins, 1992).

Fogel, Y., *I will be Sanctified: Religious Responses to the Holocaust*, trans. E. Levin. (New Jersey: Jason Aronson, 1998).

Shepkaru, S., *Jewish Martyrs in the Pagan and Christian Worlds* (Cambridge: Cambridge University Press, 2006).
van Henten, J. W., *The Maccabean Martyrs as the Saviors of the Jewish People: A Study of 2 and 4 Maccabees* (Leiden: Brill, 1997).

Martyrdom in Islam

Asad, T., *On Suicide Bombing* (New York: Columbia University Press, 2007).
Cook, D., *Martyrdom in Islam* (Cambridge: Cambridge University Press, 2007).
Firestone, R., *Jihad: The Origin of Holy War in Islam* (Oxford: Oxford University Press, 1999).
Gambetta, D. (ed.), *Making Sense of Suicide Missions* (Oxford: Oxford University Press, 2005).
Khosrokhavar, R., *Suicide Bombers: Allah's New Martyrs*, trans. D. Macey. (London: Pluto Press, 2005).
Reuter, C., *My Life as a Weapon: A Modern History of Suicide Bombing*, trans. H. Ragg-Kirkby. (Princeton: Princeton University Press, 2004).
Wicker, B. (ed.), *Witnesses to Faith? Martyrdom in Christianity and Islam* (Aldershot: Ashgate, 2006).

INDEX